🐾 Skeet
Shooting
for
Astrologers

Skeet Shooting for *Astrologers*

A manual of practical instruction and advice

by David R. Roell

Astrology Classics

On the front cover: Michèle la belle Strasbourgeoise, and Judith the Englishwoman, Colorado, Thanksgiving 1973. PHOTO BY NUSBAUM.
On the back: Photo of the author BY KATE.

Pages 25–29, extracts from
SYNASTRY, A GUIDE TO HUMAN RELATIONSHIPS, by Ronald Davison
excerpted with permission of **Aurora Press Inc.**
Copyright Aurora Press 1983
ALL RIGHTS RESERVED www.AuroraPress.com

All other materials quoted herein are
believed to be in the Public Domain.

Illustrations were taken from:
Old Fashioned Transportation Cuts, edited by Carol Belanger Grafton, published by Dover Publications, New York, 1987
Treasury of Art Nouveau Design and Ornament, selected by Carol Belanger Grafton, published by Dover Publications, New York, 1980

ISBN: 978 1 933303 29 1

Copyright © 2011 by William R. Roell.
All rights reserved.

Published by
Astrology Classics

The publication division of
The Astrology Center of America
207 Victory Lane, Bel Air MD 21014

On the net at www.**AstroAmerica.com**

❦ Table of Contents

On Skeets ix
Preface xi

Essays

Houses, and what to do with them 1
Yogas of the East, Aphorisms of the West 3
Politicians and Astrology 5
Be a professional Astrologer and make lotsa money! 7
La Rentrée—How the French get back to business 9
How to read intercepted signs 11
Towards a new history of Astrology 13
Transmission, oral and written 20
The excitement of hope—The 2009 Inaugural chart 22
Rectification 31
Dear Dave 32
On Charles Carter's *The Principles of Astrology* 35
Hot tips in real estate 36
Dancing Lessons: How the world sees you 40
Dancing Lessons: Where the money comes from 43
Astrology and number 46
State of play 48
Gardening 51
Fertility / On Zodiacs 52
Dancing Lessons: Techniques 54
Eclipse season 56
Eclipses: Mundane 57
Vive le Bastille 58

Tropical *versus* Sidereal 60
Astrology in the news 63
What is Pseudoscience? Doppler dogma 65
Astrology and weather 67
Cosmobiology 70
Science or Pseudoscience? Craters of the Moon 71
The best books on Progressions 74
AstroAmerica's retrograde technology roundup 75
Pseudoscience proudly presents: The 5000 year old
    theory of the Sun 77
More on the Antikythera mechanism 81
Astro*Carto*Graphy at your fingertips 89
NASA lays an egg, *and,* Pain management 92
Rules for Operations, *by H.L. Cornell* 95
More on A pill in the hand 97
The Introductory from AstroAmerica's
    Daily Ephemeris 100
Make money with astrology ! 101
More on Make money 103
Friday the 13th of November is good for you ! 105
Book of the week 106
Thee kinds of astrologers, *by Sepharial* 107
Retrogrades 111
Merry Christmas 2009 114
Reincarnation: Astrology and karma 115
Aphorisms 117
Reincarnation: Intercepted signs 120
Intercepted signs and reincarnation 123
More on houses 126
Initiation, *and other new books* 129
More Fun with houses 140

Table of Contents

Neptune returns 143
Climes 144
Another birthtime for President Obama 145
George Washington's Birthday 148
Sun versus Moon, *which is stronger?* 151
Help save astrology ! 154
Mozart's birthday 155
A Dream 158
Easter 159
How to set up a chart 162
How to calculate Tertiary Progressions 165
Spring planting 166
The new health care legislation
    Easy astrology 167
New books for spring 170
VOTE 171
Porphyry the Philosopher 172
Charles Carter *versus* Adolf Hitler 173
Odds and ends 175
A Charles Carter festival ! 177
A new theory of astrology 180
The Pre-Copernican World 193

Epilogue: The Author's Lament 194

Appendix: Natal charts mentioned in this book 195

Bibliography 207
Index 211

On Skeets

Many years ago Sam N. asked me to photograph his collection of German sniper rifles, with a view to publishing them in a book. In the end his collection was combined with that of another and in the resulting book I got no credit for my efforts. Such is life.

Skeets are small clay disks that are used in target shooting. There are people who still practice this arcane sport, but modern aficionados do much the same with video games.

This kind of competition focuses the mind and body, training it to respond rapidly to varying conditions.

I would have larded the cover with pictures of old guns, but the society in which I live is far too soaked with guns, cheap guns, vulgar guns, and the attendant violence, destruction, despair and death, for any such foolishness.

So instead of thinking of astrology and astrologers as members of a distinguished sporting club, think of us instead as middle aged, potbellied, naked jaybirds, in an English garden, late on a Tuesday afternoon, sadistically attacking each other with flyswatters.

Preface

Most of the essays in this book were written for my monthly, and then, weekly on-line newsletter, 2007–2010. Some others were taken from my website, and some from contributions I have made on-line elsewhere. And there are a couple of excerpts from other authors as well. My excuse for collecting them in a book is that essays and articles written for magazines and newsletters are often lost to posterity. Those written for on-line publication have even more grim prospects.

These are, for the most part, in order of date of publication. I have left them mostly unchanged.

Not included are essays on the Aquarian Age, as well as some of my more seriously metaphysical stuff. I am not certain these deserve posterity, and am, at any rate, not satisfied with them. They need work.

I have also set aside my solution to Mozart's death, as well as various essays about Ludwig van Beethoven, as these, as well as my notes on Ferdinand Ries, deserve a book of their own.

There are themes in this book. One is that the astrological techniques in use in any given region are the product of the underlying number system, combined with the latitude north of the equator. Thus, northern climes, combined with decimal notation, produced European astrology, whereas, the lack of a workable number system left the Chinese with stems and branches, which, if Tibetan astrology is a guide, might best be expressed with the fingers of the hand. Compare to India, where semitropical latitudes combined with a fabulous number system produced an astrology that is more about numbers than it is planets. The Mayans, as far north as the Indians but lacking a simple number system, created yet another astrology.

A second theme is that knowledge can be transmitted, century by century, either orally or in writing. Each system has its advantages and disadvantages, and leaves behind unique traces. Astrology is not the only discipline that has been transmitted both ways, at different times, by different cultures.

My own personal delight, which you will find here and there, concerns the use of rulers and dispositors in the reading of a chart. These amplify the meanings that can be extracted from any chart and if pursued to their logical ends will most likely lead to breakthroughs in forecasting.

Some parts of what follows will contradict some other parts, or will appear to. For this I make no apologies. Life is a process. We believe what we believe, until challenge or stress makes us reconsider. Whereupon we may suddenly find ourselves with new ideas and new beliefs. Readers who want consistency can wait until they are dead and then ask their God. Who, if I know him, and I think I do, a little, will merely laugh at our folly. Until then, humans are entitled to believe three or more things at once. Why not?

As befits a book of essays from a bookseller, there are many books referenced in the following pages. They are all listed in the bibliography. Where space permits, I have included charts as part of the essays. Where not, you can find them in the appendix.

One of the charms of compilations is that they are dated. Like an old newspaper, or an old diary entry.

Enjoy!

David R. Roell

February 10, 2011

❧   Essays

The same goes for a possible lack of order in presentation. I shall relate the events as they occur to me; should the reader be of a mind to do so, he will find it easy enough to put them in order. And so without further ado I will begin. — Ries.

HOUSES,
and what to do with them
(How I read a chart)

I'm Aquarian. Tell me what the rules are, and I'll go looking for some other rules. So I wasn't satisfied with aspects, no matter how finely the were diced, and midpoints were too much fuss. But hey, what about that empty house over there? What can that tell me?

Sakoian and Acker, in **The Astrologer's Handbook**, tease with Rising Sign Overlays. With Leo on the 3rd house cusp, Gemini ascendants express power through creative thinking. Except that I have Cancer there. So much for cookbooks.

Have you ever tried reading a friend's *second* house cusp? Everyone knows his sun sign, a lot of folks know their ascendant, some even know their moon. The second house is what folks value, but if it's empty, then, nobody knows. Read just the sign on the cusp and they'll sit up and take notice.

And it's not hard. Second house are your personal possessions, what you value. Cancer on the second? You're possessive. Leo? You're proud of what you own. Virgo: You're fussy about your things. Libra: Your partner tells you what to like. Scorpio: It's a secret! Sagittarius? Something foreign or exotic. Capricorn: Antiques. Aquarius: A souvenir of a group, or a symbol of an idea. Pisces: Everything, or nothing. Aries: Getting it. Taurus: Having it.

But now think about the planet that rules the sign on the second. Its sign and house placement will tell you the specific kinds of things that you value.

Aries on the second, ruler Mars in Gemini in the fourth? Your house (4th) has lots of noisy telephones (Gemini)! Move that Mars to Cancer and the 5th, and your aggressive children (5th) are your prized possessions. Put Mars in Leo in the 6th, and you could end up collecting kitchen (Leo = fire) equipment. In Virgo in the seventh, and every new partner will clean house upon arrival (Virgo = fussy).

The next phase, if you want to go there, is to look at the ruler's ruler, again, by sign and house. Are you a Pisces rising with Aries on the second, with Mars in Virgo in the seventh? Are you tired of every new person you meet throwing out all the things you value? Well, that Virgo is ruled by Mercury.

So let's look at Mercury. Suppose it's in Scorpio in the 9th. If so, then your partners will base their intense (Scorpio) criticisms of your possessions on philosophical or religious grounds, or on what country they came from (all 9th). So if this is your private nightmare, one way to defeat it is to buy only what is made in your own country.

But notice that if Aries is on the second, Mars in Virgo in the 7th, Mercury in Scorpio in the 9th, there is a mutual reception between Mars and Mercury. (Leave Pluto out of this for the moment.) Which has the effect of binding the two houses, 7th and 9th, together, with a secondary focus on the 2nd (Aries, ruled by Mars) and the 4th (Gemini, ruled by Mercury). What does this mean?

Travel to a foreign country, find a new partner. They arrive with their own unique religion or philosophy. With a secondary focus on the 4th house, they set up housekeeping, possibly abroad, even when you don't want to.

And then there's Saturn. Saturn always makes a mess of whatever house he's domiciled in. But that's only the surface gloss. What's the sign on the cusp? What planet rules it, and from what sign and what house?

In my case, Saturn is in Libra, in my 5th, which meant no fun and no girlfriends. But the sign on the cusp was Virgo. Ruler Mercury was in Aquarius in the 9th. So I fled the small towns of my youth and found solace with exotic foreigners. I got good at flirting (like these newsletters). But I didn't really figure me out until Uranus conjuncted my Mercury some years ago: I suddenly (Uranus) took to writing (Mercury) love poems (5th house) that did not rhyme (Virgo). I emailed them (Aquarius) to a woman in France (9th). I also had fun phone encounters with fair sex. Only one of whom I ever met. All in all, the Uranus transit was a revelation.

Is there a book? Yes: Karen Hamaker-Zondag's **House Connection**.

Yogas of the East ~ Aphorisms of the West

In Vedic astrology, a yoga (union) is an association of two or more planets that produce a predictable effect in a natal chart. Vedic astrologers have collected hundreds. They give them names. The A*dhi Yoga* forms when Mercury, Jupiter and Venus occupy the 6th, 7th and 8th houses from the Moon. It makes the native a king, a minister, or commander of an army. (K.S. Charak, **Yogas In Astrology**, pg. 113)

Vedic astrologers presume these sorts of things do not exist in western astrology, and western astrologers haven't challenged them on this point.

But in fact, they do. In the west, Yogas are known as Aphorisms. Until recent times, astrologers assiduously collected and passed them down, generation to generation.

They're treated much as Vedic astrologers treat Yogas: As simple formulas to be memorized and applied in a mechanical fashion. So far as Yogas go, the rote approach might actually be the best they can do, since Vedic astrology does not have a strong concept of aspects, nor does their sidereal zodiac give them usable astrological sign values.

(I know we're supposed to bow to the superiority of Vedic astrology, but after 12 years selling books on the subject, I've begun to wonder. Vedic astrology is a fabulous system, but western astrology can more than hold its own.)

Western aphorisms often include zodiacal sign values, along with dispositors, which is another factor largely missing from Vedic. An example, from Robson, will suffice:

"147. Moon in Libra, Capricorn or Aquarius in conjunction with the Sun, and in square or opposition to Saturn denies marriage." (**Astrology and Sex**, pg. 219)

Let's think about this. Moon conjunct Sun in Libra or Aquarius is a debilitated Sun. Moon conjunct Sun in Capricorn is a debilitated Moon. Saturn opposing Libra, Capricorn or Aquarius puts it in signs of its fall. So of the three planets that make up this "yoga", opposition places two of them in debility, by default. The square is not much cheerier, since squares amount to unresolved tension. Since Sun, Moon and Saturn are the major building blocks of formal relationship (Mars and Venus are just hot dates), an unhappy relationship between these three (i.e., "yoga") may well result in no formal marriage. One way or another.

Understand the dynamics, and you can invent your own aphorisms. I was working out an example of Cancer on the second house cusp, with the Moon ruling it from various houses and signs. Cancer on the second cusp is someone who may be compulsively insecure about his possessions.

Suppose, I said, that the Moon was in Gemini in the first house. The first house / ascendant is how we project ourself in the world. The Moon in Gemini is unsteady and talkative. Combine Cancerian 2nd house insecurity with the tell-everyone-everything-about-you of a first house Gemini Moon, and you have a beggar. Neat. And all you did was simple, basic astrology. No fancy midpoint tricks. No obscure aspects. No fly-by-night asteroids. No galactic center. Just plain nuts and bolts astrology.

Still with Cancer on 2, put the Moon in the 10th and you get some one who begs for a living. If in Pisces, they weep for effect. Now you've gone from simply reading a natal chart, to indicating profession.

A profession which, if it ever arrives at your door, will come begging.

Here's another one you won't find in a book: Capricorn rising, mutables Gemini on the 5th, Virgo on the 8th, with Mercury in a feminine sign under stressful aspect from Saturn or Mars, in a man's chart, produces homosexuality. In this case, Capricorn is the set-up. Asexual Mercury rules both houses of sexual expression, but is in the wrong gender for the native, and is stressed as well. Result: Heterosexual relations are of no interest. (Nope. You don't need Uranus.)

— *April–May 2008.*

Politicians and Astrology
Be an Astrological Patriot!

Charts, pgs. 196-206.

Neptune, Neptune, Neptune and did I mention, Neptune? ... but I don't want to bore my readers.

In a politician's chart, look first for hard aspects from Neptune to his personal planets. Some examples:

Barrack Obama: Mercury square Neptune. Sun square Neptune. Jupiter (not a personal planet) square Neptune.

Tony Blair: Neptune square Mercury. Squares to Neptune are aspects of delusion. One paints rosy pictures. One fools himself. The deluded politician sees the world as better than it is. In Tony's case, those delusions got manipulated into a war by someone with a different agenda. But, happily, Tony is still so deluded as to not know.

Maybe we should call Neptunian squares the Sucker Aspect. When Plutonians (George W. Bush) manipulate deluded Neptunians, the people in Neptune's charge (in Tony's case, British subjects) become victims. A Brazilian electrician's horrible death on a tube platform comes to mind.

Bill Clinton: Neptune conjunct Mars. Conjunctions with Neptune are an inability to sense reality. In this case, as it's in his first house, everyone thinks he's not doing the right thing, because, well, maybe he's not.

Richard Nixon: Neptune opposite Mercury. Oppositions to Neptune are outright deceit. Lies. You lie because you are lied to, you lie in equal measure.

Pluto is power for its own sake. Be ware the politician with Pluto in the first house who lacks oppositions in his chart. He will run roughshod over everyone and everything, since, by definition, he knows no opposition: **George W. Bush**.

Hillary Clinton: Mars-Pluto conjunct, with Saturn

making a stellium. Mars and Sun are in mutual reception as well as widely square.

John McCain: Sun/Neptune conjunct: The swindler. And don't they all claim to be "straight talkers"! Neptune-Venus conjunct. Neptune opposite Saturn. Pluto in the 10th.

This is too easy. Name a prominent politician, look for his Neptune. Then look for his Pluto.

So let's look at some more. Your heroes, or mine? Could Neptune rule clay feet?

Ronald Reagan: Neptune opposite Mercury/Uranus. Widely opposite Mars.

Jimmy Carter: Neptune/Node/Venus conjunct, opposite Mars. Lust in his heart.

Mike Huckabee: Stellium in Leo: Uranus, Jupiter, Pluto, Mars, Venus.

Ron Paul: Neptune/Mercury conjunct, opposite Saturn.

Mike Gravel: Uranus conjunct Mars, Neptune square Mercury.

Hard Neptune aspects do not make people bad. They do make them different. And just for the fun of it:

Bobby Kennedy: Pluto/Mars square. Pluto/Jupiter opposition.

Franklin Roosevelt: Stellium in Taurus: Saturn, Neptune, Jupiter, square Sun and Mercury in Aquarius.

Abraham Lincoln: Neptune conjunct Saturn (by far the best configuration for Neptune), square a Mercury/Pluto conjunction.

Mao Tse-tung: Neptune/Pluto conjunct, opposite Mercury.

A client walks in the door, you find Neptunian aspects, this is not what you should think of him. He's an ordinary working stiff. Political office attracts the dishonest as well as those who crave power for its own sake. Astrology can easily unmask both. Then we can decide if we like them.

— July 2008.

Be a Professional Astrologer and Make Lotsa Money!

So you've just read your first good book on astrology (Rae Orion's **Astrology for Dummies** was an excellent choice) and you want to make it a career. You're not the first. Here's some useful advice:

Natal readings aren't the way to go. Lots of reasons. 1. There's just not that much demand for it. 2. For the number of readings you can expect in a week, you have to charge $150 - $250 per reading, and not that many people want to pay that much. 3. They're exhausting, grueling set pieces.

But try it. Most people give up in 6-12 months. Robert Blaschke wrote the ultimate guide to life as a self-employed natal chart reader (Astrology, A Language of Life vol. 3: **A Handbook for the Self-Employed Astrologer**). Noel Tyl offers single-shot advice in **The Creative Astrologer: Effective Single Session Counseling**.

What makes money in astrology? Horary makes money. People have questions. Horary gives answers. You set up the chart for the moment you hear the question, you study it until the answer emerges. Once you get the hang of it, most questions won't take more than 15 minutes of your time. From start to finish, 30 minutes with the client. What's that worth? $50. You can see upwards of a dozen clients a day. Do the math.

If you're good — which means, right — clients will remember and come back. They will, dumbfounded, tell their friends, the best advertising there is.

Questions like, *Who stole my money? Should I buy a new house? Is my spouse having an affair? Should I send my kid to college?*

And these aren't abstractions. My favorite example is a

cheating husband. One fine evening, out with his secretary, he has lost his wedding ring. His wife already suspects. It's now 12:30 am and he's desperate and you're his only hope. If you can tell him to look on the left-hand side of the rear seat of his car, next to the door, and if he finds the ring there, he will be your friend for life.

Is this moral? No, it's not moral. Not at all. A lot of horary is like that. You have to be okay with that. It's part of your job.

But learning horary can be hard. It's not for everyone. It's eluded me, and I once edited William Lilly's famous book (**Christian Astrology**). For those of you who have the resources, you might consider a teacher. Among the good ones, John Frawley, J. Lee Lehman, the late Olivia Barclay's Qualifying Horary Diploma Course (now run from Tokyo), Gilbert Navarro, Carol Wiggers. Indeed, horary is such a powerful tool, and such a fundamental use of astrology, that I am hard-pressed to suggest any other kind of astrological teacher.

But, fear not. There is a halfway-house, halfway between the bottomless pits of natal reading, and the dizzying heights of horary. What is this twilight zone?

It has become known as the **Consultation Chart**. Which, before it was a book by Wanda Sellar, was a technique employed by the famous Evangeline Adams. You note the time your client arrives, you determine the degree rising on the eastern horizon, and then you find that degree (an "ascendant") in the client's natal chart. In other words, you make an impromptu horary chart of your client's natal chart. The natal house that contains the ascendant of the moment becomes the topic at hand. You then steer the discussion in that direction.

If that degree turns up in the client's 7th house, it's a partnership, or a thief. If in the 6th, a matter of health, or his pet, or his diet. In the 5th, pregnancy or romance. In the fourth, his house, etc. I am certain Lilly would have used this trick, had he clients with birth data.

Astrologers who use these techniques are rarely short of clients — or income.

— *August, 2008.*

Let us now praise
La Rentrée — How the French get back to business

The most civilized people in Europe, perhaps all the world, are at this very moment getting back to work. It is not often seen by outsiders for the simple reason that it is one of the craziest times on earth.

It started in 1936, in the deep dark days of the Third Republic, when France briefly elected a Socialist government. They didn't last long, partly as the big money boys hated them, and partly as they hadn't a clue how to govern, but before they left, they passed a law giving every employee, regardless of time on the job, a paid vacation. Each and every year. That law still stands today. The French started with two weeks. Eventually it became four.

I'm not sure exactly when it happened, and I'm not sure exactly how it happened, but it came to pass that the month in question came to be August, and it was August for everyone. Rich and poor alike. One story I heard is that all those imposing stone buildings in Paris have, by August, been thoroughly heated by the summer sun and radiate raw heat to all inside. Which is why they're happy to rent them out to us at inflated prices. *Plus ça change, plus c'est le meme chose*, or something like that.

Well, if you're looking for work, you can imagine your prospects for getting hired in, say, June of any given year, are rather slim, and you'd be right.

But then there was the Bastille. Perhaps driven crazy by an excessively hot summer and a shortage of cakes to eat, the French stormed the Bastille, a prison fortress similar to the Tower of London, on July 14, 1789. Ripped it to pieces. It's now a park. Bastille Day was first celebrated the very next year. It has been a national holiday since 1880, and, by law, the French are to "celebrate with all the brilliance that the local resources allow."

Well, to celebrate on that level you need at least a day to prepare, and after you've had such a good time, you need at least a day to recover, or may be two or three. So Bastille Day was always an expansive holiday.

But then people thought, heck, why go back to work after "Bastille day" if *vacance* starts only a week later. Why not just go *en vacance* on *Quatorze Juillet* and come back the end of August? And, Presto! Four weeks turned into six.

And then there was the start of school. In order to give people time to get back and get ready, the first day of school – *La Rentrée* – was set for September 15. And parents thought, well, heck. I don't need two weeks to get the kids ready. We can get back late on the 14th and we'll manage somehow.

And so it came to pass that the French – not all of them, mind you, but quite a lot of them – got themselves Two Full Months Paid Vacation. Each and every year. In the entire civilized world, it doesn't get better.

In my younger days I once spent the month of August hitching in France. The French hate hitchers, or so I've heard, but I didn't have a problem until one morning on the north side of Bordeaux. Overnight it had become *La Rentrée*. One hundred cars a minute chugged passed me, for eighteen continuous hours. No one stopped. Packed-out caravans, mostly. Mom, pop, five kids, the grandparents and maybe an aunt or two, all crammed inside. Luggage strapped to the roof. Towing a trailer. Went on for three solid days. No astrology this month, just this story. *La Rentrée* is going on now!

— *September, 2008*

How to read intercepted signs

An intercepted Sign is a chart containing a sign of the Zodiac that has no house cusp. In other words, when two houses sandwich a sign between them. See the example to the right, from 8th house of the President-elect's official 7:24 pm birth chart. These always come in opposing pairs, and elsewhere in the chart there will be two pairs of houses with only two signs on them, but that's a story for another day.

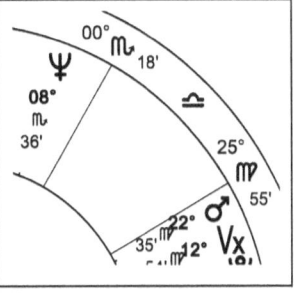

Houses with intercepted signs inside them have two distinct stories. The Main Story is the sign on the cusp, its ruler and its sign and house. But early in life the individual finds this story doesn't work. The degree on the cusp – always a late one, as shown here – "runs out of gas", forcing the individual to find some other way of handling the affairs of the house. After a bit of fussing about, that new way turns out to be the intercepted sign and its ruler and the house and sign that ruler is in. Remarkably, most individuals are unaware they have two approaches to the affairs of the same house. I have intercepted signs in my 5th and 11th and until I discovered this rule a few weeks ago, I was unaware I had two different approaches to children and romance. Here is another example:

Jane, born January, 1966, has 29 Scorpio on the cusp of the 5th. Mars, the ruler, is at 29 Aquarius from the 8th, exactly square to the cusp. Jane is unable to carry a baby to term, and she has tried many times. She miscarries, in a heavy loss of blood. Her desire for children (Sagittarius intercepted) drove her to adopt. So where was Jupiter, the ruler of Sag? In Gemini in the 11th. Jane adopted a baby from friends. He's a cute kid, I've met mother and son. But as Jupiter opposes the fifth house, and is debilitated (and intercepted) in Gemini, I fear she will adopt only one.

So what about our new president? The promise of Obama's 8th house Mars, as hinted in Sakoian and Acker's **Astrologer's Handbook**, pg. 159, is denied by the dispositor, Mercury, debilitated in Leo and placed in the 6th house: There will always be self-appointed people looking out for his best interests. The events of Mr. Obama's 8th house will play out through his children, as the intercepted sign, Libra, is disposed by Venus in Cancer in the 5th. As Venus is itself disposed by the Moon in Gemini in the 4th, Mr. Obama will unconsciously (Moon) verbalize (Gemini) his concerns, but only in private (4th house). What a great home life!

The Voids

Obama announced for the Presidency on a void (Feb. 10, 2007). The rules change that got him the primary votes of Michigan and Florida was on a void (June 8, 2008), the election, Nov. 4, was void. Inauguration moment, noon on Jan. 20, will be a void. This is *prima facie* evidence that Mr. Obama was born prior to 1:06 pm on the day, but I digress.

What do these voids mean? That Barrack Obama could use them to become president at this time hints the Constitution of 1787 may be at an end, and that a transition period, of unknown nature and duration, has begun.

— *Thanksgiving, 2008.*

Towards a new History of Astrology

Astrological histories are based on two presumptions. One is that astrology was derived from observation and deduction. The second is that it was transmitted by written means.

The first is easily demolished. Hellenistic astrology cannot be explained by means of observation, as Robert Schmidt's work with Hindsight brilliantly proves. Hellenistic astrology from the Classical period goes far beyond what can be developed by means of observation.

If astrology was derived from observation, ancient astrologers had better eyes and better brains than we do. In this regard, there seems to be an inverse relationship between brainpower and diet. Those of us who care about these things clearly eat better now than at any previous time in history, but I digress.

So how about the early books? Many of the best have survived. Which of these early ones, I wonder, were most prized? Answer: What do the following books have in common?

Tetrabiblos, by Ptolemy: Written, c. 140 AD, for Syrus, his patron. Unknown for at least a century.

Carmen Astrologicum, by Dorotheus of Sidon, first century AD. Unknown to Vettius Valens, a century later.

Mathesoes Libri VIII, by Julius Firmicus Maternus. Written, c. 340 AD, for his patron, Mavortius. It was largely unknown before the 12th century.

What do these books, and many others from the same period, have in common? They were not written as manuals of instruction. They were not written for students. They, like Bach's Brandenburg Concertos, were written for the idle amusement of a lord or noble. Or at least, that was the authors' fervent hope. They ended up, unread (and in Bach's case, unplayed), in libraries.

Where they were discovered decades, even centuries, later.

So if these early books, these masterpieces of the genre, were not used as teaching manuals, were not, in fact, eagerly snatched up by aspiring students, then how, and with what, were early astrologers taught?

Here's another set of "what do these have in common?"

Carmen Astrologicum, and,

Astronomica, by Manilius

Answer: The word, Carmen means song. But a song on a printed page is what, exactly? A lyric. What are lyrics? Poetry. So what is Astronomica? Answer: A Latin didactic poem.

So what do poems have that ordinary prose does not? Meter. What is meter? Meter is a form of rhythm based on syllabic order. What can meter and rhythm do that ordinary prose cannot?

Quickly, again: How many verses of The Star Spangled Banner, the US national anthem, do you know? Only the first? How many stanzas of Poe's The Raven?

Now for the hard question: **WHY** do you know these verses? Why do you know them better than, say, Lincoln's Gettysburg Address? Many of us had to memorize and recite it in front of class. Why do you remember the song but not the Address?

What can meter and rhythm do that ordinary prose cannot? Meter can be memorized and recited, word for word, years, even decades later. How much can be memorized?

The Iliad is a Greek epic poem, dating to the 9th century BC. Written in dactylic hexameter, it comprises 15,693 lines of verse. It is known to have been transmitted orally for centuries. The only reason we know the age of the poem is because we know the approximate date of the events it records, the Trojan War: Around the 12th century BC.

So could astrology have been orally transmitted? Yes. It could have. For how long? We do not know, but the Indian Vedas give hints of staggering age.

Towards a new history of Astrology

Next question: Why oral transmission? Why not read a book?

Answer: Before the printing press, books were written by hand. Which meant there were not very many of them. It also meant they were expensive. Students, then and now, are poor. Consider also the format of early books: Individual leaves that were glued or stitched together to form long scrolls. Long term storage, or mere casual use, would risk leaves separating from other leaves. Which would result in a scroll in fragments. Once in pieces, it would not necessarily be clear which piece went where. Individual pieces were easily damaged, and just as easily lost altogether, which accounts for the lacunae in many of these scroll-based books. Early inks were subject to fading over time, and not just from exposure to sun and air. This is quite apart from accidental loss due to rain or fire, or deliberate destruction, as with the sack of the library at Alexandria. Remember, before the printing press, there were few copies of any book.

Now think of oral transmission. I presume the author started with words on paper, an outline at least, and gradually found the meter, the rhythm, the poetry, to express his ideas. Gradually his poem got longer and longer, more and more complete. Until finally he was finished and was happy, and began to recite it.

He did not recite his poem for idle amusement. Homer recited his to entertain a crowd and make a living. Astrologers recited theirs in order to answer questions and make a living. What did these memorized books amount to, in actual practice?

In actual practice, an astrologer would search the verses, in his mind, until he came to one that described the situation as he understood it. He would then recite it verbatim. This is where proverbs come from: Fragments of a forgotten whole.

I regret the following are not astrological. (If anyone knows where I can find pithy astrological proverbs, in English, I would be grateful.)

Absence makes the heart grow fonder.
A bird in the hand is worth two in the bush.
A stitch in time saves nine.
One bad apple spoils the bunch.

— Etc., etc. —

By such means, an astrologer could instruct his pupil. A father could teach his son. Word for word, preserved, intact, for centuries. Up to the fall of the Roman Empire, this was, in fact, how knowledge was transmitted, from generation to generation, century to century. This was why all notable Romans wrote in verse. They were hoping to achieve immortality by means of oral transmission.

I spent some time with the Introduction in G.P. Gould's translation of Manilius's **Astronomica**. In his Preface, Gould complains that Manilius is virtually untranslatable:

> Moreover, he frequently embarks on an audacious plan of rendering diagrams, tables, and maps in hexameter form; and in these places even the best of translations would need visual aids to be readily comprehensible. (pg. vii)

You can almost hear his complaint: If only Manilius had written in Plain English, it would be so much easier to translate! But this gives the game away. **Astronomica** was intended to be memorized and recited. Tables in meter, however clumsy, could be recited and therefore remembered. Those in prose would be forgotten and lost. The author's challenge was to set his entire text not only in meter, but in the same meter, from first to last. The fate of Manilius's book was unlike that of Ptolemy's, or for that matter, Firmicus'.

At several places in his Introduction, Gould draws parallels between Manilius and Firmicus Maternus, at one point remarking that Firmicus had Manilius open in front of him as he wrote. Why did Firmicus favor Manilius, but not Ptolemy or Dorotheus?

Because Manilius was, by 340 AD, in oral transmission. Firmicus did not "have a book open" in front of him. Firmicus was reciting Manilius from memory. Which also accounts for the variations in early written copies of **Astronomica**. Different people, when they came to set the book down in writing, had been reciting it differently.

So far as I can tell, oral transmission in the west ended, and was lost, starting with the fall of the Roman Empire. The outpost in Jerusalem fell in the Crusades, the one in

Constantinople in 1453. (In India, oral transmission continues to this day, as it does in China.)

Worse, the unfortunate consequence of early Islamic conquests, the unfortunate consequence of Charlemagne's persecution of pagans, of Genghis Khan's slaughter of entire cities, was the further eradication of oral transmission in the areas that fell under the control of these ideologies.

Islam became a religion of the Book, in this case, the Koran. From Koranic studies, Islam became a religion of scholars, which it is to this day. These scholars, lacking an oral tradition, invented a new kind of learning by means of the physical books they salvaged from here and there. These they carefully copied and preserved. They then added many new works of their own. These they transmitted the to the monks of Europe and the early scholars of Spain and Italy, who also got assistance from the loot plundered by returning Crusaders. These became the basis of the first printed books centuries later.

By the time of William Lilly (17th century), all memory of oral transmission had been lost.

By these deductions, I establish the existence of an astrological oral transmission. I suspect the bulk of it verged on doggerel.

Academics will say that, well, oral books were not written down and are therefore lost and what is lost cannot be known and so cannot be studied, so what we have is the best we can do, so, please, dear Dave, get over yourself. But this is merely the excuse of weak minds. Textural analysis will prove that many early written books were transcriptions of oral books. Firmicus may well be Manilius embroidered – pieces of Manilius were actually found in Firmicus's text. More recently, my analysis of Richard Saunders' **Astrological Judgement and Practice of Physick** showed it to have been written at least 50 years prior to its first publication, which was 1677. Many early printed books were in fact centuries old hand-me-downs, but that's another story for another time.

So to return to an earlier question, how did early astrologers learn their craft?

Ancient astrologers were unanimous: They learned from Hermes Trismegistus, the mythical Egyptian sage. Holden states that Hermes was credited with 42 books, of which four concerned astronomy and astrology. All attempts to date, or even to establish the existence of Hermes, have failed. If we combine modern research with ancient opinion, we are left with the possibility that Hermes is of very great age indeed.

Next: How is oral knowledge different from written knowledge?

I have already noted that oral knowledge, in the form of proverbs, is often a doggerel recited mindlessly. From this we may conclude that oral transmission discourages analysis while it promotes conformity and consensus. Oral knowledge becomes a form of ancestor worship.

So what if, trained in the oral transmission while a youth, we grow restless as the years pass and want to actually understand what we have endlessly recited? What about the times when there was no verse for the situation at hand? When we stood naked in front of the community and our verses made us look like fools? That sort of failure can sting. It can lead to loss of position, even loss of life.

So what do we do when the verses fail? How do we avoid being the fool?

Our only hope is to look again at the verses, as those are all we know. Maybe there is some combination that will give us the answer we seek?

But here we run into problems with meter, with the very means that enabled us to memorize so easily and so precisely. If the solution is to run verse 214 into verse 65, the process will forever scramble the original verses, which will be lost. This is what commonly happens when we try to remember music in the back of our heads. We get stuck in repeats, where the music loops back on itself, rather than carry us to the final cadence.

The musical solution is to get out the score, i.e., refer to the printed page. The solution for the itinerant savant is to write out what he thinks he knows. Write out the verses. *Et voilà*, a book.

Once we have a written book in front of us, we, like Firmicus, can analyze. We can deduce. We can arrive at conclusions. We can go beyond the limitations of memory and verse. But it is a time-consuming process. Best to wait until we have that cushy appointment, the patron and his annual stipend. Let us set our deductions down in a book that will earn his undying respect, and perhaps in reward, a slave, or a daughter's hand in marriage.

The ideal solution would be oracular pronouncement, backed up, when necessary, with written analysis. A learned man should have both tools at his disposal. The modern world equates literacy with intelligence, illiteracy with poverty and deprivation. Study of oral transmission proves this to be simplistic. The ability to use the mind is the key.

Aside from rote learning of letters and numbers, many literate people have minds that function poorly. Many have short attention spans and an almost complete lack of memory. Illiterates, by contrast, often have highly developed minds and well-developed memory.

Oral tradition could be the solution for a long-standing mystery: It is known the New Testament was not written until nearly a full century after the Crucifixion. No one knows how the original Evangelists could possibly have lived so long.

But if Mark, Matthew, Luke and John composed their works in verse, those words would then have entered the oral tradition of the day. This was, after all, how most knowledge was spread at the time, since only the wealthy had actual books, and the wealthy, then as now, can rarely be bothered to read them. (I am a bookseller by profession, I know these things.) Individual sentences in the Bible are termed "verses", but I am unable to determine if the earliest versions were actually written as verse. I would appreciate help by a Biblical scholar.

Oral transmission of the new Christian doctrine would have worked fine, up until the moment it began to spread so fast that memorization could not keep up. At that point, popular demand would have forced the early Church leaders to set the Gospels down in writing, along with various other teaching materials (Paul's Letters, etc.). That they did this grudgingly is evidenced by the fact, to this day, they have set almost nothing else down. Protestants notably failed to realize there was more to the Church than the Bible, but this is enough of a digression.

— *Christmas, 2008.*

T R A N S

Oral

The Raven
by Edgar Allan Poe (apologies for being a fragment)

Once upon a midnight dreary, while I pondered weak and weary,
Over many a quaint and curious volume of forgotten lore,
While I nodded, nearly napping, suddenly there came a tapping,
As of some one gently rapping, rapping at my chamber door.
`'Tis some visitor,' I muttered, `tapping at my chamber door -
Only this, and nothing more.'

Ah, distinctly I remember it was in the bleak December,
And each separate dying ember wrought its ghost upon the floor.
Eagerly I wished the morrow; - vainly I had sought to borrow
From my books surcease of sorrow - sorrow for the lost Lenore -
For the rare and radiant maiden whom the angels named Lenore -
Nameless here for evermore.

And the silken sad uncertain rustling of each purple curtain
Thrilled me - filled me with fantastic terrors never felt before;
So that now, to still the beating of my heart, I stood repeating
`'Tis some visitor entreating entrance at my chamber door -
Some late visitor entreating entrance at my chamber door; -
This it is, and nothing more,'

Presently my soul grew stronger; hesitating then no longer,
`Sir,' said I, `or Madam, truly your forgiveness I implore;
But the fact is I was napping, and so gently you came rapping,
And so faintly you came tapping, tapping at my chamber door,
That I scarce was sure I heard you' - here I opened wide the door; -
Darkness there, and nothing more.

Deep into that darkness peering, long I stood there wondering, fearing,
Doubting, dreaming dreams no mortal ever dared to dream before;
But the silence was unbroken, and the darkness gave no token,
And the only word there spoken was the whispered word, `Lenore!'
This I whispered, and an echo murmured back the word, `Lenore!'
Merely this and nothing more. . . .

MISSION

Written

The Gettysburg Address
by Abraham Lincoln

Four score and seven years ago our fathers brought forth on this continent, a new nation, conceived in Liberty, and dedicated to the proposition that all men are created equal.

Now we are engaged in a great civil war, testing whether that nation, or any nation so conceived and so dedicated, can long endure. We are met on a great battle-field of that war. We have come to dedicate a portion of that field, as a final resting place for those who here gave their lives that that nation might live. It is altogether fitting and proper that we should do this.

But, in a larger sense, we can not dedicate -- we can not consecrate -- we can not hallow -- this ground. The brave men, living and dead, who struggled here, have consecrated it, far above our poor power to add or detract. The world will little note, nor long remember what we say here, but it can never forget what they did here. It is for us the living, rather, to be dedicated here to the unfinished work which they who fought here have thus far so nobly advanced. It is rather for us to be here dedicated to the great task remaining before us -- that from these honored dead we take increased devotion to that cause for which they gave the last full measure of devotion -- that we here highly resolve that these dead shall not have died in vain -- that this nation, under God, shall have a new birth of freedom -- and that government of the people, by the people, for the people, shall not perish from the earth.

    Lincoln's Gettysburg Address is a masterpiece of prose writing, which means it is more easily memorized than the usual best-seller. Most prose writing is so poorly done that after the passage of a few years, authors themselves do not remember what they have written.

The Excitement of Hope:
The 2009 Inaugural Chart

While we have had 44 presidents and 56 inaugurals, we have had, to date, only three Inaugural Charts. The first was on April 30, 1789, in New York. The second, from 1793 to 1933, was for Noon on March 4*, at the nation's Capital, which was originally New York. Since the 20th Amendment to the Constitution, which first took effect in January, 1937, Inauguration has been at Noon on January 20.

As the festival is once every four years at precisely the same time, the degree ascending, the degrees on the MC, and all the other house cusps, are exactly the same, from inaugural to inaugural. As the year is exactly 365 and a quarter days long, the Sun's degree and minute position is exactly the same as well. The current Inaugural Chart, the one used since 1937, now has 14°03' Taurus on the ascendant, 26°10' Capricorn on the midheaven, with the Sun at 0°47' Aquarius. Those positions, angles and Sun, advance about 30 seconds of arc per year, or about two minutes per presidential term. If you're curious, at noon on January 20, 1937, the Sun stood at 0°15' Aquarius.

The other house cusps change at the same rate. For the 2009 chart, the Placidus positions are:

ASC	**14 TAU**	**03**
2nd	12 GEM	30
3rd	04 CAN	33
IC	**26 CAN**	**10**
5th	21 LEO	52
6th	27 VIR	24
DSC	**14 SCO**	**14**

*Hat tip to an alert reader. Not March 20 as I originally wrote. I should do my homework!

The 2009 Inaugural chart

8th	12 SAG	30
9th	04 CAP	33
MC	**26 CAP**	**10**
11th	21 AQU	52
12th	27 PIS	23

Note that Aries and Libra are intercepted in the 6th and 12th.

This makes the Inaugural Chart, the chart of the incoming administration, an exercise in planetary positions, aspects and house dispositors. So let's begin:

VENUS rules the Ascendant, which represents the people, in general.

SATURN rules both the MC, in Capricorn, and the Sun, in Aquarius. The midheaven represents the Office of the President. The Sun represents the man who holds it. Note there are four degrees separating the two. Since 1 degree equals 1 year, the four degrees represent the first term.

MARS, planet of war, rules the 7th, of foreigners and foreign lands.

The MOON rules the 4th, land, weather, mineral resources. Such are the four angles.

The other mundane houses:

The 2nd house represents money.

The 3rd is transport: roads, rails, air.

The 5th is entertainment. Hollywood.

The 6th is labor and the military.

The 8th is the death rate.

The 9th is law, religion, shipping.

The 11th is Congress.

The 12th is prisons, hospitals, spies,

crime, charity.

— adapted from Raphael's **Mundane Astrology**, part of our compilation of three books on the subject.

We have a basic idea what the houses mean, and we have the signs on the cusp. So let's put them into play.

TAURUS on the ascendant, the American people love the good life, but are lazy. "Couch potato," anyone?

GEMINI on the second, financial double-dealing, budgetary slight-of-hand.

CANCER on the third, commuters.

CANCER on the 4th, "Not in my back yard."

LEO on the 5th, Presidents as entertainers, and/or babysitters.

VIRGO on 6th, fussy, complicated weapons of war.

SCORPIO on the 7th, fear of the sneak attack, i.e., Pearl Harbor, or 9-11. NORAD, in other words.

SAGITTARIUS on the 8th: In mundane astrology, the 8th is inheritances. The hopes of getting something for nothing. The stock market. Other People's Money.

CAPRICORN on the 9th: Legal and judicial systems that are bureaucratic, formalistic, and, overall, strict. Don't expect sympathy from the police.

CAPRICORN on the 10th: This is where Capricorn would be if Aries were rising. It is traditionally the house of the king. Capricorn on this cusp tends to view the President as a Sovereign, or king.

AQUARIUS on 11: Alliances and treaties based on ideals rather than realpolitik, and with a tendency to be willful and abandon them when it suits.

PISCES on 12: A belief that we are better than we are. A tendency to neglect affairs of the house (prisons, hospitals, espionage) until they are out of control.

Now we add the planetary positions for the day in question, January 20, 2009. Which were:

Sun	00 AQU	47	
Moon	29 SCO	45	*Void*
Mercury	00 AQU	41	*Cazimi/retro*
Venus	17 PIS	47	
Mars	18 CAP	29	
Jupiter	03 AQU	32	
Saturn	21 VIR	24	*Retrograde*
Uranus	19 PIS	56	
Neptune	23 AQU	05	
Pluto	01 CAP	56	
N. Node	09 AQU	20	*Retrograde*

Sun conjunct Jupiter, both in Aquarius, is exciting. Obama will be larger than life, and embody Aquarian ideals, both good and bad. Remember that Aquarians, as bright as they are, are aloof, impersonal and live in the future.

Mercury is exalted in Aquarius and Cazimi, i.e., "in the heart of the Sun" as well, which would be good for its rulership of the 2nd and 6th houses, except that it is retrograde and may therefore be expected to work, powerfully, against the best interests of American finance, defense and labor.

Ascendant ruler Venus is conjunct Uranus, both late in the 11th. Venus in Pisces is transcendental, Uranus adds a touch of the messianic. Which is hopeful, though I confess I've seen too many "saviours" in my day not to be a little on guard.

With Venus, ruler of the ascendant, in opposition to Saturn, ruler of the MC/Sun/Jupiter/Mercury/Node, expect fussy, day-to-day details to get in the way of hopes and ideals. Note that Saturn has at his disposal the Office of the President itself, as well as the laws of the land (9th house). January 20 inaugurals always give Saturn these powers, which might be why the hopes of so many administrations fail. For Obama's first term, Saturn's placement in the 6th gives Saturn the military as well.

When I added Obama's chart to the mix, things got hairy. I wrote what I thought was straightforward, but when I passed the gist of it around, I was shot down. People are in the mood to party, I was raining on the parade. So let's try something else.

The relationship of Obama's natal chart to the Inaugural chart is essentially a synastry. So I will look at it in that way. To simplify matters, we will declare Obama to be the male, the Inaugural chart to be the female. For a referee, one of the best books: **Synastry**, by Ronald Davison.

If you believe, as I do, that Obama has a void Moon in Taurus, then you will note, as I have, the Inaugural Moon, void in Scorpio, which opposes it. The Moon in the Inaugural chart represents the American people. The Inaugural chart came into effect at 11:00 pm EST on Election Day, November 4, 2008, when Senator Obama was declared the winner and won it. Of the Moons, Davison says,

> "*The unfavorable aspects* [i.e., square and opposition] *suggest conflicting habit patterns and a failure to appreciate each other's instinctive reactions to a problem situation.... The opposition can provide piquantly contrasting habit patterns, unless squares or conjunc-*

Inaugural 2009

January 20, 2009
12:00 pm (noon)
Washington DC

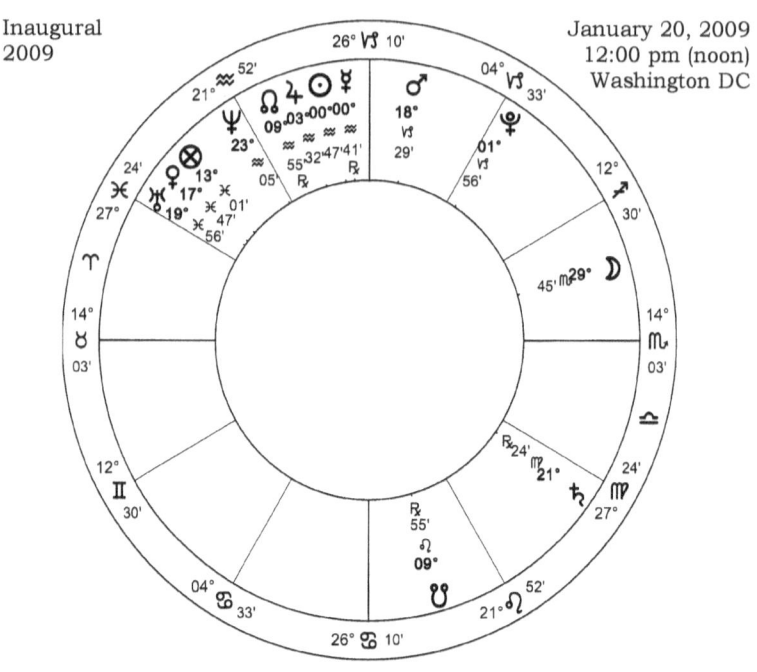

Barack Obama

August 4, 1961
7:24 pm
Honolulu, HI

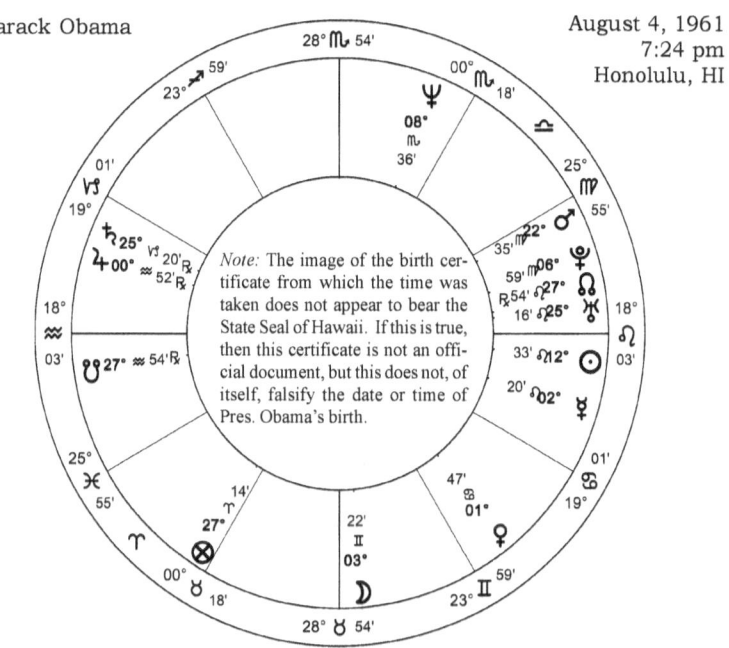

The 2009 Inaugural chart 27

tions from malefics afflict either Moon. The quincunx can indicate some fundamental lack of unity between the feelings and instincts of each partner which is difficult to counteract." (pg. 114)

If Obama has a Gemini Moon, then the Inaugural Moon is inconjunct, by sign. We get the opposition when the Inaugural Moon goes to Sagittarius. Which is in a week, by secondary progression, or in about 3 months if by solar arc. If he has a Taurus Moon, then we have an immediate lock on the piquancy of contrasts, for better or worse. In either case, look for the mood of the country to change by May, 2009.

Obama's Mars is conjunct Inaugural Saturn. Since Saturn represents the government itself, you could say that Mr. Obama's Mars has to get the government going again, and that it won't be easy. It's made harder because Saturn is retrograde (and in Terms) and so not likely to pay a lot of attention to Mars's efforts. Of this pairing, Davison says,

"No combination of planets has achieved a worse reputation in astrology." (pg. 136) and, *"When frustrated, Mars can resort to vigorous.... action to cut loose from anything that is holding him back, while Saturn may take a special delight in suddenly applying the brake to Mars in order to demonstrate his power."* (pg. 137)

And there's a flip side. Inaugural Mars in near conjunction with Obama's Saturn, both in Capricorn. So it's a double whammy of Mars and Saturn. Davison continues,

"Saturn may consider the enterprises of his Martian partner to be ill-considered and under-prepared, while Mars may consider that his Saturnian partner should do the tidying up, rectifying any omissions or mistakes committed as a result of Mars being in too much of a hurry. **The best working arrangement may be for Saturn to draw up the plans and for Mars to put them into execution.***"* (pg. 137, my emphasis)

Obama's Venus in Cancer is opposed by Inaugural Pluto in Capricorn, both at 1 degree. Here is Davison:

"If the planets are in adverse aspect or either is debilitated, this awareness [sexual] can be embarrassingly increased and Pluto's advances may become uncomfortably pressing to Venus, who always likes to act in a way pleasing to others if it can be accomplished without too much loss of comfort and composure. The con-

junction and opposition may produce situations in which the partners seem to be irresistibly drawn together for better or worse, according to the natal aspects of each planet. In some cases, Pluto may attempt to block any intimate overtures from Venus, preferring to remain aloof or to terminate a relationship that threatens to produce an emotional involvement..." (pg. 134)

Obama Mercury, debilitated in Leo, opposite Inaugural Mercury, which is retrograde:

"This contact is the main index of compatibility at the mental level... A difficult aspect between two Mercurys signifies that there is a basic difference of approach to mental problems, with the result that the thought patterns of one partner may differ radically from those of the other. There can be an element of challenge inherent in this combination leading to spirited arguments or even disagreements over fundamental intellectual issues." (pg. 122)

Obama Mars opposite Inaugural Uranus:

"This is a high tension combination that may prove a fascinating stimulus to partners who thrive on excitement, but if they should prefer a quiet life the difficult aspects can prove particularly disruptive... When the planets are in opposition, both partners have room for maneuver, so a good deal of fencing may take place, each trying to establish his position at the expense of the other. Mars usually favors the direct approach, while Uranus usually does his best to throw his opponent off guard, relying on the element of surprise." (pgs. 138-9)

So what do you think it will be? The excitement and hope of Uranus/Venus and Mars, or the frustration of Saturn/Mars? There seem to be two opinions about Mr. Obama. One, sensing the exciting aspects, is drunk on hope, the other, sensing the impotence of Mars/Saturn, is sour. Time will tell.

But no prize for noting the opposition between Obama's Leo Sun and the Inaugural Aquarius Sun, by sign. Do opposites attract, or will it be Bill Clinton (another Leo) all over again?

Now for the fun stuff. You knew it wasn't going to be all

bad. Obama Jupiter, retrograde, conjunct Inaugural Mercury, also retrograde. Here's Davison:

> "*Jupiter can support and encourage Mercury, so that it is not surprising to find that this aspect is often present in parent-child relationships. When the child's Mercury contacts a parent's Jupiter, this may denote that the child's education is likely to be a source of expense.... This is also a contact frequently met with in business partnerships, where Mercury contributes the ideas and Jupiter supplies the necessary capital and encouragement. When there is an adverse aspect or Jupiter is debilitated, Mercury's ideas and abilities may be exploited by Jupiter, who may be out to capitalize as much as possible on the relationship.*" (pg. 124)

With both these planets retrograde, whatever the two cook up will not be of practical value. This is the usual result of paired retrogrades.

Obama retrograde Jupiter conjunct Inauguration Sun:

> "*This is another aspect frequently found between the horoscopes of marriage partners.... Jupiter may know exactly how to enhance the Sun's self-esteem, though if there is an adverse aspect between the two bodies or either is debilitated* [Sun in fall, Jupiter retrograde], *Jupiter may use this factor to his own advantage, employing flattery in order to deceive or the Sun may be led astray by Jupiter's over-confidence. As a result, a lack of good faith may develop on either side.*" (pgs. 106-7)

Obama's retrograde Jupiter conjunct Inaugural Jupiter:

> "*A good aspect between two Jupiters indicates that both partners can agree on matters involving philosophy, ethics and general moral standards... If one or both Jupiters are debilitated* [i.e., retrograde], *there may be a difference of outlook on philosophy or religion or they may have different moral standards. Such differences may occasionally be the cause of disagreements. Any tendencies toward over-expansiveness in one partner may remain unchecked by, or even be encouraged by, the other, with the result that extravagances may be recklessly multiplied.*" (pg. 142)

Here ends Mr. Davison. I am hopeful a few of you will buy his book (from me, from anyone) and put money in his publisher's pocket , as payment for my abuse of his work and your enjoyment of it.

QUERIES

Q. So what about the economy?

A. To me, the charts look murky, but to Paul Krugman, the situation is clear: Obama's recovery plan, so far, at any rate, is wanting.

Q. What about war?

A. Disentangling the military is not on the cards. This is a 6th house Inaugural chart matter. Its ruler, Mercury, is retrograde. Saturn, which is in the military's house, is also retrograde, and the two planets are in mutual reception, which means they conspire to block effective action. Bill Clinton, unpopular with labor and the military, had his debilitated Mars here. Obama has his Mars conjunct the military's retrograde Saturn. Both military and labor will resist the efforts of the new president. The retrogrades mean the issue of gays in the military, gays in the workforce, will quickly return.

Elsewhere, there's Obama's Jupiter/Saturn conjunction smeared across the Inaugural MC, there is the Inaugural Sun/Moon midpoint = Pluto, which you can look up in Ebertin's **Combination of Stellar Influences** if you like. It's not exactly rosy.

Such are some of the things you can do with an Inaugural chart. You don't need astrology to know that President Barack Obama has huge tasks ahead of him. He will need all the strength, all the skills, all the wit that he can muster. He will also need our help. I wish him much success.

Extracts excerpted with permission of **Aurora Press Inc.**
from **SYNASTRY, A GUIDE TO HUMAN RELATIONSHIPS**
by Ronald Davison
Copyright Aurora Press 1983
ISBN- 978-0-943358-05-5
ALL RIGHTS RESERVED www.AuroraPress.com

— *January, 2009.*

Rectification

Last month I needed Evangeline Adams' chart. I got the place wrong (it should have been Jersey City, NJ), but there was no birth time, and I wanted that. So I rectified it to 2 pm, February 8, 1868. How did I do it?

Start with a noon chart. Note the Sun and Moon, and any stelliums. Here's a rule: People are known by their dominant house. One dominant house is typical. Two you find on occasion. More than that is rare. That house will contain the Sun, or Moon, or stellium, or possibly the ruler of the ascendant.

This makes rectification similar to horary. In horary, we first establish the house that rules the question at hand. We do the same with rectification. Evangeline Adams was known for being intelligent. That's a 3rd house/9th house thing. As Miss Adams was a full moon birth, I could set the Sun in 9 and the Moon in 3. So I did.

Which put Cancer on the ascendant. Cancers are known for having big chests. I looked at the picture on the cover of Karen Christino's book (**Foreseeing the Future**, One Reed Publications, 2002) and it looked chesty to me. I then noticed Venus in Pisces in 10, which would seem to account for her popularity. Neptune was further along in 10, which would be her fame on early radio. Moon, ruler of the ascendant in 3, and in Leo, Adams would be busy about town, a prominent person in her city of residence. Consider also angular vs: cadent houses. Angular makes for aggressive people, according to the angle. Cadent are those who blow with the wind.

Et voilà: Adams rectified to 2 pm. Is this definitive? No. More work, more questions, will produce better results.

Dear Dave

Dear Dave,
    My brother and sister-in-law have just arrived. Both have Gemini rising but sis may be Cancer, as she has the moon face of a Cancer rising.
    — *Curious in Chicago*

Dear CC,
    Check also the sun/moon. Full moons have round faces. This is from Marc Penfield, who looked at me and nailed mine at a glance.

Dear Dave,
    Bro-in law-has has Saturn on his Mars! The in-laws always talk about how laid back he is as if it were a good thing but my husband says he has no initiative, no forward momentum, squashes every plan that anyone comes up with almost as a matter of course.

    Driving with the brakes on, as Oken observed. (**Alan Oken's Complete Astrology**, *Bantam, 1980.)*

Dear Dave,
    It is little surprise that she rules the roost. I wondered about the conjunct ascendants. I guess that would make their outlook on life similar as there would be house cusps in common.

    Conjunct ascendants/identical signs on house cusps mean they experience a lot of things in the same way. They also get hit with the same house-based transits at pretty much the same time, so their lives are often in sequence. For areas of harmony and conflict, look to house-based, mundane aspects. Is what's in her 4th house compatible with what's in his 4th house, for example. If one has Mars in 4 and the other has Saturn in 4, they're going to grate, even if there's no traditional aspect between them. If they're near the same age, then the outer planets should all fall in the same houses, which gives them a feeling of being in the foxhole together, facing the world as a team. Differences come from the relative house placements of Sun, Moon, Mercury, Venus, Mars, Jupiter and Saturn. Houses, not sign to sign (or degree-based) aspects are what you're looking for. Robson gets into this, in **Astrology and Sex** *(Astrology Classics, 2004). — Dave*

— March 24, 2009

Dear Dave,
I want to ask what book(s) you recommend to learn about the Decile, Quintile, Tridecile, Sesquiquadrate, Bi-quintile, Vigintile, etc.?
— Heather in Hollywood

Dear Heather,

Minor aspects were invented by Kepler, but in my judgment they are weak. Every now and then I hear of Cosmobiology astrologers who get results with 45° and 135° (which is 3 x 45). Aspects are based on sign-to-sign relationships, and as there are only 12 signs, the number of workable aspects will be limited. Signs provide the "atmosphere" or "environment" or "framing" for planet to planet aspects. When you strip them out it doesn't leave a lot for the planets concerned to work with. Think of signs like rooms in a house. If the two of you are in the same room, you're "conjunct". If you're close enough to touch, you're in (technical) aspect. If you're close enough to kiss, well!!

If you're in adjacent rooms and if the doors are open, then you're in aspect if you're in hollering distance (trines and sextiles). If there's rooms in between, then chances of miscommunicated hollers abound (i.e., squares). If you are on opposite sides of the house, chances are good that reports of cheerful sunshine on one side will be met with reports of shade and gloom on the other.

Then there are rooms with doors that are kept closed while people are in them. The bathroom is one. The attic another, the cellar a third. I once lived in a house with four bathrooms. These are rooms in which aspects, i.e., relations between people in other rooms, are not possible.

And, of course, if you live in an apartment building, you will share at least one wall with another apartment, about which you may know little or nothing at all.

All of which is to say that "aspects" are not simple measurements of distance. The kind of aspect you have depends on the kinds of rooms (signs) you find yourselves in.

Why are squares stressful? It isn't "90°". It's the fact that both parties will be in signs of the same quality. Aries, a cardinal sign, wants to charge out in one direction. Cancer, another cardinal, wants to be cautious in another. Neither will compromise. It's not their nature. Trines and sextiles work with elements. Air gets on well with air, as well as with fire.

Happy Birthday:—
SIKKIM, born April 4, 1965, 9:52 am INT, Gangtok, India. Data from Nicholas Campion's **The Book of World Horoscopes**: Although self-governing, Sikkim is a protectorate of India, which is therefore responsible for the tiny Himalayan state's foreign affairs, defense and communications ….

— March 31, 2009.

On Charles Carter's
The Principles of Astrology

One of the best written, most masterful books on astrology is Charles Carter's **Principles of Astrology**, but it's been out of print for decades. While many of his other books are still in print – **Aspects, Foundations, Symbolic Directions, Mundane, Encyclopaedia**, etc., Carter's **Principles** is the book that puts them all into context.

The **Principles of Astrology** was first published in 1925, with revisions in 1931 and 1939. The type in my 1939 edition is cramped and ungainly, so I am resetting it in modern type. I should be finished by May. The book is intended for learners, but scattered throughout are keen insights and hard-won lessons. Here's an example:

The Grand Trine
It sometimes happens that two bodies are in trine and a third body is in trine with each. Such a configuration was considered very evil by medieval writers and unfortunately this view appears to be often correct. Often there seems to be too great dependence upon others.

Think about this for a moment. We've all been told, the more trines the merrier, and, Grand Trines, Kites (where a planet is sextile to two and opposed to the third) is Even Better. But have you ever seen that to work in practice? Carter hasn't. And I haven't. My youngest sister, 44 this January, has a fabulous kite: Mercury, Venus, Jupiter, Uranus, Pluto all within 2 degrees, Neptune 4 degrees out, with Moon, Mars and Saturn wide, all in earth and water. (Work it out.) Yet she lives in a trailer and has no family of her own.

This is just one of many surprises Carter has in store. Why this book was ever out of print is beyond me.

Hot Tips in Real Estate
an occasional feature

There's so much work to be done house training the psychological crowd, that I was happy, darn happy, when Hindsight and the Back to the Past crowd came along. Hellenistic astrology might not have all the answers and might not be to everyone's taste, but they were doing yeoman's work.

Or so I thought. Turns out, they've no better idea what to do with houses than their immediate predecessors. This shocked me. I thought the Greeks knew. Turns out, they didn't, and their proponents don't, either. Houses are where signs and elements, qualities and dispositors, individual degrees, faces, sect and even aspects all come together and dance. Houses are the essential framework we've all been looking for. Houses are of extraordinary importance. If the Greeks didn't "get it", I wanted to know why.

As Hellenistic astrology is currently understood, Greek houses are based on the rising sign. The entire sign, starting at 0 degrees, ending at 30. The other eleven houses are the other eleven signs.

Hellenistic astrology makes no use of the midheaven. Why? Because the Greeks had no reliable means of finding it, and, in their experience, it was rarely more than a few degrees different from 90^0 anyway.

This was in part because they had no clocks. Daytime could be had with a sundial, but at night, or on cloudy days, there was only the clepsydra, the water-clock. To have any accuracy, water-clocks had to be set to a sundial, either at commencement, or at some point before they ran out of water. When the water ran out, time-keeping ended. Even among the nobility, timed births were rare. Which is why

Hot Tips in Real Estate   37

the Greeks had so many (mostly useless) rectification techniques. They had to. (If you were wondering how they knew where the planets were, the answer is they had mechanical computers. The rusted remains of a handful have been found, though, to date, they are misidentified.)

Then there was the matter of latitude above (or below) the equator. In tropical climes (23° N/S of the equator), the sun rises straight up out of the ground, goes directly overhead, then dives straight back in at sunset. In this area of the world, it makes no difference what house system you use. All house systems are equal. Literally.

Which is a good thing, because the math needed for the fancy spherical trig to calculate houses was unknown to the Greeks. And you will never guess why.

The Greeks, like the Romans, had no practical numerical system. The Greeks had Attic numerals. These were hash marks, combined with the first letter for the words, "five", "ten", "fifty", "hundred", etc. Four was IIII. Forty was TIIII ("T for ten"). 257 was IIH-F-IIIIIII. Or some such. Roman numerals were actually an improvement, and for the rest of this example I will use them in place of the Attic.

A simple house division system is to trisect the angle between ascendant and midheaven. So, suppose the ascendant is CXV, and the MC is CCCXXII, where [ ] is 0 Aries (remember, neither Greeks nor Romans had a zero). The arc is CXVII. Trisecting this (the Porphyry method) gives cusps that are XXXIX degrees each. All you need do now is add XXXIX to the observed MC, CCCXXII, to get the XI house cusp. Which is CCCLXI. As this is more than CCCLX, we subtract CCCLX to get I. Which in modern notation is 1 Aries.

In the Attic system of numbers, this house system, as simple as it is, was impractical to compute. It did not arise until the 3rd century, by which time Attic numerals had been replaced, among the Greeks, by the somewhat easier Romans.

The upshot was the Greeks weren't all that interested in computing actual house cusps, even presuming they could find the MC to start with. And they didn't need to, anyway. Despite what you might think, Greek astrology wasn't based in Athens, but in Alexandria. Athens is 38° N. Alexandria is

31°. At 31°, equal houses work well-enough that the alternative – dealing with all those cumbersome Roman numbers – wasn't worth it. This is just as true with Vedic astrology. Ujjain, the traditional center of Indian astrology, is 23°N. In India, all house systems produce equal houses. All hours of the day. All days of the year. (Try it!) Which means that house development in India and Greece was stunted. It never got started.

The Europeans developed many house systems. The first question is, why?
Rome is 42°N. Paris is 48°N. London is 51°N. The sun simply doesn't work the same way in these climes, as it does further south. It wasn't that they didn't know about Hellenistic houses. The only astrology books the Europeans had were Hellenistic, as handed down to them by the tireless Arabs. It was that, for the Europeans, equal houses did not work. They needed a midheaven and houses calculated with it, but they were stuck with useless Roman numerals.

This changed abruptly with the introduction of "Arabic" numbers (actually Hindu) and their promotion by the Italian, Fibonacci, starting in 1202. Immediately came Campanus houses. Regiomontanus, the first "modern" system, arrived in the 15th century. Morin devised his own system in the 17th century, though it seems he was the only one who ever used it. About the same time Placido de Titis developed the (very sophisticated) Placidian system. These were the results of steady advances in mathematics, made possible by the modern number system. In the 20th century, A.P. Nelson Page and Vendel Polich jointly developed Topocentric, a system almost identical to Placidus. Both were intended to flesh out Ptolemy's sketchy ideas about Primary Directions. Which is to say, the Greeks would have got here ages earlier, if only they had clocks and a decent number system!

It is therefore alarming that modern Hellenistic astrologers are ignorant of these essential facts. Equal houses do not work in the latitudes in which most people are born, live, work, and die. That's why they were abandoned.

The development of a true house-based astrology cannot be done using crude Hellenistic and Vedic charts. It is critically dependent on proper house division. It only got underway in the late 19th century, and is still far from generally known. We first needed a proper house system (Placidus). Then we had to puzzle out how to use it, and then we had to integrate the rest of astrology to it. This has taken, so far, the better part of 300 years. The resulting system, which I myself know well, is based on simple, fundamental astrological basics. It is the most powerful system of astrology I have ever found.

Yet, modern ignorance abounds. For most astrologers, houses are simply things that "turn up", like gum on the bottom of your shoe. The German school (Witte, Lefeldt, Ebertin, along with Geoffrey Dean) is emphatic. Houses do not exist. The "modified" German school of the 1970's – Walter Koch, et al – is of the opinion that house cusps should mark transiting planet ingresses, and this is, indeed, a limited, but good use of them (see Joyce Wehrman's **What Are Winning Transits**). Modern Hellenistic astrologers spring from these roots. They have 2000 years of catching up to do!

April 16 birthdays:
Anatole France, 1844
Wilbur Wright, 1867
Charlie Chaplin, 1889
Merce Cunningham, 1919
Joseph Alois Ratzinger, 1927. *Happy birthday to the Pope!*

— *April 14, 2009*

Dancing Lessons

1. How the world sees you

Dancing is what I call the interplay of houses, their rulers, and the sign and house their dispositors are in. Learn to dance and charts will tell you amazing things. Let's start at the beginning. All else being equal, the house and sign of the Ruler of the Ascendant, aka Ruler of the Horoscope, is one of the most important points in the entire chart.

Ruler of the First in the FIRST:
This reinforces the sign on the ascendant. A Leo Sun, born at sunrise, is more of a Leo. Mercury in Virgo, Virgo rising, is more of a Virgo. Venus rising, Venus in Libra in the first, is always pleasant and good natured, at least on the surface (Bill Clinton, anyone?).

Ruler of the First in the SECOND:
Known for their money. What kind of money, you ask? Depends on the signs and rulers. Gemini rising, Mercury in Cancer in 2, a petty thief, perhaps. Work it out: Gemini is two-faced, Mercury makes for small-scale and light fingers, Cancer takes its money personally, and the second house is money. A pickpocket. Virgo rising, Mercury in 2 in Libra? Donates exact amounts.

Ruler of the First in the THIRD:
Is big shot. You don't follow? Third house is day-to-day life. Running around town, brothers and sisters, ordinary smarts, etc. First house magnifies that, so we run around town big-time. How? Look at the planets and signs

involved. Libra rising, Venus in Sag in 3, with grace and flair and a touch of *je ne sais quoi*, i.e., the exotic. More pronounced when ruler is sextile to the rising degree.

Ruler of the First in the FOURTH:
Is a homebody. What kind of home, what kind of body? Suppose it's Sag on the ascendant and Jupiter in Pisces in 4: A messy house full of religious icons and foreign souvenirs. Signs in square tend to fight each other, when the ruler is square the house it rules, things are stressful. More so when the ruler is actually square by degree to the ascendant.

Ruler of the First in the FIFTH:
Is a playboy, but not one you've ever heard of, as Hef had to work at it. When the ruler of the first is in the 5th you don't have to, you just are. Lucky with kids. Natural at gambling, but look to aspects to the ruler to know if they win or not. The closer to a perfect trine, the "smoother" they are.

Ruler of the First in the SIXTH:
Has a life of work. Likes small animals. Might be a cook. If the aspects to the ruler bring skill sets, could take up medicine. If the ruler is stressed, look for hypochondria.

Ruler of the First in the SEVENTH:
When the ruler is in the house opposite, that ruler is, by definition, in debility. It's going to wish it was in the house (sign) opposite, where it would rule. Ruler of the first in the seventh, the spouse is the boss, precisely because the debilitated ruler wants the spouse to run his chart. What kind of boss? Libra rising, Venus in Aries in 7, partners are aggressive, so, as a result, you (Libra rising chap) come with baggage and are never as nice as you seem.

Ruler of the First in the EIGHTH:
Other people's money, for better or worse. Capricorn rising, Saturn in Leo in 8, I'd be careful letting that man handle my money. Leo rising, Sun in Pisces in 8: known as a clairvoyant.

Ruler of the First in the NINTH:

Lives abroad if he can. Is brilliant and/or weird in any case. This is more pronounced as the aspect from ruler to rising degree gets closer to a trine.

Ruler of the First in the TENTH:

Lives in public. Has little private life. The closer the ruler is to exactly square the rising degree, the less he likes it, but the less control he has over it.

Ruler of the First in the ELEVENTH:

Lives for his friends. What kind of friends? Again, look at the ruler and the signs involved. Scorpio rising, Mars in Virgo in 11, picks fights with friends. Thinks he can do better than they can.

Ruler of the First in the TWELFTH:

Lives in secret. Is this good or bad? Depends on point of view. In a weak chart, there is frustration at being "held back". In a strong chart, there is cunning.

Aspects to rulers are critical. Why do people think I'm smart and put their trust in me? Ascendant ruler in the 9th is smart. Ruler trine Saturn is trust. Both trine to the ascending degree makes it certain. Never mind that it always amazes me. **Note well:** Rulers and dispositors work regardless of "aspect". Dispositors define houses by relating one sign to another sign. The better you know signs, as distinct from houses, the better this works.

April 22 Birthdays:
Glen Campbell, 1936
Marilyn Chambers, 1952. (*Died, April 12, 2009.*)
Ryan Stiles, 1959

— *April 21, 2009*

Dancing Lessons

2. Where the money comes from

Learn to read the second house and even jaded astrologers like me will sit up and take notice. There are more self-serving excuses, lies and outright denial associated with the money house than in all the rest of the chart.

Start with the element on the cusp. An earth sign on the cusp of 2 is practical. A water sign is emotional. A fire sign burns through money and doesn't care, an air sign has trouble connecting with it altogether.

The house and sign of the ruler of the 2nd tells you where the money comes from and how the individual handles it.

Ruler of the Second in the THIRD

The smarter you are, the richer you will be, or so you think. (The education trap.) Or, the more you run around town (local transport), the richer you will be. Or financial partnership with brothers and/or sisters.

But in practice it doesn't always work that way. Suppose Cancer is on the 2nd. Cancer says it's MY MONEY, keep your mitts off! (i.e., is possessive). Moon in Leo in 3, the more education you get, the more money you feel you should make. Both proud and possessive. Now look at aspects to that ruler. A 9th house opposition to a 2nd house ruler in the third means your smarts are unappreciated and you are eternally passed over. Squares to the ruler mean that, however smart you are, you never quite get the money you think you deserve, and the problems, in this specific case, stem from planets in the 6th and 12th houses, as planets in those houses are in square to 3, which is where your money (2) comes from. You're either sickly (6th) or are stuck in an institution (12th — the army?) where the bureaucracy limits your ability to make the money you desire.

Robert Blaschke is an interesting case. He published his horoscope in his **Volume 3**, but I will not give it here. Using my methods, where the whole sign is the house, the (Placidus) cusp merely the most intense degree of the house, Mr. Blaschke has 2nd and 3rd house rulers in mutual reception. Mutual reception binds the houses together. (Binds the houses, not the signs! This is an important distinction.) As a result, the more Blaschke tours (3), the more books he publishes (3), the more readings he gives (3), the more money (2) he makes. When he doesn't, he goes quickly broke. **Mutual disposition make for intensity between the two houses in question.**

Ruler of the Second in the FOURTH

If the second house is water, the fourth house will be earth. Farmers. Landlords. The relationship is a sextile. This often works very well, as one would expect of a sextile. Cancer on 2, Moon in Virgo in 4, a fussy landlord. Scorpio on 2, Mars in Capricorn in 4, an ambitious one. Pisces on 2, Jupiter in 4 in Taurus, a lazy one that makes lots of money. Note the first pair is cardinal/mutable, the second is fixed/cardinal, and the third mutable/fixed.

Shift this a bit. Put a fire sign on 2, the ruler (Sun/Mars/Jupiter) in an air sign in 4. Farming is out, because air and fire signs are infertile. Intellectual activity in the home becomes a source of income.

Ruler of the Second in the FIFTH

Income is from gambling, speculation, or sex. I.e., prostitution, to put it bluntly. Why are these avenues of income frowned upon? Consider that the 2nd and 5th houses are in square to each other. If one can handle the stress, much money can be made — or lost.

Ruler of the Second in the SIXTH

Income from food/cooking, or medicine, or from small animals, such as pets. Since the relationship between the two houses is a trine, this can sometimes be too much of a good thing. The doctor who has too many patients, or the chef who is his own best customer, can both experience health problems. Which are 6th house! Both houses in earth, we have the practical chef or simple doctor. Both in water, the chef specializes in sauces — or booze. Both in air, the doctor is an intellect, more interested in technique than healthy patients. Both in fire, a great deal of enthusiasm, but a tendency to burn out in one's career.

This "Dance of Rulers and Dispositors" produces an amazing amount of detail. Aspects, by contrast, are vague. Alan Oken, my favorite aspect delineator, can only say, *Will Unites With Consolidation!* or, *Will Challenges Expansion!* or, *Will Versus Consolidation!* Which are all fine as far as they go, but tell you little by comparison to what you will get from house rulers and their dispositors.

Astrology and Number

Not an article on numerology, apologies

Two weeks ago in the April 14 issue, I touched on the Greek way with houses (**Hot Tips in Real Estate**). Turns out, Greeks didn't have sophisticated house division because they didn't have the numbers that would generate them.

And then I thought, what about the Chinese and their strange astrology? Animals and stems and branches. What were their numbers like? Turns out, Chinese numbers were even worse than Greek numbers. To express the number, 863, for example, the Chinese would write, (8x100)+(6x10)+3. Which isn't a notation system at all, actually. In practice, the Chinese would write, 8H-6T-3, where 'H' is hundred and 'T' is ten. This was so unwieldy that, for multiplication and division, the Chinese invented the abacus. Which they also found useful for simple sums.

So let's take a quick and dirty look at Chinese astrology. Beijing is 40 degrees north – same as Philadelphia. At that latitude, equal houses won't work. (*Sorry, Hellenists!*) Lacking a proper number system, the best the Chinese could do seems to have been what they actually did. Chinese astrology is unique and for mundane affairs, effective, but it has only a tenuous connection to the sky because they had not the numbers to represent it. So far as the demanding uses, Chinese astrology fails.

But then, what about Vedic astrology? In equatorial climes, houses never got developed at all, but on the other hand, the combination of clever minds and a fabulous number system (which India, not the Arabs, invented) resulted in purely mathematical astrological representations. In other words, Vimshottari and Yogini and all the other dasa systems, along with Ashtakavarga and myriad other number (not sky) based systems.

Which means that Europeans, blessed with India's number system and cursed with northern latitudes, have created a unique, sky-based astrology. This is not to fault the Vedic, the Chinese, the Tibetan, the Mayan, the Persian, the Native American and all the many other variants. But it is to say that if you're a western astrologer, you have nothing to apologize for. Get out there and learn it! There's more than you ever suspected, waiting for you.

April 30 in history:
1812, Louisiana becomes the 18th state.

Birthdays:
Willie Nelson, 1933.
Bugs Bunny, 1938.

State of Play

*Dave's heavily revised view of things,
as of the moment*

In the Christmas 2008 newsletter, I proposed a revised history of astrology, one based on poetry and centuries of oral tradition.

Over the last three weeks, I have shown the importance of number as it relates to houses and how house delineation relates to the ongoing development of Astrological Theory. In real time.

What happens if we combine these?

First, we see that astrology neither began, nor ended, with the Hellenists. Nor is Vedic astrology "better" than European. Both of these were developed for local conditions. Not planet-wide use.

Instead, we see medieval Europeans developing Alexandrian astrology (a more accurate term than Hellenistic) not only to suit the needs of Europeans, but in the process, furthering astrological theory in general.

Strictly speaking, Alexandrian astrology was an offshoot of Vedic, since Vedic was suited for the equatorial climes where it was practiced, whereas Greek astrology was clearly not. Greek astrology was an unsatisfactory adaptation.

The Greek system initially failed to make much impression with the Europeans — or anybody else — precisely because Europeans lacked a counting system that would enable them to describe their northern skies in a convenient fashion. This was solved in 1202 with the introduction of "Arabic" numerals. Which, in the centuries since they were developed in India (sometime prior to the 4th century AD), has displaced all other counting systems. Utterly and without exception.

The Europeans used the Indian number system to develop astrological house theory, first by struggling to find a house system which would support Primary Directions. Which the Greeks themselves had observed, but were largely unable to make use of.

The next step, which has been underway since Jean-Baptiste Morin, uses sophisticated house delineation to augment the existing, incomplete astrological structure, the one based on signs and aspects (which we know so well), to develop one that puts houses, and house delineation, in the very center of things.

What's curious about this is that the twelve houses themselves, the ignored and forgotten corner of astrology, have been waiting patiently ever since astrology first arrived on the scene, thousands of years ago. When I read a chart using rulers and dispositors (and in the process, amazing everyone in the room), I am not inventing anything new. I am not reaching out for unknown bodies and ascribing magical powers to them. I am not using murky psychological constructs. I am using the purest, the simplest, the plainest nuts-and-bolts astrology. Yes, it's sophisticated, and, yes, the exact details of any delineation are open to opinion, but this is nothing different than the structure of a great novel, or the struggle to compose — and then perform — a great symphony. All are sophisticated. All require mastery of, and attention to, minute detail, in order to produce the final result.

And what amazes me is that this seed, this kernel, in other words, the houses I know and use so well, remained hidden until recently. How could this possibly be? Was astrology a divine revelation? Hindus think so, to this day. Increasingly I agree.

So where do we go from here? Seems to me that first we delineate the personality, using Tropical house rulers and dispositors as the primary means. In the process we easily rectify the chart, should that need to be done.

Next we employ Sidereal Vedic forecasting methods, supported by Gochara (i.e., transits) and whatever symbolic methods (Directions) as we may desire. We do things this way because only when we know the native can we make forecasts for him. Late medieval astrology, not Hellenistic, becomes our starting point. Then we add Vedic. And then Hellenistic. Why not? The more tools, the better. The result will truly be a WORLD ASTROLOGY.

— April 28, 2009

Gardening

The dates apply to 2009.

Gardening has some simple rules: Things grow from new moon to full (waxing). Not so much from full to new (waning). Plant in a fertile sign when the moon is waxing, you will get better results. Conversely, harvest in an infertile sign when the moon is waning and you will avoid rot.

The fertile signs are the water signs:

Cancer, Scorpio, Pisces, and,

Taurus, which, while earth, is almost as good.

Put fertile signs with waxing moon and you get April 28, 29 and 30 (Cancer), and May 7, 8, 9 (Scorpio) as good planting days.

Looking ahead, May 26 and 27 (Cancer), and June 4 and 5 (Scorpio) will be good days.

Root crops, such as potatoes, carrots, beets, onions, etc., where you want underground growth, are best planted in fertile signs when the moon is waning, such as May 14 and 15 (Pisces), June 11 and 12 (Pisces).

Pretty things, like flowers, are planted in a waxing moon in Taurus or Libra, signs of pretty things: May 5, 6 and 7 (Libra), June 1, 2 and 3 (Libra).

The late Louise Riotte, of Oklahoma, wrote books on planetary planting, but they are all out of print, though other books of hers remain in print. She said to plant trees under Taurus, and vines in Virgo.

My garden has yet to be started. Strawberries survived the winter and have white flowers. I just have to rescue them from drowning in massive dandelions.

♀ Fertility ♂

Human, that is, has almost the same rules. You're more likely to get pregnant when the Moon is in a fertile sign, especially if the exact degree is conjunct, square, or opposed to the exact degree of your 5th house cusp (use both Koch and Placidus), or the planet ruling the 5th, or any planets in the 5th.

You are less likely to end up in a family way if the Moon is in air or fire signs, which are (mostly) infertile, or when the Moon makes no aspects to the 5th cusp, or to the relevant planet(s). **These rules apply to boys just as much as girls,** so if you're planning a hot date, beware!

— *May 4, 2009*

On Zodiacs

My daughter is home schooled, which is not what you might think. The local home-schoolers arrange numerous field trips and special events.

Which is how I found myself, this past Tuesday, in a middle school planetarium listening to a teacher telling us that *your sun sign isn't your real sun sign* and that *there's really 13 signs in the zodiac, not 12.* We've all heard this before.

But he had a point, however murky. Astrologers have been lazy in not defining the zodiac for ourselves (as well as for the rest of the world), and it's past time to sort out some basics.

On Zodiacs

Such as, is the zodiac made up of stars in the sky, or do equinoxes and solstices trump them?

Based on the observation that sidereal astrologers seem to make little use of signs, I came to the conclusion that Zodiacs, in general, show the relationship between two bodies, one of which is in orbit around the other. Zodiacs are then expressed in numbers and units that are appropriate to the location of the observer in question.

This formula can produce unique zodiacs for Mars, for Jupiter, for Saturn, as well as for each and every moon in the solar system.

It also means the *"constellations of the zodiac"* are merely a convenient backdrop upon which the Earth/Sun relationship was projected some 2000 years ago. This also makes sense. Why should an arrangement of stars in the sky have any meaning at all? (With the exception of the Pleiades, which actually are physically close to one another.) Name me a star that embodies any of the signs of the zodiac. There isn't one!

So how many zodiacs do we have on Planet Earth? Two? Tropical and Sidereal? No. The Earth has a Moon. It goes around every 28 days. The Earth and Moon have a relationship and therefore a zodiac. We know it as the Lunar Mansions, aka Nakshatras. There are 27 or 28 of them, depending on who you talk to.

So next time the man says, *There's really 13 signs,* tell him, **Signs have nothing to do with constellations.**

May 13th: HAPPY BIRTHDAY Mike Gravel, 1930

— May 12, 2009.

Dancing Lessons

3. *Techniques*

Dancing is what I call the interplay of house cusps, signs, ruling planets, dispositors, aspects and more. Dancing happens when we use the framework of the twelve houses to integrate and combine otherwise isolated astrological features. When we do that, we get, for the first time, the whole. Learn to dance and the world will never be the same!

Because there are a lot of pieces to keep track of, I use keywords. Simple keywords. Sun is life, or men. Moon is feeling, or women. Mercury is information, or youth. Venus is what is pretty. Mars is aggressive and pushy. Jupiter is a lot of. Saturn is NO.

Cardinal signs are active, fixed signs stay put, mutable signs are confused. Conjunctions push the two planets together; with sextiles and trines they wave at each other, squares are stress, oppositions are confrontations. Early degrees are youthful and inexperienced. Middle degrees are solid and dependable. Late degrees are old and senile.

So when I see Capricorn on the cusp of 2, with Saturn ruling from Gemini in 7, I take keywords and string them together in a sentence. The process goes like this:

Capricorn on 2 is a busy worker bee. For instruction it looks to its ruler, Saturn, which it finds in the 7th. Seventh is wife (or husband), Gemini is mindless chatter, Saturn is NO. Which becomes:

Efforts to make money (Capricorn) are undermined (2 to 7 is inconjunct) by the wife's constant chatter (Gemini) and useless ideas (i.e., Saturn says, NO).

But this takes practice. I got it with Astrodice. Which

are three 12-sided dies, one with planets (including nodes), one with houses, one with signs. Roll all three of them, give yourself 30 seconds (5 *seconds!*) to synthesize and orally state the result. *Hint:* Stream-of-consciousness-wild-guesses are usually better than you think. Fun at parties (or meetings) where the first one to shout out a solution wins that round.

Happy Birthday William Lilly!

Born April 30, May 1, May 5 AND May 6, of 1602. (See John Gadbury's notes in **Collectio Genitorum**, London, 1662.) As those dates are in Old Style, add ten days to get proper Gregorian dates. Which are: May 9, May 11, May 15 AND May 16, of 1602. Let's just give Bill the whole month of May.

— *May 12, 2009*

Transits were unknown to the ancients because they had no ephemerides. The most obvious things!!! That's what I learned this week peeking at Wilson and DeVore. Primaries, secondaries, solar arcs, were all make-dos.

At the rate of 1 degree every 72 years, stars change signs every 2160 years: Alcyone changed from Taurus to Gemini in 2000.

HAPPY BIRTHDAY
May 20:
Cherilyn Bono, *née Sarkisian*

— *May 19, 2009*

Eclipse Season

(*The dates are for 2009.*)

It's eclipse season! Lunar eclipse the 7th, solar on the 21st. Everyone wants to know What The Eclipse Will Do in My Natal Chart. Old hands will say they don't often do very much of anything. Two important points:

If the solar eclipse of 21 July, at 29 ♋ 27, is exactly on your ascendant, but months pass and "nothing happens", your birth time is wrong, by at least a degree, if not more.

If it is exactly conjunct a planet which is NOT angular, nothing of consequence may happen. Such is what happened to Bill Clinton in 1998: Solar eclipse directly on his 11th house Sun. A notable Arizona/Minneapolis operatic astrologer (is that enough of a hint?) publicly predicted that Bill would resign. Bill refused to follow the script. Had it been on his Libran Venus, which is Bill's chart ruler and disposes virtually every planet in his chart, I suspect it would have been a different story.

Want to find out if you've ever had a solar eclipse directly on a sensitive point in your chart? If the period from 1800 to 2000 will do, see pages 155-164 in DeVore's **Encyclopedia of Astrology**. For more recent dates, grab your ephemeris and look them up. There aren't that many.

Eclipses: Mundane

The effects of eclipses in mundane astrology, i.e., politics, can be huge. Raphael's delineations, by decanate, which I think he cribbed from Lilly (who may well have cribbed himself) are standard. For Tuesday's lunar eclipse at 15 ♑ 24, Raphael says, *"Brings frequent incursions and assaults of soldiers, robberies and captivities."* Which I presume means bad news from Iraq, Afghanistan and Pakistan. Let's hope not. As Capricorn is opposite Cancer, and as Cancer is the American Sun, the soldiers and incursions might be to the USA's favor. Time will tell.

— July 7, 2009

Vive le Bastille!

France is another country. I love the place. I love the people. I love the culture. The first Bastille, a riot that destroyed a hated prison, was July 14, 1789. Ever the ultimate arbiters in matters of taste and style, the French had their first Bastille day celebration the very next year.

July 14, 1789 had almost as powerful an impact on Vienna as it did on Paris. Here is why: The French queen, Marie Antoinette, was the youngest daughter of Maria Therese, the most powerful monarch Austria ever had. Marie Antoinette's eldest brother, Joseph II, was in fact the Austrian ruler (1765-90) at the time. During his reign Vienna came to resemble Weimar Berlin, i.e., immorality and political unrest became problems. He was succeeded by his brother, Leopold II. Horrified and panicked at the fate of their sister in Versailles and fearing they could be next, they set about cleaning up Vienna. In typical Viennese fashion.

Vienna quietly "encouraged" the worst of the miscreants to leave town. Lorenzo Da Ponte, one of Mozart's librettist's, fled. He ended up in America and is buried in Brooklyn.

Mozart, a prime target, thought he could tough it out. That he was bigger than they were. So, all through 1791 he put on ceaseless concerts and operas. He did this in the face of government rumors that he had been poisoned, while falling for the inspired joke of writing his own funeral music.

At last patience ran out. Just after midnight on December 5,1791, a fake death certificate was served (tuberculosis), Mozart was manhandled into a public hearse and spent rest of the night in terror at Vienna's public cemetery. He fled for Prague at dawn.

Vive le Bastille!

He returned 18 months later as a phony Dane and thereafter played cat and mouse. When the Danes found out, he spent 1812 to 1820 as their "guest" in Copenhagen. Mozart ultimately died, aged 70, on March 24, 1826, in Salzburg, where he is buried. Such is what the Bastille did to Wolfgang Mozart. *Vive le Bastille!*

July 14:
1789: 7 prisoners freed.
1790: 7 prisoners celebrate.
1862: Gustav Klimt born.
1881: Billy the Kid shot.

Tropical *versus* Sidereal

Dr. H phoned this past week. He told me of a new book on Primaries, to be published by Wessex Astrologer. He also told me about Michael Erlewine's ACT Astrology blog, which he said was moribund, except for a lively Hellenistic Astrology section.

So I went and had a look. There I found T.H. and D.K. hashing out Tropical vs: Sidereal.

I had thought this settled long ago. Tropical is an arbitrary, make-believe system that has nothing to do with the actual zodiac. Such is what everyone believes. Sidereal is based on Spica as the fiducial star (i.e., marker) as being 30° Virgo.

It's said that Tropical is based on the Spring Equinox, when the Sun's declination crosses the Earth's equator and goes north, which is declared to be 0° Aries. But this is not the whole story.

Tropical also notes the Sun's maximum northward declination and declares this to be 0° Cancer. Tropical therefore marks the Earth's four seasons by means of the Sun's declination. Where it gets tricky is the fact the Earth's seasons are not equal in length.

The reason they're not equal is because the Earth's orbit, like that of all planets, is not circular. It's elliptical. Sometimes we're closer to the Sun (perihelion). Sometimes we're further away (aphelion). The exact dates, i.e., positions of perihelion/aphelion, like the Moon's nodes, change over time.

At perihelion (closest), we're going faster, which means the Sun travels more than a degree a day. At aphelion (furthest), we're travelling slower, which means the Sun appears to move less than a degree a day. Expressed in zodiacal notation, these days are pretty much opposite. Do you understand so far?

Now: If perihelion/aphelion dates fall around the dates of solstices (December/June), spring and fall are of equal length.

When perihelion/aphelion fall around equinox dates (March/September), winter and summer are equal.

Tropical, which fixes the Earth/Sun relationship at four distinct times every year, shows this. Sidereal, based on a single star, does not.

According to Neil Michelsen (**Tables of Planetary Phenomena**), in 2009, perihelion was January 4. Aphelion was July 4. The dates advance at a rate of about 2 days a century. This past winter was exactly 2126:40 hours long, or 88 days, 12-some hours. This summer will be 2247:32 hours, or 93 days, 15-ish hours.

Expressed in astrological terms, currently, in winter, the Sun moves, on average, a hair under 59 minutes a day. In summer, the Sun moves an average of 60 and one half minutes per day, but *only* in the Tropical zodiac. In Sidereal, the Sun moves at a uniform rate, a hair over exactly 60 minutes per day, all year 'round. Again, this is because Tropical is based on Sun's declination, as well as speed, which is based on the perigee and apogee of the Earth's orbit. Sidereal is based on Spica, or Aldebaran.

So you could say that Tropical is Geocentric, while Sidereal is Heliocentric. And though you would not be exactly right, you would not be far wrong.

So what does this mean for your typical Leo?

We presumed signs of the zodiac were stars in the sky, but if the Tropical zodiac is based on the Sun's declination, then Tropical signs are, too. Zero degrees of Cancer is the Sun's maximum north declination. In Tropical, that's what it's always been and what it always will be. The distance from a Tropical degree, to any star, is a variable.

In other words, in the Tropical zodiac, signs show the relationship between Earth and Sun and are projected against a backdrop of stars, in the same way a movie is projected on a screen. The stars that make up the constellation "Leo" are no more "Leo" than your local movie theatre is "Humphrey

Bogart" merely because your grandmother once saw Casablanca on it. You can say that if it's 8 o'clock on a Saturday night, there's a movie on every screen, just as you can say that every star within 23° N/S of the equator is in one or another of the signs of the (Tropical) zodiac. Exactly which movie is on which screen, which star is in which sign, depends on the date. Check your local listings.

Signs of the Tropical zodiac are symbolic, not actual They represent the annual, on-going relationship between the Earth and Sun. The Sidereal zodiac is entirely different. T.H. says there's some things that Sidereal just does better, and I think she has a point. Give each their due!

July 14:
1927: John Chancellor born.
1938: Jerry Rubin born.
1939: Alphonse Mucha dies.
Feast day of St. Ulrich of Zell.

Birthdays
July 21: Ernest Hemmingway, 1899.
July 22: Rose Kennedy, 1890.
July 23: Pee Wee Reese, 1918, and Don Imus, 1940
July 24: Amelia Earhart, 1897.
July 26: Aldous Huxley.
July 27: Confucius, 550 B C

— *July 14, 2009*

Astrology in the News

This week, it's the ancient Greek Antikythera mechanism, a strange assortment of gears found by sponge divers off a Greek island in 1901.

What brings this ancient find back into the news is a new animation, by Massimo Mogi Vicentini, of how it was constructed and employed. It's impressive. Jo Marchant is using it to further promote himself and his new book, **Decoding The Heavens**, at the expense, it seems, of other envious researchers. ("Science" as an ego trip.)

Doing a bit of background reading on Wiki, I learn this was not the only machine of its type, but is, to date, the only one that has been found.

The purpose of the machine, which calculates the positions of sun, moon, planets and eclipses, is said to be a "mystery", but it is a mystery easily solved.

Given that astrologers need accurate planetary positions, and, (my own observation) given the Greek number system was unsuited for the advanced computations necessary for accurate planetary positions, given there were no such things as printed ephemerides, we may therefore guess that a clockwork mechanism, such as this, was the astrological software of its day. The only question is, how many charts did it calculate, in other words, what percentage of its use was astrological? And I have an answer, of sorts.

From March 1986, to February, 1990, I ran charts at Henry Weingarten's New York Astrology Center. These were not interpretations. They were 3 pages of raw data that sold for $3.00 each and were made to order for New York's consulting astrologers.

By my estimates, in four years I ran more than 10,000

charts. ACS, in San Diego, did vastly greater business, as many of you well-know. Which means the Antikythera mechanism was primarily a money-making device. It, or a machine very like it, produced the charts shown in Dorotheus's **Carmen Astrologicum**.

Not surprisingly, no one wants to hear it. Admit the finest mechanical device known to the ancient world was constructed and used by astrologers? Never! The bias is so great, we are denied our own tools. This is not a mystery, but an old story.

Happy Birthday!
August 4:
1821: Louis Vuitton, French designer
1901: Louis Armstrong.
1912: Raoul Wallenberg.
1920: Helen Thomas.
1930: Grand Ayatollah Ali al-Sistani.

August 5:
1887: Reginald Owen.
1906: John Huston.
1930: Neil Armstrong.

— *August 4, 2009*

Friday, the 13th of August, falls on Thursday this month.
On this date:
3114 B C - According to Lounsbury, the start of the Mayan calendar. (*Ends soon!*)
1521 AD: Tenochtitlan (Mexico City) falls to Hernan Cortes
1889: Zeppelin patents the Zeppelin.
1820: Birth of George Grove.
1860: Birth of Annie Oakley.
1899: Birth of Alfred Hitchcock.
1926: Birth of Fidel Castro.
1995: Death of Mickey Mantle.

— *August 11, 2009*

What is PseudoScience?
Doppler Dogma and The Big Banger

Never denigrate someone without hurling that insult first and foremost at yourself. See if you can make it stick – to you. And even if you can't, you should still tread carefully.

Astronomers, more than any other scientists, have thrown the word "pseudo science" at us. It's time to put the shoe on the other foot. Astronomy, yes, astronomy, the guys with the giant telescopes and Ph.D.'s and all that scientific knowhow, are not as innocent as they claim.

Let's start with the Doppler effect. Astronomers use the shift in a galaxy's spectrum to judge how fast it's moving away from us – the famous red shift. This works very well in determining the speed of gases in the Sun's corona, and it works well in determining the orbits of binary stars in the Milky Way.

It breaks down when it comes to intergalactic distances. With distant galaxies, not only do we find that everyone is moving away from us (*do we smell that bad?*), but the farther away they are, the faster they're fleeing the room. We must stink so awful, galaxies on the very fringes are at or near the speed of light. Since Einstein says that nothing can go faster than light (and also says that objects approaching that speed are infinitely massive) Doppler, as it's presently understood, is leading astronomers in some uncomfortable directions.

I will give the solution in a moment, but the problem is that science, in the "Enlightenment" abandoned its philosophical underpinnings and instead adopted a "first past the post" system: If it sounds good, if it looks good, we'll believe it. And because we, as Scientists, are Enlightened

Paragons of Logic and Truth, if it looks and sounds and smells good, then as far as we're concerned, it's The Truth.

Normally when such truths are established (driven home with a lot of personal ego behind them) – and then later found not to work so very well, a generation or two later Young Turks rise up and throw the old garbage out and replace it with their own. Eventually this new garbage begins to smell and so is thrown out in its turn. The excuse they use is "scientific advancement", but that's just to snow you. Religions used to claim that God Said So. Science simply copied them. They are both dogmatic, which doesn't mean they're not actually right every now and then.

It turns out that what passes for "science" is merely the fad of the moment. Someone's ego got his name in the history books. Someone else's ego replaces it. That's the real game. Ask any librarian. Twenty-year old science books are routinely discarded. "We know more now than we did then" is the invariable excuse. If that were true, science would be building upon earlier foundations, rather than throwing things out wholesale. Lobotomies, anyone?

But this process does not work all that well with astronomy, because astronomy, unlike all other branches of science, never has to confront engineering, i.e., actual human experience. Uncomfortable details that arise can be swept aside indefinitely. Pseudo-intellectual equations can be devised to explain variances. Even better, new, ever more warped theories can be built upon these tortured foundations. Dark matter? Black holes? Anyone? Astronomy is riddled with problems, which is why expensive space probes return conflicting data. But enough of this. Here is the Doppler solution:

Doppler presumes space to be a perfect vacuum. Which means that shifts in the spectrum can only be accounted for by changes in speed. And locally, which is to say, in the Milky Way, this works just fine. But there is no such thing as perfect. In space there are cosmic rays, various forms of radiation, solar winds that, locally at least, are strong enough to drive giant sails, wisps of gas and dust – some so thick we can see them.

In other words, why isn't space like the atmosphere?

Clear and transparent at short range, but, if you stack it up and look through a billion trillion of miles of it, why shouldn't it have its own unique color?

Factor out the inherent color of space (red, anyone?) and the paradoxes of speed and distance disappear. The cosmic soup of galaxies then resembles the ocean depths, with an abundance of fish and marine life, some moving this way, some moving that, each going about its own business.

But this destroys the Big Bang, which says that everything started in one place (gee, right where we're standing now?) and is expanding ever outward. Factor out the color of space and you get a relatively static, but much more dynamic cosmos. And you're thrown back to that fundamental question, How did it all begin? I have a surprising solution, but that's for another time.

09/09:
9 AD: Six German tribes wipe out 3 Roman legions
1379: Treaty of Neuberg, splitting Austria
1569: Pieter Bruegel, the Elder, dies
1739: Stono Rebellion, the largest slave uprising
1839: John Herschel makes first glass plate photograph
1899: Neil Hamilton, American actor, born *("Batman")*
1919: Jimmy "the Greek" Snyder, a bookie, born
1999: Catfish Hunter, American baseball player, dies

Happy Birthday NORTH KOREA!
September 10, 1949, Pyongyang, Corée du Nord. *Implacable Enemy of America!*

— *September 8, 2009*

Astrology and Weather

Skeptics say we just make it up and suckers fall for it. Well, they claim to be scientists and they've been making stuff up for a long time. What's the latest "scientific miracle" that you've fallen for?

On Friday we had buckets of rain and a flood in the basement. Which made me think about astrology and the weather. Ever wonder how the old farmers did it? They did it with astrology, of course!

So will the winter be long and cold, or short and mild? Do it yourself! Here's a primer. Set these charts for your location:

The Temperature Chart is drawn for the entry of the Sun into Cardinal signs. Which next happens on September 22, 2009 at 21:19 GMT, when the Sun enters Libra.

The Air Movement Chart is drawn for the entry of Mercury into each of the signs of the zodiac. Which next happens on September 18, 2009, at 3:26 am GMT, when it retrogrades back into Virgo.

The Moisture Chart is based on phases of the Moon, set as charts for your locale.

In each, angular planets (4th house stronger than the 1st) and aspects to them determine overall weather patterns. Transits to the ascendant degrees indicate weather changes, according to the transiting planet, the sign on the ascendant and the fundamental nature of the chart (temperature, wind, moisture).

And according to your area. If the town where you live is normally hot and dry, it won't take much of a temperature chart to produce hot weather, but only an exceptional moisture chart will produce rain.

Planets:

Sun: dry.
Moon: cool.
Mercury: cold.
Venus: moderate.
Mars: hot.
Jupiter: warm.
Saturn: stormy.
Uranus: cold.
Neptune: weird.
Pluto: cool.

Signs:

Aries: hot.
Taurus: moderate.
Gemini: cold and drafty.
Cancer: cold.
Leo: hot.
Virgo: cold.
Libra: cool.
Scorpio: extreme.
Sagittarius: warm.
Capricorn: storms.
Aquarius: cold.
Pisces: cool.

Study the books: **Weather Predicting**, by CC Zain, and, **Astrometeorology**, by Kris Brandt Riske.

For extra credit, follow the extended forecast on the Weather Channel. Every eight minutes they give The Week Ahead. Take the last day listed and follow it as the days pass. Did the weather they forecasted seven days in advance actually come to pass? Myself, I have never seen it to happen. Last Saturday they said this coming Friday would be sunny with a temperature in the mid-80's. As of Wednesday, Friday is now forecast to be 71, with rain, and Friday is still 48 hours away. By contrast, I have seen the Old Farmers to be one or two days out, with forecasts they publish a year in advance. Good thing we keep this astrology stuff a secret, don't you think!

Cosmobiology

Cosmobiology amounts to an intensification, and an intense reduction, of the astrological chart. As befits the work and intensity behind this system, its originator, Reinhold Ebertin, had Capricorn rising and Scorpio on the MC: February 16, 1901, 4:45 am MET (-1), Goerlitz, Germany: 51N09, 14E59.

Cosmobiology eliminates both houses and soft aspects, in favor of hard aspects, midpoints, and hard and tight aspects to those midpoints, known as Planetary Trees. To make hard aspects easier to find, the zodiac is folded upon itself, twice, to form a dial of 90 degrees. The first 30 degrees represent all four cardinal signs (Aries, Cancer, Libra, Capricorn). The second 30 degrees are all the fixed signs (Taurus, Leo, Scorpio, Aquarius), the final 30 degrees are the mutable signs (Gemini, Virgo, Sagittarius, Pisces). So a planet or point at 20 Cardinal could be at 20 degrees of Aries, Cancer, Libra or Capricorn – the Cosmobiologist does not care which. Whatever you find on the dial that is opposed to that is, by definition, half of 90, which means it's a 45° aspect. Squares on the dial are 22°30'. In other words, all your hard aspects, laid out at a glance.

For the basic Sun, Moon and planets, there are around 100 midpoints in total. How to sort? Look first at those midpoints which are conjunct, square, opposed, or in semi-square or semi-semi-square to planets. Those are the important ones. Transits to such a midpoint may set off both planets at once and if you weren't watching your midpoints, you would never know.

The basic books are by Ebertin himself: **Combination of Stellar Influences**, and, **Applied Cosmobiology**. See them, and more, on our Cosmobiology page. Dials? Yep. We got 'em.

Science or Pseudoscience?
The Craters of the Moon

This one is easy. Easy, easy, easy. Like stealing money from a bank. Easy, easy easy. The Moon has craters. Mercury has craters. Moons of Jupiter and Saturn have craters. Even asteroids have craters.

We first saw craters nearly 400 years ago when we first looked at the Moon with telescopes. And we knew then, just as we know now, that craters are caused by meteorite impacts. There are thousands of meteorites in museums around the world. Most of them are made of nickel and iron. Simple stuff.

And we have actual samples of lunar soil, and while it's not available to you or me, its basic chemical properties are known. Since we've walked on it, we could probably substitute ordinary dirt. After all, all we need to do for this week's challenge is :

MAKE A CRATER

We have the rocks that flew through space, we have the material they hit. HOW HARD CAN IT BE?

The great claim of Science is that we only believe what has been proven to be true. None of this "God told me so" stuff. No Old Wives tales. Science is rigorous! Science is methodical! Science is exact! Science is True! Science Examines Everything! So if meteor impacts created the craters of the Moon, then surely someone, somewhere, has proven that?

Would you believe me if I said that in nearly 400 years, NO ONE, no "scientist", at any rate, has attempted to make even one?

While I think this is a staggering oversight, surprisingly, craters-from-meteorite-impacts falls apart as soon as you look at it. Here is what must be duplicated:

Every crater ever observed, tens of thousands in all, are all perfectly circular. Which can only happen if the meteorite lands at a perfect – or near-perfect – right-angle to the surface. A straight vertical drop. And while the Earth may be big enough to draw meteorites into us, and while our atmosphere may be dense enough to slow meteors to the necessary perfectly vertical trajectory, none of this applies to the Moon. It has no atmosphere, and its gravity is weak. So why is every extraterrestrial crater ever observed perfectly circular? Where are the glancing impacts? Elliptical shapes? Straight line gashes? Shouldn't they be in the majority?

All extraterrestrial craters, every single one, are shallow. How can that be? The crater in Arizona, which actually seems to be an impact crater, is roughly eight times as wide as it is deep. It shows signs of significant erosion, which would imply it was once even deeper. The Moon's Tycho Crater is 17 times as wide as it is deep. Seventeen times. And Tycho is one of the Moon's deeper and supposedly newer craters.

All extraterrestrial craters, all the one's we've had a really close look at, are badly eroded. "Melted", if you like. Supposedly this is because of later meteorite impacts, but if this were true, the Moon's surface should be littered with meteorite debris. It is not. Astronauts could find none.

And then there is the problem of lunar domes. Big flat round domes. Meteors didn't create them, nor were they created by lava flows, since there is no evidence of lava vents, and a lava flow isn't a soap bubble. It never flows round. Go look at Hawaii. Super-hot lava goes where it likes. I will leave aside the fact that the Moon is believed to have gone cold long, long ago and so has no lava, inside or on the surface, which means those domes should have been smashed to pieces eons ago from all those meteorites.

An alternative theory, first proposed by a rabbi in 1950 (who shall remain nameless), says that both the craters, as well as the domes, were formed when the Moon (and, presumably other similar extraterrestrial bodies) were superheated from an outside source, until their surfaces boiled. I liken it to the bubbles that form in sugar solutions, like fudge.

The Craters of the Moon

Bubbles are always perfectly circular. If the heat was intense, but brief, it would not penetrate more than a few hundred feet into the surface, which would explain why extraterrestrial craters are shallow. Gas pressure inside the bubbles would eventually burst them, shooting material in all directions, forming the mysterious rays. Sudden removal of the heat would leave unexploded bubbles, which would collapse and form domes.

What did astronomers do upon hearing of this theory? Pseudoscientists all, they condemned the rabbi, declaring he was not a member of the club.

Next time: The 5000 year old theory of the Sun.

On September 22:
1499: Switzerland becomes independent
1692: Last witchcraft hanging in America.
1761: George III crowned king of England.
1776: Nathan Hale hanged.
1784: Russia colonizes Alaska.
1823: Joseph Smith finds gold tablets.
1888: National Geographic appears.
1893: Victoria lasts longer than George 3.
1908: Bulgaria declares independence.
1927: Jack Dempsey loses to Gene Tunney
1975: Sarah Jane Moore tries to kill Gerald Ford.

Born September 22:
1961: Michael Torke, composer.

— September 22, 2009

The Best Books on:
Progressions

I was asked this week for Nancy Hastings' book, **Secondary Progressions, Time to Remember**. Which, I regret to say, is out of print. When it was new two decades ago, it was almost the only book on progressions in print.

The best book on progressions, better than Nancy's, is Sophia Mason's **Delineation of Progressions**. It's detailed, comprehensive, written by a working astrologer, and nicely laid out. I have heard complaints the delineations are excessively harsh, but exactly how much sugar coating do we really want, or need? Better to know the worst, even if it's not likely.

I myself reprinted Alan Leo's **The Progressed Horoscope** a few years back. The book dates from 1905. It is full of an English sense of Pep! and Vigor! and Pull Yourself Up and Do Something, which can be annoying. Unique to this book, delineations include parallels, semi-squares and inconjuncts. Leo ran a mail-order chart business, it seems he profited from the volume.

Leigh Hope Milburn's **The Progressed Horoscope Simplified** dates from 1928. It uses the old good vs: bad aspect, which, in fact, is not in any way shabby. (Leo, by contrast, may have been the very first to explicitly write conjunctions, sextiles, squares, trines, inconjuncts, oppositions, etc.) As progressions show trends, not actual events, keeping up with them gives a necessary framework to transits.

Finally, there's Robert Blaschke's **Astrology, A Language of Life, vol. 1: Progressions**, a staggeringly brilliant compilation of techniques. A must-have.

— September 22, 2009

Time for AstroAmerica's Retrograde Technology Roundup:
FiOS Arrives

EARLY August, there were Verizon cable-laying trucks all through town. When I saw a truck parked half a block down from my desk here at AstroCentral, I strolled over.

"Is it Fios?"
"Yep!"
"When?"
"Last week of August, maybe first week in September."
"Sign up on-line"?
"Nah! Wait for the college kids to come 'round."

Heck, jobs are hard to get. Who was I to cheat someone out of honest work? So I waited and while I waited, I cheated and went on-line anyway. It was indecipherable gibberish. Like everything Verizon. They're a communications company, naturally.

The Verizon team showed up the evening of Monday, September 14. Was Mercury retrograde? Sure was, but Verizon has never talked straight in their entire existence. Retrograde, everything they said curled back on itself like oodles of tiny little donuts. I plucked a few out of the air, sliced them open and had a look.

And wasn't that the week — yep. You guessed. Saturn-Uranus duking it out from the corners. New Lamps for Old, anyone?

Installation was on Wednesday, 16 September. And was quick and painless, even though it was two computers, two phone lines and three TV sets.

So how's it compare? We had Comcast for internet and TV. Comcast gave 16 mb download speed. Fios is 25. Which in practice is not significant. The basic Fios TV package gave a few new channels and maybe a better guide (it's clunky). Lack of subscribers means that Fios Weather isn't as good as Comcast, but that may change as more sign up. Fios picture is fabulous, but that only matters if you're fussy, and if you can find anything much to watch. (Old Hee Haw on RFD is a hit.) Price? Fios replaces about $200 in other services. The rep gave a price of $168. His phone rep gave me $113. I said to the reps, You all look like Three Stooges to me. — Did you know Moe and Larry were grinding it out up to 1970? Hey! It's a job!!

Update, May 2010

So, how did it work out? Turns out that a FiOS line is incompatible with a standard credit card terminal. Which Verizon repair techs should have known but didn't. I asked Verizon to convert the line back to copper. When three weeks went by and they were still thinking about it, I cancelled the line. Fortunately I had kept a copper line in reserve for this kind of emergency.

The FiOS line terminates in a transmitter in the basement, which broadcasts to a receiver on a shelf behind my desk. I'd not previously had wireless in the house. This let us put the Wii on-line. Which meant we could download movies from Netflix.

And that made it all worthwhile. Instead of paying for Verizon's premium channels or movie package, Netflix offers vastly greater downloads, with more to come, at a very good price.

Pseudoscience proudly presents
The 5000 year-old theory of the Sun

In its natural state, uranium is mildly radioactive. Find a good ore ("yellow-cake"), turn it into a gas, send that gas through a thousand cascading centrifuges, precipitate the result back into a solid, and, if you can get enough of it and shape it just right, the resulting enhanced radiation makes the substance naturally explosive. In other words, matter becomes energy at the speed of light.

One of the parlor tricks that has been done with this substance is to shape it into a hollow sphere and then put things inside which, when the uranium explodes, will be superheated and super compressed.

Such as hydrogen. Edward Teller, an insane Hungarian scientist with a pathological hatred of everything Russian, insisted the US develop the hydrogen bomb, where a nuclear bomb serves as a trigger to a much more powerful hydrogen core.

This was of interest to astronomers. It solved, or seemed to solve, a long-standing problem: From where does the Sun get its light and heat? From spectroscopic analysis, astronomers knew the Sun was a giant hydrogen gas bag but how that made the sun a Sun and kept us warm and toasty they had not a clue.

For centuries astronomers had played a guessing game. Is the Sun like a glowing coal? Coal would be put in a brazier and observed. X amount of coal burned for Y amount of time. If the Sun were coal, then as the Sun has a mass of X^z, then the Sun would burn for Y^z period of time. (We'll pretend that we, like Edison, know nothing of oxidation.) Unfortunately, when the numbers were crunched, coal wasn't it.

But the Sun is big and massive and so at its very center

there was certainly enough pressure to make the hydrogen fuse. So that was it. Problem solved.

Except it wasn't. Nuclear furnaces have certain characteristics and it was darn hard, harder by the year, to make the Sun behave as scientists knew it to be. I won't trouble you with tales of missing radiation, of impossible temperature gradients, of winds and particles that the Sun produces in abundance but that nuclear fusion does not. You'll have to look that up for yourself.

In 1981 in London, I bought a book of science essays and was amusing myself reading a nearly incomprehensible (to me) story of the electrical properties of the Sun, when I was amazed to read,

> "It seems astonishing that in the course of half a century of studies of the sun in context with the thermonuclear theory, very few professional astrophysicists have ever expressed the slightest discomfort over discrepancies between observation and theory, or even over the fact that an ad hoc extra theory has had to be devised to explain practically every individual feature of the solar atmosphere.
>
> "I can find no way to state this diplomatically, so let me be blunt: The modern astrophysical concept that ascribes the sun's energy to thermonuclear reactions deep in the solar interior is contradicted by nearly every observable aspect of the sun.
>
> "Apparently with a steady hand, Fred Hoyle wrote some years ago: 'We should expect on the basis of a straightforward calculation that the Sun would "end" itself in a simple and rather prosaic way; that with increasing height above the photosphere the density of the solar material would decrease quite rapidly, until it became pretty well negligible only two or three kilometres up... Instead, the atmosphere is a huge bloated envelope.' And today we know that this 'bloated envelope' extends out among the planets.
>
> "Even the photosphere, where theory would suggest the sun ought to 'end,' fails miserably to conform with expectations. Its opacity almost conspires

The 5000 year old theory of the Sun 79

to prevent the sun from radiating away its internal energy, if that is indeed where the energy comes from. The granular structure of the photosphere is still attributed to 'non-stationary convection,' even though Minnaert pointed out decades ago that the Reynolds number of the photospheric gas exceeds the critical value by eight powers of ten—which is to say, by a factor of 100 million—and therefore convection currents in the photosphere should be completely turbulent."

— Taken from **Reconciling Celestial Mechanics and Velikovskian Catastrophism**, by Ralph E. Juergens, 1972, from **Velikovsky Reconsidered**, by the Editors of Pensee. Juergens was a retired civil engineer who got interested in Velikovsky's theories late in life. Velikovsky is far too large a topic for these pages, but for an alternate reality (one that can be applied surprisingly well to astrology), I urge you to read Juergens's entire article. I will summarize, as best I understand:

The Sun is an electrified body. Its light and heat are generated at its surface by means of its relationship to the "empty" space around it. In other words, the Sun does not exist in a vacuum. The Sun and surrounding space are in relationship. They are interdependent. From this comes plasma, and with plasma, gigantic electric "sheaths" that enrobe the Sun and planets. Among other things, Juergens's electric theory easily explains the otherwise inexplicable tails of comets.

While this may or may not be The Answer, it is an order of magnitude better than the thermonuclear theory. It is, at the very least, a radical departure from the traditional theory, that the Sun's energy is a product of the biggest and hottest thing of which we know. In other words, a change from the Sun as Glowing Coal, or Swamp Gas, or Superheated Iron Bar or Thermonuclear Furnace or Whatever Important People Think is Hot This Week. Juergens's theory has actual observation to support it. Which is a novel thing! Do I have to tell you it met, not with sound scientific refutation, but rather, deafening silence?

But Juergens is still treating "space" as a nonentity, as

something which has no existence apart from what is projected upon it. I want to go a step further. What if "space" is a substance in its own right? Consider this:

I have previously refuted the expanding cosmos by suggesting the Red Shift to be an optical illusion. Now, Juergens gives us a theory that puts stars and planets in relationship to the space around them. So, which came first? Space, or matter?

Suppose we look again at Einstein's famous equation of matter, energy and light. Suppose we add a fourth variable, for space? Suppose there is a way in which "empty" space suddenly produces, brings forth, if you will, energy and matter, which of themselves then produce light? Looking out at the non-Big Bang, relatively static cosmos, we see unimaginable expanses of "nothingness" with, here and there, a galaxy or two, appearing as of out of the darkness itself. Are galaxies like eddies in a stream? Why is modern science so flabby that such speculation as this even merits attention?!

— *September 29, 2009*

More on the Antikythera mechanism
*from my notes on Wiki,
with comments from others.*

Found here: http://en.wikipedia.org/wiki/
Talk:Antikythera_mechanism#
The_Antikythera_mechanism_was_for_producing_astrology_charts

To a working astrologer, it is self-evident the Antikythera mechanism was intended to produce astrology charts. The earliest published charts are found in Dorotheus of Sidon's **Carmen Astrologicum**, which dates from the first century AD. Its charts are dated 13 AD, 22 AD, 29 AD, 36 AD, 43 AD, etc. David Pingree translated the book in 1976. The eight charts in it are generally accurate, but are quirky. Modern calculations show individual planets shifted far from their proper positions. This is easily explained if an individual gear in a clockwork mechanism had come out of alignment.

The question arises, how did ancient astrologers calculate charts? There were no printed ephemerides, nor were Greek or Roman numbers suitable for complex calculations. (The modern number system was centuries in the future.) One could always make his own nightly observations, but the best method, by far, would be to construct a clockwork mechanism. Such as the Antikythera mechanism.

Such a machine would be expensive, but also very lucrative. The owner of such a machine could make money supplying data to astrologers far and wide. Make a good deal of money, if I am not mistaken. A bit of extra money could be had by providing precise dates for games and other events. That eclipses were a part of it indicates that the machine calculated the Mean Node in addition to the Sun, Moon and five planets. Such machines would command a high price, and would be handed down through the generations, until they physically wore out. Why was the Antikythera mechanism found at sea? Presumably its owner was on a voyage. As has been remarked already, it is unsuitable as a navigation aid.

Pingree's translation: **Carmen Astrologicum**, published by K.G. Saur Verlag GmbH, Munich, 1976. Reprinted by Astrology Classics, Abingdon MD, 2005. Which is me, by the way.

Everything about this device is easily explained by its use as an astrological calculator. Without doubt, it was not the only such machine in existence. — Dave of Maryland (talk) 23:49, 19 September 2010 (UTC)

> *Comment by Green Wyvern:*
> It is a common misconception to think that Roman numbers were not suitable for complex calculations. Romans used the abacus (or alternatively the counting board) for arithmetic, and were able to perform large and complex arithmetic operations very rapidly. Roman numerals simply describe the state of an abacus or counting board representing a number.   The Romans were the great builders of antiquity. Without being able to do arithmetic quickly and easily, it would not have been possible to create a vast, elaborate civilization with architecturally complex public buildings everywhere, roads, bridges, aqueducts, canals, reservoirs, dams, harbours, fortifications; do complex commercial transactions and accounts, run banks, do land surveying and mapping, do tax planning and budgeting, run commercial farms, mines, and manufacturing industries, etc.
> Green Wyvern (talk) 08:26, 20 September 2010 (UTC)

My reply:
Orbital vectors & spherical trig are the issues at hand. These calculations are messy in Arabic numbers, which is

why no one, to this day, attempts them. Kepler was one of the first to solve that problem, and that was 400 years after the introduction of Arabic numbers in 1202. Greek astrology was centered on Alexandria (32 degrees north), which, up to at least 30 BC, and probably long thereafter, presumably used Attic numbers, which were somewhat inferior to Roman.

The problem with numbers also includes how astrological houses were calculated, which gets into the problem of latitude, which the ancients solved, not by calculation, but by noting the length of the longest day of the year, presumably with water-clocks. The earth, from equator to pole, was divided into seven or twelve climes, based on length of day. This inability to make what we would consider basic calculations kept astrology confined to tropical (23 degrees north latitude) and near-tropical areas of the world, and also limited accurate map-making in northern latitudes.

These problems were not solved, in Europe at least, until centuries after the introduction of Arabic numbers in 1202. (China and Tibet never solved them, India & the Maya had no need. The abacus has limitations.) By 1600, there were a handful of printed ephemerides, for a few years at a time, laboriously hand-calculated & set for the author's home town. Nothing comparable is known to have existed in Classical times.

I was asked a few moments ago how ancient astrologers calculated charts, as they are uniformly silent on the matter. Over the past 50 years, we now have good translations of several dozen texts from the period. While many of them give instruction for calculating the ascendant, and some for Dodecatemoria (12ths), not one covers zodiacal calculation. Moreover, the kind of mistakes we find in ancient charts is not compatible with actual calculation. Compare Dorotheus to William Lilly's **Christian Astrology**, Book 3, of 1647. In Book 3, written under great duress, a number of the charts have mistakes, but these are mistakes of degree, or wrong house placement. Not whole sign. — Dave of Maryland (talk) 11:34, 20 September 2010 (UTC)

Reply from Green Wyvern:
I fully agree that astrology would have been one the

major uses of the device, and that it would have been a lot more convenient to use such a device for astrological calculations than to do the calculations by hand.

However, a high degree of mathematical and observational knowledge of the motions of heavenly bodies was needed in order to construct the device in the first place. The designers of such devices had the knowledge not only to predict the motions of the sun, moon and inner planets very accurately, but also to design a complex set of gears to simulate those motions.

That means they were certainly able to do calculations by hand which they built the device to do more conveniently. No doubt it was a great time saver to turn a handle and see the positions of the planets at a future or past time, but the ability to get the same results by manual calculations obviously existed, or else the device itself could not have been constructed.

I agree that astrology should be mentioned prominently in the article among the uses of the device - I think that it was mentioned in some earlier versions of the article, but was unjustifiably removed.
Green Wyvern (talk) 13:09, 20 September 2010 (UTC)

My reply:

It might be that somebody could make Roman or Attic numbers work, or it might be that a clockmaker took many years of actual observations (from an observatory in Alexandria, for example) and made his gears fit those observations, supplementing that with laborious calculations as a crosscheck. There are general patterns in planetary data which have long been known. The resulting clockwork would probably not be accurate to a degree of arc. We know this because the astrological texts of the period base their delineations on decans (10 degree sections of a sign), or, from time to time, faces, which are 5 degrees. With a bit of luck, the ascendant could be known to the degree, but ascendants were not part of the Antikythera mechanism, as ascendants are based on the axial rotation of the Earth.

Which means that machines like the Antikythera mechanism were accurate, more or less, only over a certain range of dates. Beyond that range—which might be as little as a decade, and probably not more than a century—it would become progressively more inaccurate. This is another argument in favor of hodge-podge observational construction, rather than grinding through a lot of Roman numbers. This is also a caution to modern model-makers, that they do not inadvertently make a better Antikythera replica than what actually existed. Which, as I think of it, gives us another possibility as to its ultimate fate: It might have become so old, and, consequently, inaccurate, as to be worthless. Which might also explain why such devices, which should have been common, simply disappeared. Could they have all been thrown away?

You might be surprised to learn that astrologers, to this day, do not actually calculate a chart. Not from scratch, at any rate. They never, ever have. Open any medieval textbook – Lilly, Gadbury, Partridge, Coley, Ramesey, etc., and you will read the same instructions: Get a table (aka ephemeris), find the date, look up the positions you find there, do the necessary calculations to adjust for clock time, and set your chart. My own experience in this matter is clear: When astrological computer programs first became available nearly 30 years ago, there were businesses set up expressly to provide astrologers with charts. I was hired to run charts at the New York Astrology Center, 1986-90. I estimate I ran 10,000 charts during that period, the vast majority of which went to astrologers in a 50 mile radius. Astro-Computing, in San Diego, did several times that volume, as they had a national business.

The accepted opinion of astrology—that it is a belief system at best—should not blind us to a larger study of cultures and how they expressed themselves. If analysis and logic proves the Antikythera mechanism to have been astrological, we should not hesitate to say so. The scientific objection to astrology is that it seems to have no theoretical foundation. This is flimsy objection, as, at any moment, such a theory might well be found. (I in fact have one.) The previous religious objection—that astrology usurped the role of God in man's life—was more solid, although still flawed.

Astrology does not usurp "God" (whatever that might be). Astrology usurps the role of the priest as self-appointed intermediary—which it does. Astrology exposes, and, consequently, usurps, all authority. Which is the real reason it has been, is now, and forever will be, banned. — Dave of Maryland (talk) 17:39, 21 September 2010 (UTC)

> *Reply from The Eskimo:*
> Very interesting. Do you know of sources that put forth this theory? — The Eskimo (talk) 13:34, 24 September 2010 (UTC)
>
> *Reply from Steve Baker:*
> We don't know what it was used for—we can only just barely infer what it could do. Everything that Dave says could be true—but we have no way to know that it was true. My laptop could be used to produce astrological charts—but it most certainly has never been used to do that. The same exact thing is true of Antikythera. Without solid references saying that it was used in this way—we cannot, should not and must not add this into the article—no matter how reasonable it seems—because it is both OR and SYNTHESIS. — SteveBaker (talk) 17:08, 24 September 2010 (UTC)
>
> *Reply from The Eskimo:*
> There is an entire section of the article dedicated to speculation of its uses. In fact, the "probably had" or "was likely to have" which are nothing more than assumptions. Dave, if you can provide a source that passes wp:rs, and reports the opinion of a notable researcher that says it may have been used for astrological purposes, then you should add it.—The Eskimo (talk) 20:01, 24 September 2010 (UTC)
>
> *Reply to Eskimo & SteveBaker:*
> Hello Eskimo & SteveBaker, my thanks for your comments. While computers have other uses, the Antikythera mechanism had NO other use. (The sporting calculator is

clearly an add-on. A clever person could estimate the cost of the machine by deducing how much money could be made by providing such dates, but I digress.)

Devices identical to the Antikythera mechanism are used by astrologers to this day. Printed ephemerides being the most obvious, but also Maynard's annual **Celestial Influences Wall Calendar**, which sells in the many thousands, despite the fact that it never appears before mid-November. It sells for full price in January, February & March, right up to the moment when it has sold out. Looking at today, December 24, 2010, the calendar, which is set in Eastern Standard Time, tells me the Moon is in Leo, that it will sextile Saturn at 11:16 am, square Venus at 12:10 pm, and trine Mercury at 8:45 pm. In London can be found the annual **Raphael's Ephemeris**, which has been continuously published since the late 1820's. It has many times the sales of Maynard. Please remember that in classical times there were no printing presses, so far as is known. Clockwork mechanisms were in fact the means by which astrological positions were known.

Computers have, in fact done the Antikythera mechanism one better. Many astrology programs have a routine that will display the current planetary positions on-screen, in real time, along with the local horizon. Which produces exact times for the rising, culmination & setting of the Sun, Moon & planets. For details about these programs, contact Hank Friedman at http://soulhealing.com/. He's been reviewing & selling astro software for 30 years.

For these reasons, a test of Dave's theory, that the Antikythera mechanism was intended for astrologers, can easily be made. Give replicas of the device, with modern names for planets & signs & dates, with modern planetary positions, to astrologers & see what they make of it. Don't give them any instructions, as I don't think they will need any. (Yes. To a working astrologer, the machine is that obvious.) Have them keep a month's diary. See what turns up.

Yes, a few ephemerides are sold to people who are not astrologers. A small handful buy Maynard, even though they do not understand it. Some people will spend $200 for astrology software but then never use it. But in fact, by far the majority of interest in this area comes exclusively from astrologers, and always will.

Skeptics should be aware of two other factors. One is Occam's Razor, which is to say, if it looks like a duck, then it's probably a duck. You might have been expecting a peacock. Hitler was expecting the Pas de Calais. We all know how he ended up.

The other factor is observer bias, in this case, the Cargo Cult factor. Cargo Cults (Wiki has a nice article on it: http://en.wikipedia.org/wiki/Cargo_cult) are what happens when artifacts specific to a single culture are taken out of context and dumped on unsuspecting rubes. The reactions of those natives are surprisingly similar to modern speculation about the Antikythera mechanism, or, for that matter, modern speculations as to the remains of the giant stone battery that can be found on the Wiltshire plains (apologies for the digression). In the case of south seas Cargo Cults, any American teenager could sort the natives out, but the islands' wise elders will hear none of it. Their ears and eyes are closed, they will consider nothing that contradicts their theories of long standing. I fully expect to suffer a similar fate at your hands.

In 110 years, the Antikythera mechanism has gone from puzzle to puzzle. The best modern guess, according to Wiki's main article, is that it was for public display, or for use by sea captains. Both are clearly wrong. Is that the best that academics can do?

The study of Hellenistic astrology, of which the Antikythera mechanism is a critical component, has come a long way just since 1990. At some point it won't just be me. The astrological community will move wholesale to reclaim what was always rightly theirs. In the end, the fate of the Antikythera mechanism might be one of the consequences of Europe having banned "astrological superstition" some 300 years ago. — Dave of Maryland (talk) 16:37, 24 December 2010 (UTC)

— At this point the conversation became uninteresting. —

Going Places
Astro*Carto*Graphy at your Fingertips

Years ago I thought I would make a good test case for Astrocartography. Which says that even though your natal chart is mediocre, that Jupiter and Venus are simply nowhere near the angles, that you can cheat fate by moving to those locations where, at the moment of your birth, such planets were exactly angular.

In my case, that's 133W, 56S, which is far to the west and south of Easter Island, in the middle of the freezing far south Pacific, where Jupiter is exactly on my ascendant and Venus exactly on the midheaven. But, alas, a sailor's life was not for me. I have lived in Kansas, Los Angeles, New York, Santa Fe, Maryland, Paris, London and Montpellier, with special guest appearances in Strasbourg. While I agree with the deduction that places where planets are angular are magnetic and will suck us helplessly into their grasp, such a location (Kennebunkport) has yet to befall me. And I have tried.

Astrocartography is the Astrologer's way of planning a holiday. Use of Astrocartography will get you off the beaten track, away from tacky tourists and ensure a unique trove of holiday snaps that your friends are certain to enjoy. And if it's a Venus line you're following, you might even find true love. All you need are the right books to guide you. And this is the right place to find them. *Behold—*

Of the various authors, I most like Martin Davis. His book, **Astrolocality Astrology, A Guide to What It Is and How to Use It,** combines Astrocartography (moving your birth chart from here to there) with Local Space. Local Space is a souped-up version of a more ancient technique, where *a)* the natal chart is reduced to a compass, *b)* you are to go off in the direction of your most favored planet until c) you come to a location which is ruled by it. Traditional Local Space fails at part c) as no one now knows how to figure out what planet or sign rules where. Penfield's and Campion's chart collections only tell us about governments, not the people who actually live there. So the modern method is to wander off in the direction of, say, Venus, until you get to an agreeable ACG line. Davis will give you the details.

Michael Erlewine, founder of Matrix Software, once published his birth data. Once, for fun, I ran his chart with both ACG and LS and discovered he had wandered along one particular LS line until it intersected an ACG line, exactly at Big Rapids, MI, where he lives to this day, so far as I am aware. I once asked him about this and he corrected me. His birth in Pennsylvania was an accident, he was in fact raised in Big Rapids, his boyhood home town. Those of you who like karmic explanations, go ahead!

For a detailed presentation of Astrocartography itself, get David Meadows' **Where In the World With Astro*Carto*Graphy** (sadly, now out of print). Meadows expands the subject to tell you when to pack your bags, in other words, Cyclo*Astro*Carto*Graphy. While ACG has long been used to tweak solar return trips (an enjoyable way of spending a birthday), the Cyclo technique expands this greatly. Got an upcoming transit? Want to make the best of it, or avoid the worst? Get David's book and study closely.

Here is yet another method, one first proposed by Sepharial. It goes like this:

Suppose the Meridian of London, 0 degrees, is 0 Aries. One degree east of London is 1 Aries, two degrees east is 2 Aries, three degrees east is 3 Aries, etc. This is taken as the local midheaven.

The Ascendant is drawn for your latitude north or south of the equator. A table of houses (Koch, Placidus, Regiomontanus, Porphyry, etc.) will give intermediate house cusps. This produces a unique map for every location on the planet. Looking over a range of possibilities, you then pick a place where LS or ACG lines, in combination with the local chart, all seem agreeable. New York, for example, has a geodetic ascendant of 29 Aries and a geodetic midheaven of 16 Capricorn. To date, this technique has mostly been used for mundane work, but there is no reason it should be so limited. For more details, get Chris McRae's book, **The Geodetic World Map**.

Local Space is handled best by Steve Cozzi, in his classic book, **Planets In Locality**. LS is, in fact, the western version of Feng Shui and compares well with it.

So as the salesman says on TV, Stop Having A Boring Life. But rather than buy his product, get out and explore the world!

— October 6, 2009

October 12 (*Columbus Day?*) :
1582 - This day does not exist in Italy, Poland, Portugal and Spain.
1692 - Salem witch trials end.
1773 - Virginia opens first insane asylum.
1810 - First Octoberfest, Munich.
1823 - Charles Macintosh sells first raincoat.
1933 - Alcatraz becomes a federal prison.
1960 - Khrushchev pounds shoe on desk.
1964 - Soviet Union launches Voskhod 1.
1986 - Elizabeth II visits China.
1999 - World reaches 6 billion population.
2005 - Chinese launch Shenzhou 6

NASA lays an egg

Early Friday morning America time (is there any other time, really?), NASA slammed the LCROSS (Lunar Crater Observation and Sensing Satellite) into the Moon. On board were one visible camera, two near-infrared cameras, two mid-infrared cameras, a visible light spectrometer, two near-infrared spectrometers, and a photometer. A hundred million bucks sacrificed in the belief that violent impact would discover water just under the surface of a deep crater at the lunar south pole. If only a big enough splash, I mean, hole, could be made.

I wasn't on tenterhooks. I knew what the result would be. If lunar craters were formed by boiling, as some suspect, then the intense heat drove off lunar waters long ago. It was said that a lunar orbiter had detected hydrogen (i.e., traces of water) in the bottom of the Cabeus crater. Well, yes. You will find a microscopically thin film of water in most permanently shady places on the moon. It comes from the Earth. It is the net result of lunar tides. And that ain't rocket science.

Nor was I surprised to hear there wasn't a big splash or plume of debris. The Moon boiled because there wasn't oxygen to burn. Burnt things have no springiness. Here on Earth there are how many hundred pounds of lunar soil available to study? Did anyone bother?

NASA is a crystal-clear example of brilliant engineering enslaved to dumb science. Engineering excellence brings the probe to its distant destination. Whereupon "scientific" experiments fail. Repeatedly. Over and over again. And every time they do, there is the same excuse:

"The LCROSS science instruments worked exceedingly

NASA lays an egg

well and returned a wealth of data that will greatly improve our understanding of our closest celestial neighbor," said Anthony Colaprete, LCROSS principal investigator and project scientist at NASA's Ames Research Center in Moffett Field, Calif. "The team is excited to dive into data."

Except they didn't find any water. Just another dry hole. If NASA can come up with a use for theirs, maybe they can come up with a use for some of ours.

Engineering is the ceaseless struggle against the elements, the endless tinkering, the trials by error, the original do-it-yourself brigade, invention itself. Engineering in fact built every civilization known to man: Egyptian, Babylonian, Sumerian, Indian, Chinese, Mayan, Incan, Roman, Greek, Moslem, European, and, yes, our own. Without exception. Engineering is the study of What Works. The same engineering principles that built the Pyramids, are today at work building skyscrapers in the Persian Gulf, as well as the next generation of rockets to the Moon and to the planets and distant stars beyond. Engineering it is that claws Knowledge from the darkness.

Science, by contrast, is its shabby stepsister. It guesses, it supposes, it builds elaborate houses of cards, it is "logical", it "deduces", it is full of preening egos. All fighting for attention. Which leads me to:

Dave's Formula for Pain Management
which I discovered last night. Wracked with pain from a broken molar, the end result of an accident 30 some years ago, I succumbed to the necessity of taking Vicodin. It's nasty stuff – go Wiki. I put a pill in my left hand but couldn't make my self swallow. Five minutes went by. I was out of pain. Not a lessening of intensity. The pain was gone. I held the tab in my hand for two hours. No pain at all. There's very good metaphysical reasons why holding a pain pill in your left hand may take the pain away, but rather than bore you with that, know that I taped the pill to the palm of my hand and had the best night's sleep in three days. (Being worn out after 24 hours of intense pain helped.) This morning I could eat again. Drink liquids. Chew. That same pill, now in pieces, is taped to one of my fingers.

American medicine is expensive not because of greedy

insurance companies, though they don't help any. Medicine is expensive because of all the engineering gizmos that cost millions of dollars each but which, like NASA's space probes, don't actually work, nor even give a worthwhile diagnosis. And for the same reason: While the engineering is excellent, the science behind it is shoddy. "Science" says the body is a machine made up of independent parts. This obsession is the best that "science" can do. The best it will ever manage. Next time I will tell you why.

You want medicine? There is Saunders, Culpeper, Blagrave, Cornell, there is Brother Aloysius, there are many, many more, all shunned. I turned a pill into a poultice. Next time you're in pain, hold the pain pill in your left hand. If in five minutes it's brought solace, you've discovered something. If not, get relief! Swallow it!

— *October 13, 2009.*

October 15
1582 – First day of the Gregorian Calendar
1815 – Napoleon begins exile on St. Helena
1863 – CSS Huntley sunk (1st submarine)
1888 – "From Hell" sent by Jack the Ripper
1894 – Alfred Dreyfuss arrested
1917 – Mata Hari executed
1945 – Pierre Laval shot by firing squad
1946 – Hermann Goering poisons himself

Rules for Operations
as taken from the
Encyclopaedia of Medical Astrology, by H.L. Cornell, M.D.

Statistics show that operations are more successfully performed when the Moon is increasing in light, between the New and Full Moon, and heal more quickly, and are less liable to complications than when the Moon is past the full and decreasing. Note the following Rules:—
1) Operate on the increase of the Moon if possible.
2) Do not operate at the exact time of the Full Moon, as the fluids are running high at this time.
3) Never operate when the Moon is in the same sign as at birth.
4) Never operate upon that part of the body ruled by the sign thru which the Moon is passing at the time, but wait a day or two until the Moon passes into the next sign below, and especially if the Moon be in conjunction, square or opposition Neptune, Uranus, Saturn or Mars at the time. This rule should be especially followed in major operations. Ptolemy says, "Pierce not with iron that part of the body which may be governed by the sign actually occupied by the Moon."
5) Do not operate when the Moon is applying closely to the square or opposition the Sun, Saturn or Mars.
6) Let the Moon be increasing in light, and in sextile or trine Jupiter or Venus and not afflicted by Mars.
7) Let the Moon be in a fixed sign, but not in the sign ruling the part to be operated upon, and such sign of the Moon also not on the ascendant.
8) Do not operate when the Moon is applying to any aspect of Mars, as such tends to danger of inflammation and complications after the operation.

9) Avoid operations when the Sun is in the sign ruling the part upon which the operation is to be performed.
10) Never operate when the Moon is combust, or within 17 degrees of the Sun, and with the Moon opposite Mars at the same time.
11) The Moon should be free from all manner of impediment.
12) Jupiter, Venus, and the ruler of the ascendant should be in the ascendant or in the M.C., if possible, and free of Mars affliction.
13) Fortify the Sign ruling the part of the body to be operated upon.
14) A Mars hour is evil for surgical operations.
15) Do not cut a nerve when Mercury is afflicted.

— The above from page 609. Immediately preceding the above, Cornell warns (pg 608-9):

Undesirable Elemental Spirits are often present at Operations to absorb the life force from the blood of the patient, introduce Astral infections, and prevent recovery. Every operation should be preceded with prayer to prevent the presence of Elementals, and to place an Aura of Protection about the patient.

And, a paragraph later: **Operations Dangerous** – Performed when the Sun is in the 12th house, in conjunction Saturn or South Node, and Mars afflicted in the 6th House at the same time.

Dave adds: It's also known that a prominent Neptune may lead to complications with anesthesia and that Jupiter in hard aspect to the Moon can cause too much bleeding.

— October 13, 2009

More on A Pill in the Hand

Surprising response to my note last week, that holding a pill in my hand had brought relief from pain. Thanks to John C. for the neat tag, "a pill in the hand." He reports the same unwillingness to swallow the things. Karen K., who does energy work, wondered why she hadn't thought of it. I wondered that of myself.

I can't tell you that a pill in the hand will work for you, because we're all different, but there is more to it than mere hand-holding.

Underlying and interpenetrating the physical body is an energy body. One of the big secrets in medieval medicine —which has been lost to the modern world—were numerous ways of healing by working directly with the energy body itself. Bypassing the physical altogether.

As I've mentioned before, Blagrave constantly tells us to put three solar herbs in a small bag (such as fennel, centaury and daffodil), tie it closed and wear it around the neck. Why solar (Sun) herbs and why around the neck? Because the heart is ruled by the Sun, and "around the neck" does not imply a choker. A satchel worn around the neck will fall naturally on the breastbone, which is very near the heart, thus putting the herbs in close proximity. What strengthens the heart strengthens the body as a whole. Strengthen the body and the cure is half done already.

Since I suffer from a weak heart, once I figured out what Blagrave was up to, I wanted one of those satchels. Alas, it's too late in the season to start a garden and I wouldn't know chevril from centaury anyway. But, I thought, gold would work as well. I remembered a gold ring from a failed relationship 20-some years ago and tore through the house to find it. Nice heavy man's 18K thing, but it would need cleaning. I put it in a glass jar and set it outside at sunrise on a Sunday. I "harvested" it a week later, at sunrise on a Sunday, tied it onto a shoelace and put it around my neck, in accordance with Blagrave's rules. The water, full of solar energy, I drank.

I've been wearing it two weeks. Here's what I think:

Unlike herbs, gold has a heavier energy. The energy is expressed by the shape, so the ring functions as a flywheel. It seems to be stabilizing and strengthening my heartbeat, which is good.

The shape of an object is important. Many women wear small gold crosses around their necks, and not always for strictly religious reasons. The esoteric function of a cross is to disturb and disrupt the surrounding energies. When worn around the neck as a golden cross, it wards off infection, or it would, except the crosses women wear are too small and have too little gold to have any real impact. So far as I can tell, the Latin cross, the Celtic cross, and the equal armed Greek and Maltese crosses all have the same basic properties, in other words, they all ward off bad energies. It is for this reason the Church uses the Sign of the Cross compulsively, it is for this reason they encourage their adherents to use it, and it is for this reason those adherents so often actually do so. Much to my surprise, the fact that their Leader and Founder and Great White Father was nailed to one and died on it has nothing whatever to do with it.

Many of you are familiar with copper bracelets, which prevent arthritis. I myself wear one, after I noticed the start of this evil disease some three years ago. My father, his mother and several of my brothers and sisters have all suffered from it.

Blagrave does not use metals or precious stones in his work. He has other ideas. In the springtime he bores holes in hazelnut trees, takes pus from his patients' open wounds, mixes them with the sawdust, puts them in the holes and stops them up. As the sap rises it heals the trapped pus. Which, as it's magnetically attached to the remaining pus in the actual wound, pulls the infection from the patient, resulting in cure. Once we understand the underlying energy nature of the body, this is not hard to follow. Nor is this the only medicinal use of trees that I have found.

Even more dramatic, he takes the patient's excrement, carefully dries it in the dark, mixes it with soil, and in it plants the herbs necessary to cure the ailment. He gives the plant to the patient and instructs that as the plants are tended, so the patient will recover. The patient does not use the plant in any way. Not the leaves, not the stems, not the roots, not the flowers, as the plant physically contains the illness the patient is trying to escape. Using the plant as medicine would merely poison the patient all over again. When the patient is fully cured, the plant is burned and the soil returned to the earth.

My Chinese herbalist doctor was unhappy when she saw the ring around my neck. Wear it for a year, she said, then come back and see me. Well, yes, I replied, I expect to wear it for many years. It appears the better part of Chinese medicine was stripped away from what is now known as Traditional Chinese Medicine, leaving only the fragments that would be acceptable to western science. My daughter thinks I am a wizard, with a ring around my neck and pills taped to my fingers. She's not the first to think so.

— October 20, 2009.

Update, December 2010. In January 2010, feeling increasingly weak, I took a tip from Alton Brown, a TV chef. He said, "eat sardines, make your heart stronger." I thought, why not, and to my great surprise, immediately felt much better. Two weeks later my mother passed away. Her funeral caused me to cancel my ongoing appointment with the Chinese acupuncturist. Afterwards, the combination of herbal wine, gold ring around my neck, and a daily tin of sardines left me feeling so strong that I discontinued my bimonthly sessions altogether. Nine months later I went back for another supply of herbs. My doctor was impressed with my progress.

The Introductory from :
AstroAmerica's Daily Ephemeris

The Julian Day is calculated from noon, GMT, which means that a midnight ephemeris (such as this one) will always show it ending as a half-day. If you divide the Julian Day for January 1, 2000, by 365.25, you get a number of years a few minutes shy of exactly 6712, or, to be precise, January 1, 4713 BC (there was no year 0). This system was invented by Joseph Scaliger in 1583. It is based on the Indiction cycle of 15 years (used in dating medieval documents), multiplied times the Metonic cycle of 18 years (lunar), times the Solar cycle of 28 (in the Julian calendar, the number of years to complete one leap year cycle). The product of these numbers is 7560. Scaliger found that all three cycles were last together on January 1, 4713 BC, hence his choice of that date. Which, so far as he—or anyone else—knew, predated all historical dates.

— *October 20*

October 21
1879 – Electric Light Bulb!
1944 – First kamikaze attack
1959 – Guggenheim Museum opens

HALLOWEEN
1517: Luther posts 95 Thesis, Wittenberg
1864: Nevada admitted as 36th state.

Make Money with Astrology!!

Times tough where you are? Clients fallen off? Or are you the hot, up and coming Astro Newcomer looking to prove himself? Consider 15 minute mini-readings.

Trot on over to your favorite bar and tell the barkeep that once a week, or once a month, you would like to circulate among the patrons, giving 15 minute quickie readings. And you'd like his permission. If he's got brains, he will counter with, Why not a Zodiac night, why not set you up with a table? Which makes you the evening's entertainment. So grab your laptop!

What to wear: Something outlandish. A big floppy hat. Dress like a pirate. Beads and bangles. A monocle. Bandana. Dark sunglasses. Heavy leather. Be campy!

What to charge: You ain't doing this for free. What do ATMs dispense in your neighborhood? $20? That's good for a start. If after your first night the line is stretched around the block, consider doubling it.

Bring an assistant: Someone who can keep track of who's next, and—more importantly—keep you on schedule. You don't want to spend an hour on one guy.

How to give a mini-reading, part 1: Read the second house cusp. The sign on the cusp, the planet ruling the cusp, the house and sign the ruler is in. That impresses people no end. If there's a planet in the house, ignore it. If there's more than one, bone up on your stelliums.

How to give a mini-reading, part 2: How to deal with client emergencies, courtesy of Wanda Sellar, **The Consultation Chart**. Draw a chart for the moment (i.e., horary). Drop its ascendant into the natal. That's the house with the problem. Put the horary moon into the natal and note the house it lands in. That's how the problem is presenting itself. Make your best stab at it, and then move on.

Stream of consciousness is your friend: Most everyone you see will be at least half-drunk. Their emotions will be right on the surface. Booze will do that to them. You, as the reader (hopefully not drunk) will be reacting to that, whether you know it or not. So, Trust your hunches.

Stay cheerful: Keep the pace going. You will meet with a lot of sadness. Be prepared! Stay upbeat. Be cheerful! **Tell the truth**, give them knowledge, but always **give them hope**. And enjoy yourself!

P.S. If you're a smash success and come home with a lot of loot, if you're doing three pubs a week, consider investing in Continuing Education. Take 10% of your winnings & buy our books. Times are tough for us, too.

— *November 3, 2009*

November 5
1494 - Birth of Hans Sachs, mastersinger.
1605 - All hail Guy Fawks Day!
1872 - Susan B. Anthony votes, is fined.
1895 - George Seldon patents the automobile.
1911 - Birth of Roy Rodgers.
1940 - FDR elected to 3rd term.
1968 - Richard Nixon elected president

More on
Make Money

Last week I suggested we could all Get Rich and Retire to Florida by giving quickie readings in smoky, dank bars. C.P., of Hawaii, wanted more details. So I wrote her this, which I share with all of you:

With all respect, you go where the people are. Especially in tough times, bars are full. That's not a good thing, but that's where helpers go. Low energies in bars? Sure are. That's why you're there. You go where the need is.

Clothing is important. You have to separate yourself from everyone else. If you're a foreigner, then that will do nicely. Otherwise you need to be objectively different from everyone else, in order that they can relate to you as an outsider, and not a wannabe bed partner. And that you don't try to relate to them in that regard. In the process, you don't pick up their emotional junk, i.e., low energy. Their desperation. You need a way of staying clean of that, and that's important. My Chinese herbalist is, well, Chinese. Her patients are not. We do not think of her as "one of us". We think of her as an outsider who doesn't really understand "our problems". This objective difference permits her to heal us without taking on our garbage and, in the process, burning herself out.

If you got tired of being a Savior, it's because people saw you as one of them. It would have been better if they had seen you as a space alien. The right dress will do that. The more they're looking at your costume, the less they're weighing you down unnecessarily. Don't think of it as a "costume". Think of it as necessary armor. Whatever you do, don't go into a bar in street clothes and expect to survive the encounter.

The whole point of being in a crowded, smoky, semi-drunken bar is to generate a buzz. That buzz helps you be a better astrologer. (Trust me.) That buzz will get you a dozen people, each eager to spend a moderate amount. Which makes the night worthwhile for you. You don't need hours to prepare, and you positively DO NOT want to spend more than a few minutes with any given client—anywhere, anytime, for any reason. The best astrologers I ever met kept sessions under 30 minutes and did little if any preparation—and were quite well paid by their many adoring clients.

Clients in need are vampires. They will suck you dry. So don't let them. Keep them at arms length, by means of costume, by keeping the time short. If they come from curiosity, if they haven't got a problem, give them a dazzle and move on. If they've got a problem, FIND IT, deal with it, and then move on. That's why the horary technique with the ascendant is so vital. Do this—make it quick, make it sharp, make it pointed, get it over—and people will think you're the best reader they ever found.

If you're looking for respect, you're in the wrong field and I would guess you're not much of a counsellor. What you're looking for is to see someone's eyes light up. That's all the reward I ever wanted, and if I have to strip naked and look like a idiot moron to do it, I will. This profession has got way too many preening egos, eager to dispense Holy Writ. I'm not one of them. And, as I said last week, Stay upbeat. Be cheerful! Tell the truth, give them knowledge, but always give them hope. And enjoy yourself!

Dave

PS: Dear Donna Cunningham, Please reprint **The Consulting Astrologer's Guidebook**, or let me do it.

Friday the 13th of November is Good For You! (*really!*)

1002 – Ethelred orders all Danes in England killed.
1642 – Royalists fail to take London.
1775 – Ethan Allen attacks Montreal.
1851 – First settlers at Seattle.
1918 – Allies occupy Constantinople
1927 – NYC: Holland Tunnel opens
1941 – Ark Royal torpedoed.
1954 – Great Britain defeats France (rugby)
1971 – Mariner 9 orbits Mars.
1982 – Vietnam Veterans memorial dedicated
1994 – Sweden joins the E.U.

Born November 13:
532   – St. Augustine of Canterbury.
1814 – General Joe Hooker.
1833 – Edwin Booth, American actor. His boyhood home is not two miles from here, which is today known as "Tudor". No mention is made of his infamous brother.
1850 – Robert Louis Stevenson.
1856 – Louis Brandeis, jurist.
1953 –Andrés Manuel López Obrador - Amlo
1955 – Whoopi Goldberg.

Things to look for:
2012 – Total Solar Eclipse.

So what about the 14th ???
1921 – Communist Party of Spain founded.
1922 – The BBC begins broadcasting.
1941 – Ark Royal sinks.
2003 – Sedna discovered.

Marc Robertson
February 8, 1937 — September 26, 1984

Book of the Week

No, it's not **Gate of Rebirth**. Weiser has just reprinted Haydn Paul's 1993 book, though I don't know why. So when it showed up on Wednesday, I had to find a place on the site for it. On the House page, of course, but where? Then I saw Marc Robertson's **8th House**. I could put it next to that, make a mini-8th house section. And then, because I gave Robertson's book short shrift years ago, I could have another look at it, too.

I confess I've never really looked at Robertson's books. They're full of this fussy, obnoxious **LOOK at ⓞⒼ** typesetting that, when I was yearbook editor in 1970, was just too cute and is now entirely dated. First impressions and all that.

And I was more than surprised. I was amazed, frankly. After the evasive muddle of Paul's book, Robertson opens with investment advice. Which is 8th house, though not one astrologer in a hundred knows that. (Financial astrologers excepted, but how many of you do you think there are?) He then looks at transcendence, i.e. how the crassly physical becomes sublimely spiritual, which is 8th house. He fudges physical death (well, don't we all), but does mention that he feared September, and well he should as he had Virgo/Libra in his 8th. He died some years ago, so I looked up his date of death: September 26, 1984. October, he said, was always a better month. He was found, in fact, nine days later. The final section, Becoming an Individual Through Sex, is brilliant. Sex for the sake of amusement is 5th house. Sex as something that changes you forever, that's 8th house. In seventy-six pages, an amazing little book.

— November 24, 2009

Three kinds of Astrologers
by Sepharial

I am disposed to classify astrologers in three main groups—fatalists, casuists, and idealists—according to the various views they take of the nature and purport of astrology. The Fatalists believe, or profess to believe, that there is a planetary configuration and an event which attends it. They admit no possible intervention, amelioration, or extenuation. *Che sarà sarà,* and that is the end of the matter. They argue a certain necessity of connection between character and environment as we find it and planetary positions at the moment of birth. As regards "directions," all of which are formed within a few hours of the birth, they speak of them as " seeds sown " in the plastic soil of the human soul which spring up and bear fruit at the appointed time, as measured by the arc of direction. They are born when they are born by necessity of universal law, and they die when they die because fatal arcs of direction are then in force.

They speak of laws of Nature as if they were dynamic forces against which mankind cannot possibly contend. They forget that laws are only mental concepts induced upon our minds by an apprehension of the correlated successiveness of events, and that what we know about natural laws is an infinitesimal part of the possibly knowable. They speak of the bodies of this microscopic solar system of ours as if they were the be-all and end-all of existence. They forget that the continuity of matter is a fact only on the material plane, and that there are forces of an immaterial nature which transcend both matter and what we call the laws of material existence. The moral law is an illustration of this. It is spiritual in its origin and spiritual in its effects. If astrology teaches fatalism, its use is at an end and it becomes a suicidal science, since there is no object in knowing that which must inevitably take place. It would reduce man to an automaton and divest him of all moral responsibility.

The Casuists are those astrologers who accommodate their facts and figures to popular concepts by a discreet use of a *mélange* of spurious philosophy. They forever quote the effete adage : " The wise man rules his stars, the fool obeys them " ; and that other which says : " The stars incline but do not compel." They put a premium upon the wisdom of experience and the will-power of a purposeful character, and promptly consign a man to destruction by telling him that his horoscope indicates he has neither one nor the other. They do not suggest to him that astrology, properly conceived and applied, is in itself the very concrete of experience, nor that the will-to-be and the will-to-do are functions of the human soul which rise superior to all circumstance, outlasting life itself.

The Idealists are those among astrologers who regard the intelligible universe as the expression of a Supreme Intelligence, who regard the planetary combinations merely as symbols, knowing that the causes of all effects are within man himself, the cogniser of all experience. They regard the " signs of the times " as the driver of a locomotive regards the signals, not as " causes " of disaster, but as warnings against it, an open book to those who can read the signals, but of no value to those who cannot. They look upon the science of astrology as a wireless operator looks upon his code-book, merely as a means of interpreting the signals—a science evolved by man for the service of man.

My own view of the matter is that there is some thing to say for the materialist side of the question, and a great deal more for the idealistic. There is not the shadow of doubt in my own mind as to the material fact of the interaction of the planetary bodies, nor as to the fact that this interaction is registered by an intervening body of the system only at certain angles. The Platonic dictum that " God geometrises " is nowhere better illustrated than in the law governing the interaction of bodies belonging to the same system. The physical effects of the syzygies, and especially of ecliptic conjunctions of the luminaries, are immediately appreciable. The law of the tides is a concrete example of the fact of interplanetary action. We cannot deny the dynamic effects of planetary action on the material plane, and we have every reason for including in this category the human organism, compounded as it is of cosmic elements and in direct physical relations with a material environment. But that does not warrant us in extending our views to include the action of physical bodies upon the immaterial part of us, the only part of us that is essential and distinctively human. The only thing that can directly affect the soul of man is the soul of another human being. There is continuity of action upon all planes of existence because there is a continuity of matter upon all planes, but we have no grounds for extending the range of action from one plane to another plane, except it be by mediation or agency. Else we could say that a good soul must be possessed of a sound body, a beautiful soul of a comely body, and that our moral principles are derived from what we eat and drink—instead of which, what we eat and drink depends on our moral principles. There is sound philosophy in the words of Tennyson when he says that "Soul to soul strikes through a finer element of its own." It is capable of acting mediately through the physical body or immediately through its own essential being. These views will doubtless alter our viewpoint in regard to much that hitherto has been regarded as fundamental to a belief in astrology. The effort to accommodate the facts of astrology to the materialistic science of a generation agone has tended to this issue. Without in any way disposing of astrology as a physical science, it is high time that we learned to interpret the facts of that science in the light of the higher spiritual teaching to which we have access. Otherwise we shall debase the science and enslave our own souls. In such case it were better that our astrology had never been written. As a physical science, astrology has an immense future before it in this utilitarian age upon which we have embarked ; but as a fatalistic creed it is not worth an hour's study.

These remarks will enable the reader to understand why, in the following statement of the "Effects of Directions," I have pursued the common practice of attributing certain results or sets of conditions as accompanying the formation of " directions " or planetary combinations in the horoscope subsequent to the birth. They should not be regarded as inevitable " effects " of such directions, but rather as things signalled, as if we should hoist the red light to indicate "danger ahead," the green light for "caution," and the white light for "road clear." These signals do not cause disasters, but our ignorance of them, our inability to see them, or our wilful disregard of them may very well result in a catastrophe. Human science has harnessed many of the subtle and intangible forces of Nature and deployed them to the service of man. It may do the same with cosmic forces that are as universal as etheric action.

— Excerpted from **Primary Directions, A Definitive Study** (originally: Directional Astrology), by Sepharial. I excerpted the beginning of this in the November 24, 2009 newsletter. — *Dave*

November 26:
1789 – Thanksgiving
1922 – King Tut's tomb entered

Retrogrades
(written December, 2009)

In honor of the upcoming retrogrades of Mars (20 December) and Mercury (26 December), a quick overview of what retrogrades are, and some notes on the better books.

Viewed from a geocentric perspective, *retrogrades are a function of the angular relationship individual planets have to the Sun*. When a given planet reaches a stated number of degrees from the Sun, it goes retrograde. When the Sun's advance returns the pair to that same angular relationship, the planet goes direct. Let's consider Mercury.

On December 26, Mercury is just shy of 22 degrees Capricorn. The Sun is just shy of 6 degrees Capricorn. The difference? 16 degrees. At which time Mercury will go retrograde.

Mercury goes direct on the 15th of January. At that time it will be 5-something degrees of Capricorn. The Sun will be at 24-something degrees of Capricorn. Difference: 19 degrees. Get the picture?

Well, not quite. Up to January 27, Mercury will fall further behind the Sun, by which time it will be 25 degrees behind. For years I was unaware of this curious period of "Retrograde Hangover". Born up to a dozen days after Mercury turned direct? You're "running to catch up." Instead, the talk is of Mercury coming out of its "shadow", which is to say, catching up with where it was when it first went retrograde. Which will happen around the 4th of February, 2010.

Mercury next goes retrograde on April 18, at which time it will be at 12-something Taurus. The Sun will be at 28 Aries, the difference being 14 degrees. You can look the rest up for yourself.

Our neighboring planets, Venus and Mars, are the rarest of retrogrades, doing so only once every other year. Retrograde Venus is quite rare, lasting only five or six weeks and is always significant, one way or another. Mars is a sturdier retrograde. The upcoming Mars retrograde, which starts on 20 December, will end on 10 March next year.

On 20 December, Mars will be just shy of 20 Leo. The Sun will be 28-something Capricorn, the difference 158 degrees. We can now talk about aspects.

All the major Sun-Mars aspects, including the inconjunct, are direct, with the single exception of the opposition. But watch what happens as we move further from the Sun.

Jupiter will go retrograde at 3-something Aries on July 23. At that time the Sun will be at 0 Leo. Which is 117 degrees. So what do you think of a Sun-Jupiter trine? Did you know that Sun-Jupiter trines have a stationary (direct or retrograde) Jupiter, by definition? Does a station make an aspect "better" or "worse"? "Stronger" or "weaker"? You decide.

Saturn will go retrograde on January 14. At that time it will be at 4-something Libra, the Sun will be at 22-something Capricorn. That's 108 degrees. This brings up an interesting paradox. On the one hand, the Sun-Saturn square, said to be stressful, always has a direct Saturn, which, in most signs, is said to be good. On the other, the Sun-Saturn trine, which is said to be a good thing, has a distinctly retrograde Saturn, which, in most signs, is said to be not so good.

What's the practical result? Sun-Saturn squares give you more direct Saturn than you can probably handle, while the bashful retrograde Saturn in Sun-Saturn trines never quite delivers, even if it wants to. I have the two trine, with Saturn retrograde in Libra. Saturn in Libra is said to give a perfect sense of timing, and, trine the Sun, it certainly has the ability to manifest itself. But although I in fact have a wonderful sense of timing, I never get to use it: Retrograde. Dang!

You can work out the details on the remaining planets. Pluto, for example, changes direction at 102 degrees. A century ago, when Pluto was further out there, the number of degrees was 98. A planet infinitely far from the Sun will go retrograde at 90.

Understand the mechanics, you will better understand the interpretation. Some books:

Helen Adams Garrett's books are favorites because she has a firm grasp on the mechanics of retrogrades: **Understanding Retrogrades,** and, **More About Retrogrades.**

Mohan Koparkar deals with oppositions, house placements, and rulerships. He's notably not so good on outer planets.

What to do before Mercury goes retro on the 26th? Get Therese Francis's **Mercury Retrograde Book.** Also check out the retrograde section in Joanne Wickenburg's **Your Hidden Powers.** I'll have a few things to say about retrograde Saturn in a week or two.

—*December 15, 2009*

December 16:
1431 - Henry VI crowned in Paris.
1707 - Last eruption of Mt. Fuji.
1770 - Birth of Louis van Beet farmer, Bonn.
1773 - Boston Tea Party.
1811 - New Madrid earthquake.
1826 - Ruler of Fredonia declared.
1850 - Pilgrims arrive, New Zealand.
1893 - Premiere of New World Symphony.
1937 - Only "successful" escape, Alcatraz.

Merry Christmas, 2009!

In America, the jolly old red-suited Elf dates from an old Coca-Cola ad of a century ago. It was a right popular representation of a much older figure. Soon enough, the world-wide reach of Atlanta, Georgia, had swept all other contenders aside. Or nearly. And to think, the city is famous for its peaches.

Over at the Iceland Weather Report, ace reporter Alda has been regaling us with tales of the 13 Yule Lads: A collection of freaky guys that hold the nation hostage for the thirteen days of Christmas. Among them, Pot Licker, Bowl Licker, Door Slammer, Sausage Snatcher (horse meat, at that), Candle Beggar & more. As if they weren't enough, there is a tiger-sized Yule Cat that will eat you alive if you are not wearing new clothes on Christmas day. Not clothes received on Christmas, that's too late. You have to have a new outfit in advance of the day. And to think, all we do here in the States is shop until there is no more money, or mercy, left.

Ahhh, the Snows of Christmas! The local production of the Nutcracker, with my daughter as a soldier, was cancelled, so there was a party at dress rehearsal / improvised final production. Wonderful!

—December 22, 2009

December 24
564 – Hagia Sophia dedicated 2nd time.
1914 – World War I: Christmas truce.
1946 – French 4th Republic founded.
1955 – NORAD first tracks Santa Claus

REINCARNATION
Astrology and Karma

Last week I promised you some fun. Existing books on astrology and reincarnation are just hopeless. South node as past life is a cop-out. Problems inherited via Saturn is true enough, but is barely a start. Your last life is 12th house, your current life is first house, your next life is 2nd house, but what if, as in my case, houses 12 and 1 are empty? Does that mean no life? Isn't it true that occupied houses are More Important than unoccupied houses? What about Uranus in 2? That's sure hopeful!

For quick and dirty, I said that your present natal chart represents, more or less, conditions applying at the close of your last life. Your natal is NOT your previous death chart (that's something else entirely), but it certainly has the flavor of your life in its last days, in a general sense.

To read your current natal chart for the twilight of your last life, you read the houses with planets in them. Occupied houses represent areas of life that were of compelling interest to you. The planets were the means by which you were dealing with them. The signs they are in were the tools you were using. Aspects were planets that were helping out. Or hindering, as the case may be.

So in what house is your Sun, in this life? That's where your life, as a whole, was focused. What is the sign? That's the way you were dealing with it.

So, where's your Moon? That's what gave you peace, or, more likely, where you felt emotionally vulnerable and/or upset. The sign, again, tells us how and why. (You're going to get a lesson in distinguishing houses and signs.) The aspect between Sun and Moon tells us, more or less, what your overall success was in life.

Were you all in one place, all at the same moment, in other words, are the Sun and Moon conjunct or in the same house?

Were you stressed, born at first or last quarter: Sun and Moon in square? Look at the houses to determine the areas of life which were stressful.

You can do this with all the other planets, using simple keywords for each.

But you will say, this sounds a lot like an ordinary natal reading. And you'd be right. So let's do something more advanced.

Normally I don't use my own chart as an example, for the simple reason that if you can only read your own chart, I wonder if you can read a chart at all. But in this case, the subject is so slippery, and I have done so much personal work, that the demonstration is compelling.

So what about Saturn? Mine is retrograde in the 5th in an intercepted sign. Natally, Saturn in 5 is difficulty with children. Lack of children. Loss of children. And in fact, I have lost at least three: Two miscarriages and an abortion. I have only one, a delightful daughter. Saturn retrograde says I was never terribly concerned about the lack of children. Now, true to Saturn, I wish I could have more, but cannot (weak heart). Saturn intercepted says that women, save one, never really wanted to give me children. That's my natal Saturn.

Past life delineation of my *current natal* chart goes like this: Saturn in 5 means I wasn't a very good father, that I wasn't there *(true)*. Saturn retrograde means I repudiated them, in a most cruel fashion *(true, and don't ask for details)*. Saturn intercepted means they weren't mine. Which might explain the rest.

If they weren't mine, then whose were they? They were my wife's and I begrudgingly accepted them, as Saturn in 5 is in mutual reception to Venus in 8, where the 8th is my wife's second, of possessions. Begrudging because the two planets are square.

So who was the father? Let's look at my natal 7th. It's unoccupied, but the ruler, which represents my wife, is in the 11th, and, like Saturn, is intercepted. The 11th is friends. My wife from my last life was sleeping around—with my friends. Or people who pretended to be my "friends"—that's the "interception". But that planet itself has a dispositor, and that dispositor, Mars in the 6th, will tell me what sort of "friend": A servant. Or a doctor. In fact, I died in the arms of my wife, and a doctor. (It was so noted by the man's father, himself a doctor.) Does this mean he fathered my four children? No. We were living elsewhere when the children were born. All my natal chart can tell me is who my wife was seeing around the time I passed away. Whoever my children's father was, the intercepted opposition, from 11 to 5, says he was unable to claim them as his own.

The surprising conclusion is that parts of the chart are not ours, but rather, are the result of actions of people that we once knew. And that interceptions are dysfunctions that carry over from life to life. That's just as surprising.

—December 22, 2009

December 25:
800 – Coronation of Charlemagne
1000 – Kingdom of Hungary founded.
1066 – William crowned, London.
1223 – First nativity, by St. Francis of Assi
1643 – Christmas Island founded.
1776 – Washington crosses the Delaware !

Aphorisms —

are second-stage cookbook delineations. Instead of Mars-in-a-sign, or Venus-in-a-house, second stage delineations involve multiple factors. Such as, *Venus with Saturn or Mars in the sixth house indicates marriage to a dishonest and loose person* (Robson). They are shortcuts to reading a chart and are usually presented without their underlying rationale, which can make their application tricky. Many of my personal remarks are de facto aphorisms. Much of Firmicus is a compilation of aphorisms, as is "Ptolemy's" famous **Centiloquy,** as well as the Lilly/Coley/Cardan/Bonatus **Astrologer's Guide**. Here are some more from Vivian Robson's *(he's a guy, guys)* **Astrology and Sex.**

House position of the ruler of the 7th:

In the Tenth: Partner of high birth or position, but if afflicted, loss or trouble in the profession through marriage.

In the Eleventh: Many friendships through marriage. Happy marriage to a widow with children. If afflicted, loss of friends, or misconduct of partner with the native's friends. If Saturn is in aspect, marriage will be one of friendship and almost platonic.

In the Twelfth: Enmity and dissention with the partner, who will be of obscure birth. If well aspected, marriage to a doctor, nurse, or person connected with an institution.

Notice how this works. Ruler of the 7th in the 12, yes, that's institutions. But why doctors? Because the 12th is the 6th of the partner, which signifies servants (obscure birth), or medical people. So why enmity? Because it's still your 12th, and you have a lot of painful things hidden in there, hidden from you, but not your partner. A further deduction is that such a marriage would most likely be forced, one way or another, as I can't imagine someone wanting such a union.

—*December 22, 2009*

December 1:
1420 - Henry V enters Paris
1640 - Portugal leaves Spain
1822 - Peter I crowned in Brazil
1918 - Transylvannia unites with Romania
1919 - Lady Astor enters Parliament
1952 - Christine Jorgenson is a girl

On December 12
1812 – The French stop invading Russia
1897 – Belo Horizonte is founded in Brazil
1911 – Delhi becomes capital of India
1917 – Boy's Town founded (Nebraska)
1936 – Chiang Kai-shek is kidnapped
1941 – India declares war on Japan

Born on December 12
1745 – John Jay, 1st of the Supremes
1791 – Marie Louise, Napoleon's 2nd wife
1805 – William Lloyd Garrison
1805 – Henry Wells, founder of Amex
1821 – Gustave Flaubert
1915 – Frank Sinatra
1919 – Olivia Barclay, astrologer
1924 – Ed Koch, Mayor of New York
1940 – Dionne Warwick, singer
1952 – Cathy Rigby, gymnast

December 14:
1782 – First balloon flight, Paris.
1911– Amundsen reaches South Pole

REINCARNATION
Intercepted Signs

I was going to give you the key to finding the ascendant on your past-life chart, presuming you're lucky enough to know your past life birthday, but to my surprise, I stumbled onto something else instead. Intercepted signs.

An intercepted sign is a sign that does not fall on any house cusp. The house starts with a late degree of one sign, has all 30 degrees of the next sign inside it, and finally ends several degrees into the third sign. I had previously speculated that such a house had two distinct "stories", or delineations. The first, the sign on the cusp, was what should be, but largely wasn't, partly because the degree was late and so the sign exhausted, but mostly because there was a parasite (intercepted sign) lurking inside it. That sign constitutes a "make-do" that you're not quite aware of until it's pointed out to you. I still think that works, especially if the intercepted sign is not tenanted, i.e., there's no planet in the sign.

But in analyzing my own intercepted Saturn in Libra in the 5th, I found compelling reasons (too involved to go into here) to believe the four children I had in my most immediate past life were not mine. In this life I remember as a small child, less than five years old, before I knew or suspected anything, that I did NOT want to marry, and I did NOT want children. It is my opinion that such childish thoughts are hangovers from the previous life, as I know of no other explanation for them.

So I am now exploring the idea that intercepted signs are dysfunctions from the immediate past life. In the past week, two examples have arrived.

By accident I was directed to a page with the chart of

an English magician (the real kind, not the stage juggler), born January 8, 1953, 1:30 am, Goring by Sea, England. Here we have Sun intercepted in Capricorn in the 3rd, Saturn on the ascendant in Libra, and the Moon in the 12th. In this life, the man is said to be a recluse. Looking at the interception, with Saturn on the ascendant and ruling the intercepted Sun, I had the strongest impression of a reincarnate fugitive. Someone who was hiding in his own community (3rd house is local), someone known to the authorities (Sun disposed by Saturn), someone whose very face was known to all (Saturn on the ascendant), but who escaped capture. Moon in the 12th was another indicator.

On Monday I had a call from a woman curious about her 5th house Saturn. Turns out she had intercepted signs (I forget which) in the 1st and 7th. I had just finished delineating a chart with an erroneous time that gave interceptions in 1 and 7, so I pounced.

Interception in the first, there was a past life where she wasn't "seen" for who she really was (1st). As a consequence, there was an arranged marriage with a man who had no interest in her as a wife (7th). So, when she gave him children (5th), they weren't hers, but her husband's. Perhaps they were taken away from her, perhaps she felt guilty about having them, there are things that I just can't guess, but the net result was a pair of interceptions and Saturn in the 5th.

I stress the interceptions I've seen were all tenanted, in other words, there were planets lurking in them. Also, in every case, there was some controlling planet or house elsewhere in the chart which, by aspect, or rulership, or just because it was appropriate, was the source of the problem, or provided the outcome, or both.

A few months ago I reviewed a book by Alice Miller that claimed intercepted houses made the individual somehow "special", unique and gifted, an idea I found silly. For one thing, the further north you go, the more signs get intercepted. In India interceptions are quite rare. In Scotland, it's exactly the reverse. And now here I am, claiming that interceptions make you dysfunctional.

Could it be that we all started out in equatorial Gardens of Eden and as we made mistake after mistaeke, our penance was to be born, ever more gifted, in ever colder climes? Is our fate to be Nordic reindeer herding geniuses? Will our Ultimate Destination be as a desk clerk in that famous Swedish Ice Hotel?

I think it more likely the chart finds ways to give us what we need to experience, and that when it has interceptions to work with, it does so.

—*December 29, 2009*

January 1 first began the year:
1522: Venice
1544: Holy Roman Empire
1556: Spain, Portugal
1559: Prussia, Sweden
1564: France
1576: S. Holland;
1579: Lorraine
1583: N. Holland
1600: Scotland

January 1:
45 BC: Start of the Julian Calendar
1515: Francois 1ère King of France
1772: First travellers cheques
1788: First edition of The Times of London
1801: United Kingdom created
1801: Ceres discovered
1808: US bans importation of slaves.

Intercepted Signs & Reincarnation

I have puzzled out that intercepted signs amount to where you were a victim of abuse in a past life. This gets us into Victimology and there's a rather large body of literature on that subject already. Since co-dependency and abuse can get explosive in a hurry, I need to start with some ground rules.

Beginning with the definition of "intercepted signs". Intercepted signs are signs of the zodiac which do not appear on any house cusp. Just so we're all on the same page.

First, you need an accurately timed chart. Yes, two quadrants of your horoscope are going to be bigger than the other two, no matter what time of day you were born, but the pair of houses that have intercepted signs in them are dependent on the exact time. Interceptions in 1 and 7 are very different than interceptions in 3 and 9. If I'm not mistaken, many of you who have interceptions will go ballistic when you read my preliminary delineations, so it's important you've got the right chart in front of you.

In this regard, the time on your birth certificate IS NOT ACCURATE unless it's been PROVEN ACCURATE. And I am the example. A transcription error turned 12:52 pm into 12:32 pm (5 misread as 3). I subsequently rectified it to 12:47. In my case, the difference was interceptions in 6 and 12, instead of 5 and 11. In other words, for 25 years I had a chart which I myself could not read. That's what a time error will do.

Second. You must use PLACIDUS, or its near cousin, Topocentric. NONE other. Koch, for example, gives me interceptions in 4 and 10. Other house systems have other uses. This isn't one of them.

Third. One or both of the intercepted signs must be TENANTED. The two intercepted signs must have at least ONE PLANET between them. So what if you have interceptions but there's no planets in them? Simple. You're Over It. It was Long Ago. It's No Big Deal. It's Done and Finished. It's Old News. It's Ho-Hum. — Get the idea?

Fourth. Proper delineation requires synthesis of the signs, houses, planets, aspects and dispositors involved. If you never got beyond reading it out of a book, you're not going to get terribly far with interceptions, though you will get something.

The results are just awful. I hate myself for figuring this out. Here goes:

Interceptions in 1 and 7 are a past life as a slave (1) or as chattel (7). In both cases, you were not seen as who you actually were (ascendant), as a result, you were either a nobody (slave) or were sold in marriage (chattel). Also here are those who have no name, who lose their identity. In his next life's chart, Mozart will be here, as his identity was lost.

Interceptions in 2 and 8 have to do with property. If the emphasis is in 2, you came from a place where you had no possessions, you were destitute. If in 8, you were forced to borrow in order to survive.

Interceptions in 3 and 9 were fugitives (3) or refugees (9).

Interceptions in 4 and 10 was a life as a prisoner (4) or held to public ridicule (10).

Interceptions in 5 and 11 have to do with children (they weren't yours, that's why you're indifferent now) and/or friends who weren't true (11).

Six and 12 are confinement in a large camp (12) or forcibly drafted into an army (6). A past life as soldier on the Russian front qualifies as 6, while death in a German or Japanese labor camp qualifies as 12. As soldiers and camp laborers are often young adults, people who die in such situations often reincarnate quickly, often in less than 20 years, sometimes in as little as five. Anorexia is a possible current life consequence (12), as are vivid memories.

I just shocked myself. I know a man who is most likely a reincarnate WWII German soldier. Reliving that has been his whole life as long as I've known him, and that's nearly

30 years. So I peeked just now at his chart. Interceptions in 6 and 12 ! Intercepted Scorpio in 6 with Sun, Venus, Jupiter and Neptune in it. Intercepted Mars in Taurus in 12 opposing and disposing it all, irritates it out of him, but keeps it a secret from all but close friends. I've had his chart for 20 years, but before this moment I had never looked at the interceptions.

Intercepted planets have dispositors, and intercepted planets rule house cusps. These can be tricky. In my case, Jupiter intercepted in Aries in 11 rules Sag on my 7th: My false friends belonged to my past life wife. In another case, Sun in Capricorn, intercepted in 3, was ruled by Saturn in Libra on the ascendant. Sun in 3, a fugitive. Saturn disposing, the law was after him. On his ascendant, they knew who he was (1) and where (3), but, with Sun intercepted, could not put their hands (i.e., a cusp) on him.

Real astrology has teeth in it. It is fascinating to see it in motion.

— *January 12, 2010*

January 8
871 – Ethelred defeats Danes!
1297 – Monaco becomes independent!
1746 – Bonnie Prince Charlie in Stirling!
1790 – Washington's first State of Union Address
1815 – Andy Jackson defeats British in N Orleans.
1911 – Gypsy Rose Lee born
1926 – Abdul ibn Saud 1st King of Saudi Arabia!
1959 – Castro takes Santiago de Cuba!
1964 – LBJ declares War on Poverty!
2005 – Submarine hits mountain!

January 8, 1926 – Birth of Soupy Sales, pie-in-the-face comic. Died on October 22, 2009, little more than two months ago.

More on Houses

Houses are how astrology organizes itself. Learn to use houses and the details you will get will amaze you. Without houses as a framework, you will have only an odd collection of generalities, as that is all you can expect from aspects, planets, signs and houses, when they are out of context.

What's Your Sign?

No, let's rephrase that. What's your House? Try this: In your mind, fix a clear image of each of the twelve houses. Then think of someone you know well. What house(s) best represent him? Look at his chart. What planet(s) does he have in that house? Is it the Sun, the Moon, or the ruler of his ascendant? Or does he have a stellium in that house? In no case will it be an unoccupied house, nor will it be a house with a singleton outer planet in it.

You've heard of Cardinal, Fixed and Mutable, as they apply to signs. Apply the same idea to houses:

Angular (1, 4, 7, 10)

Succeedent (2, 5, 8, 11), and

Cadent (3, 6, 9, 12)

Planets in angular houses make you get out and DO THINGS. In the first, you do them for yourself. In the 7th, your partner does them for you (or makes you do them), in the 4th, you do it for the memory, in the 10th, to show off. Active people have angular planets. The most dynamic have cardinal planets in those angular houses. People with fixed sign planets in angular houses are determined and unyielding. People with mutable planets in angular houses drive themselves from one thing to the next.

Planets in succeedent houses (2, 5, 8 and 11) are where you want to HAVE things. Have money (2), have fun or children (5), have an intimate peer (8), have friends (11). Planets in Cardinal signs are aggressive and will pursue these things, planets in Fixed are glad to have / are stuck with — or without, planets in Mutables have no control over what they get or when or how they get it. Know someone with sex on the brain? Betcha he's got cardinal signs on succeedent house cusps and planets in Cards in 5 and/or 8. (See how simple this is?) Which is me, dear friends.

Planets in Cadent houses (3, 6, 9 and 12) make you DEFENSIVE. The world is a strange place and you must be on your guard at all times. Cardinal planets in cadent houses compel you to hunt down ambiguity and kill it. Fixed planets in cadent houses make barricades, behind which plans are carefully crafted. Mutable planets in cadent houses live in chaos. I presume that after a time, they get used to it.

Some professions are entirely dominated by just one house. Scientists come to mind. Many of them have debilitated 9th houses. Why the 9th? Because many people take up science, not in a quest for knowledge—which would be 3rd house—but from a fear of the unknown and a craving for security—which is 9th. Which makes Science a religion substitute. Such people, while repudiating "God" (whatever that may be), embrace "Science" as a god substitute. All attributes normally given to "god" are transferred to "science". Including dogmatism and intolerance. We've again run into the local high school science teacher who uses the school's planetarium to compulsively denounce astrology. Gee, I would think the planetarium gizmo would give him enough to play with, he wouldn't need to embarrass himself denouncing anything.

My neighbor, here at the Center, is a high-school physics teacher. (Is the world trying to introduce me to these people?) Who is a very nice man and a very good neighbor. For all I know, years ago he got his job and they said, Well, we need a physics teacher, can you manage? And he thought (so I suppose) Well, I'd rather be a coach, but I guess I can manage. And ever since, has just gone on.

But perhaps not. A couple of years ago he got himself ordained a minister in some fundamentalist sect or other. One that doesn't require him to knock on doors and convert the neighbors, thank, ah, well, you know.

So why do Scientists, the Clergy, and Astrologers all hate one another? Could it be they are all stuck in the 9th house and just do not get along with one another? Funny thing about the 9th. It's the house of ultimates. Compare it to the 5th, of Kinky Sex. I like kinky sex and you like kinky sex, but it's never occurred to anyone that my kinky is better than your kinky, and to the extent that it has, it's because some 9th house twit (the Church, anyone?) wants to impose outside rules (9th house) on a purely 5th house activity.

Since you asked, personally I'm convinced there's a God out there someplace, but that place is so remote and so far away that I doubt I will ever come across him. So I don't worry about him in the least. In my opinion, a male and a female, properly joined, are God (singular). So not a He, not a She, but a You'n'Me!

— *January 19, 2010*

January 15:
1559 – Elizabeth crowned queen of England
1622 – Molière born
1889 – Coca-Cola incorporated
1908 – Edward Teller born
1909 – Jean Bugatti, car designer, born
1919 – Boston Molasses Disaster
1943 – The Pentagon opens
1967 – First Super Bowl, in Los Angeles
1970 – Muammar al-Qaddafi leads Libya
2001 – Wikipedia goes on-line

January 21
1789 – First American novel, in Boston.
1793 – Execution of Louis XVI
1883 – Brisbane gets 18.3 inches of rain
1911 – First Monte Carlo rally.
1921 – Italian Communist Party founded
1905 – Christian Dior born.
1924 – Benny Hill born.
1941 – Placido Domingo, tenor, born.

INITIATION
and other new books

YOU'RE on your way to a hot date when God kidnaps you. Dangles you over the Thousand Foot Precipice of Hell. You feel the heat singing your feet. Burning your eyebrows. He asks you three inane questions:
What is the square root of Vancouver?
How many Martians does it take to land on the Moon?
And, most terrifying of all,
What is **B-FLAT** *?*
Before you can answer, with a roaring laugh, he drops you mirthlessly into the pit.

Six inches before you are to be impaled on the Devil's upraised rotisscrie pitchfork (gee, did he look like Ron Popiel?), God snaps you up, stands you beside him, says Good Job! and drops you, 30 minutes late, a quivering, hysterical blob of jell-o, smack in front of your date for the night. And it was the third date, too. The one where you were going to get lucky! She's fuming and you're a babbling incoherent mess.

Such is the cartoon that people think of when the topic of initiation comes up. For two different views, see my remarks on Delores Ashcroft-Nowicki and Stephanie V. Norris's new book, **The Door Unlocked: An astrological insight into initiation.**

Other New Books.

Friday brought a bunch. While I have them displayed on-line, I won't get notes written about them for a few more days: **Six Astrological Treatises,** by Masha'allah, translated by James Herschel Holden. This one's worth it.

Understanding Karmic Complexes, Evolutionary Astrology and Regression Therapy, by Patricia L. Walsh.

Based on Jeff Green's work, with a foreword by the mysterious Mr. Green himself. **Decanates and Dwads,** by Sakoian and Acker. Previously published as **Zodiac Within Each Sign.** The old edition is cheaper, and still in stock.

— January 26, 2010

And, just because it's such a good lead-in, here are some of my notes on Ashcroft-Nowicki's book:

The goal of initiation is to free you from the wheel of incarnation, to liberate you from the toils of the earth, to remove you from its karma, to restore you to your rightful place in Heaven, with the full awareness and knowledge you have earned, for yourself and by yourself, through an eternity of toils, trials and striving while on earth. That, and nothing more.

When Ashcroft-Nowicki said there were no books on initiation, she misspoke. Initially I thought worse of her, but I think she had a reason. So far as what she said, and what Norris wrote (the ink on paper that has been published) they are both wrong. There are dozens of books on initiation. If she knowingly lied, she's not a spiritual leader that I want anything to do with. If she had some other meaning in mind, then I still don't want anything to do with her, because I'm just not bright enough to figure it all out. (I like things simple.) Of the many books on initiation, these are certainly known to her:

Initiation, Human and Solar, by Alice Bailey

Discipleship in the New Age, volumes 1 and 2, by Alice Bailey

Krishnamurti The Years of Awakening, by Mary Lutyens.

These are well-known to all in Ashcroft-Nowicki's field.

There was a crush of people looking to get "initiated" in the first half of the 20th century. The Theosophists had their Esoteric Order. Alice Bailey, herself a member of the Theosophical Esoteric Order, founded Lucis Trust which had its own esoteric school. Students in that school, candidates for initiation all, were for a time given direct instruction by

Bailey's Tibetan contact. These instructions were compiled and published as **Discipleship in the New Age**, vols. 1 and 2. These are still in print. The names of the various individuals are given only as random initials. It is said that Dane Rudhyar was among them. And there were the Steiner people, the Moriya people, the Gurdjieff people, the CC Zain people, the Order of the Golden Dawn people, Crowley's group, Dion Fortune's group and literally a dozen others. Go Google and you will find even more.

The shabby side of initiation can be read in Mary Lutyen's book. From 1920 to July of 1929, Jiddhu Krishnamurti was put forward as the New Christ. Which, for a time, he was. He was unable, however, to surround himself with qualified people. Instead, charlatans sold "initiations" in his name, to whomever had the money, or the influence. Krishnamurti struggled in vain to control it, but gave up in disgust in 1929, disbanding his Order of the Star. Which was one of the turning points of the 20th century, though few know it.

So what is "initiation"? Initiation is a process that involves DEATH. Not metaphorical death. Not "gee I just escaped death" death. Not some sort of fancy psychic experience, regardless of intensity or duration. DEATH. By the end of the ceremony, the candidate is physically dead. Initiation is not for the squeamish. You get nothing for nothing. What will you give for this precious thing? Will you give your life? No? Then what did you expect?

I am broadly in agreement with Bailey's five initiations, and I am broadly in agreement with Benjamin Creme's list of initiates, their ray structures and Points of Evolution, which I have extensively studied. These are people from all walks of life, because, in reality, initiation in no way restricts one's free will. (Creme is a tragic figure. His great project has failed, the forces behind it—the "inner plane masters"—were false. I am hopeful something can be salvaged from his work.)

It seems to me the first initiation can take a great many forms. Of an actual esoteric order, I once heard of an initiation that went like this:

The candidate was placed in a small room, alone with a very poisonous snake. He was told that to be successful and become "initiate", he had to hypnotize the snake, render it harmless, whereupon he could leave the room. But, alas, he was given neither training, nor preparation, for this feat, and the usual result was tragic: He died by snakebite. Because, in fact, had he hypnotized the snake, he would have failed. Only by dying of snakebite could the candidate complete the process and emerge, in his next life, as an initiate. Was the school murdering its candidates, knowingly, deliberately murdering them, murder in the first degree? **Yes. It was.** That was the whole point. Now do you see why I scoffed at Ashcroft-Nowicki's book and its trivial "initiations"?

There is yet another form of first degree initiation, one handed out lavishly in many states and countries. It is the Death Penalty. This has been raised to a particularly high art in America, where "lucky candidates" often spend a decade or more on Death Row, enduring an almost (almost!) endless series of appeals and stays, hopes that are raised and then crushed. This cruel inhuman process concentrates the mind to a wonderful degree, but it also brings up a serious problem:

Once the candidate has been rendered dead, his soul and spirit are free to draw whatever lessons from the experience they wish. Will he have "learned his lesson", will he be a good and holy man in his next life? Or will he be filled with feelings of the most horrible anger and vengeance? The executioner / initiator has no way of knowing! It is for this reason alone that the Death Penalty is such a monstrous, evil act. Let people find their own way to initiation! There is no reason the state should be blundering about!

Because initiation, the first, in particular, does not make you "good". It does not make you "holy". By mastering death you become more powerful. That is all. This is why candidate selection is so very critical. To some extent, every life we live, every death we endure, are all minor initiatory experiences. But when death is raised to ritual (and executions are always ritual) the power of death to transform becomes overwhelming.

The newly minted first degree initiate, in his next life, knows that he is different, knows that something horrific has befallen him, but does not know what. He spends many years, sometimes entire lifetimes, struggling to make sense of himself. He eventually realizes he is the master of the world, that it is his servant. At this point he styles himself as "The Greatest"—often using those exact words to describe himself. This is a moment of pure ego, and it has its expected result: The Greatest is quickly entangled in the toils of the world and settles down to actual work. As a religious cleric, if that is his choice. As a ritualistic magician, if he desires. As a thespian, if that is his wish. As a loving husband and father. As a ruthless warrior or even sadistic killer, if that is his bent. As a writer, a poet, a musician, a composer, an artist, a scientist, or a politician. It is his choice. All U.S. Presidents, for example, were and are initiates. There is no possible way any lesser a person could ever attain the post. (Yes, even the wicked and stupid ones were initiate.) Whatever his occupation, the initiate will be among the leaders of his field—in company with his fellow initiates, in fact. Initiation in no way limits free will, but rather, expands it. Which is why the last thoughts the candidate has before he undergoes his ordeal are so critically important.

Once the initiate settles down to work, he inevitably becomes enmeshed into the affairs of men. Whatever he eventually decides to do with himself makes him a leader among men. Attracts the attention of the masses. Eventually their love. And no matter how shocking, how tragic, the means of his prior initiation, adulation eventually rescues his hardened heart, softens it, and brings him around. This may take a number of lives (upwards of ten, or so I've been told). Eventually he loves the attention. Ultimately he cannot live without it. Which inevitably leads him to the second of the five great initiations:

The death that creates a second degree initiate is one of selfless love. The candidate sacrifices his life for the good of another. It is the soldier who throws himself unhesitatingly on the live grenade, thereby sparring his friends at the cost of his own life. Given that the circumstances of the second initiation are fundamentally different, recovery from the event is much more rapid. Given that recovery is more rapid, the advance towards the third initiation is much faster. Those whose first initiation was of anger and rage must somehow sublimate their emotions before they can advance further. If they do not, they can, of course, reexperience the horrors of the first initiation over and over again.

Having sacrificed himself for love, the newly reincarnate 2nd degree initiate finds love flowing back to him. And while some part of that is sexual, the primary quality of love is an unquestioning openness. Not just among the people he lives with, but in all possible ways. Suddenly all doors are open. All secrets are shown. He is like a small boy in a candy shop. His eyes get big and round and he excitedly grabs at everything he can. He doesn't know anything, he doesn't understand anything, but there are so many new toys to play with! So many new places to explore! As an example, if, as a first degree initiate, he had eventually settled on a life in music, he would have ended up a pretty good tunesmith. A songwriter. A John Lennon, or a Rossini.

Now, with a lot more to play with, he expands his horizons. He takes up symphonies. He becomes a Dvorak, or a Bruckner. Mere songs are no longer a challenge. He wants symphonic complexity. And in the process something very interesting happens. When he was a first degree songwriter, he had mass appeal. Many of his fans were hardly the sort of people he'd want as friends, but there were millions of them. Now, as a "serious composer", he has the adulation of the elite, but is ignored by the masses. His horizons have narrowed, without his being quite aware.

Of course, the ultimate challenge, the one the 2nd degree initiate will always rise to, is to understand death. To make it a structured event. He will sense it coming, he will puzzle out its methods, and, one way or another, when the time comes, he will make a conscious exit. It will be his ultimate challenge. Such was how Yogananda died. Or he may die in a rage, saying to the world, Enough! I quit! Which is how Beethoven died. In the next life he expects to return as the all-conquering hero. Was not death the ultimate challenge?

Surprisingly, the next life takes an abrupt turn. Having conquered everything that was of interest, he has run out of things to do. So, he no longer has goals. He no longer has a clear purpose. Talent drips off his fingertips, but he is unable to make use of it. Many times thirds are employed as private secretaries (factotums) in their youth, to men who are their inferiors. Lacking clear direction, he may well take

Initiation

up his employer's profession, but if he does, he will most likely be branded a mere copycat. There is an interesting reason. A third is highly sensitive to the astral currents around him. As a result, he easily, and often unwittingly, picks up the thoughts and ideas of those around him. Which, having a perfectly formed mind (if you can figure out death, you can figure out most anything) he makes better use of, but still, it wasn't his own idea. Thirds are just as likely to be unwitting telepaths, verbalizing aloud the secret thoughts of their friends, which means that few will quite trust them. Fourth degree initiates have the same problems, only more so.

In an effort to regain the popularity the third degree initiate dimly remembers from his days as a first degree initiate, he may pander to the masses. Make orchestral settings of pop tunes, for example, or wander the countryside as an itinerant preacher / healer, as Jesus did. No one understands him, no one knows what to do with him. If he achieves success, he also becomes a target. Confucius, who was around this level of development, comes to mind. While briefly a governor, he increased the welfare of his people, ended poverty and brought happiness. His fellow governors promptly invaded his province and overthrew him.

Many envy the third degree initiate. Many others will fear him (fears based on their own ideas of what someone of his talents could do, rather than anything that he might actually do). Much to his surprise, the more he tries to please, the more he is shunned. What he does next is of interest.

Read Matthew with a critical eye and you will see the rabbi Jesus fell into this trap. (In other words, stop looking at him as God Incarnate and instead imagine yourself in his place.) He can heal the sick, he can perform miracles, he is wise and solemn. He entertains people as a moralizing storyteller. Why doesn't the world want him? Why is he forced to wander from town to town, unable to make a home? Unable to find a wife? Have a family? He becomes enormously frustrated. Finally he is seized with the idea that he can lead the miserable rabble to a better life, and throws the money changers out of the temple. But as soon as he flings the first one, he knows he has signed his own death warrant. Throwing the money changers out of the temple was exactly the sort of event the authorities had long feared. They moved swiftly.

The fourth initiation, known to Bailey as the Crucifixion, is when the initiate, whose life has become an enormous failure, commits suicide. This is what Jesus inadvertently willed for himself when he cleaned out the temple. Jesus failed. He died in an enormous rage, as was proven by the storm that brewed over his head. As soon as he was free of the cross, he raced back to the temple, intending to demolish it. But, lacking physical hands, the best he could do was to rip the curtain from top to bottom. Which, even so, was no mean feat. He then raced back into life as Apollonius of Tyna (such is the legend), where he was stunned to find that no one wanted him. The body he left behind, as Jesus, was, according to legend, reanimated three days later by the Christ himself. Reading the New Testament closely, you will discover that none of Jesus's followers recognized this new stranger in their midst. Which is typical of bodies that are reanimated by another entity. (Christians make such hash of their Bibles!)

The fourth initiation is suicide. It could be nothing else. The candidate, rejected by the world, in his turn rejects it. Turns his back on it. If the first initiation is a defining moment, this is a second. In all subsequent lives, he will never again be a part of the world. Which means there is no longer any point in rebirth, in a physical life.

Having been rejected by all, by the very earth itself, the fourth degree initiate comes back to life in a state of shock. He no longer sees any future. He becomes consumed in a quest to find out what had happened to him. As a child the memories are vivid. Sorting it all out, finding the WHY, even for a man of his considerable talents, can take the better part of a lifetime. This may have been Jiddhu Krishnamurti's sole defect, a desire to go back to happier days, when he was a celebrated savant, rather than progress on to his own proper fate. Once the 4th degree initiate resigns himself to his fate, he sets about constructing his new home in astral matter, such that when he eventually dies, he enters a transitory period of readjustment in his new abode. Krishnamurti did this publicly, as his "process". Which is the fifth, and for this series, the final initiation.

Such is initiation. Bailey's book, **Initiation, Human and Solar**, merely dances around the edge of all this. You must know how to read it. There is nothing, in any of this, that is ordained by inner guides. They do not move you here or there. You are not part of any school or lodge, except from your own foolish blundering. You are not, so far as I am aware, actually initiated by anyone into anything. You are, yourself, your own initiator. No one else. You are to succeed, or fail, on your own. The gifts you give to the world as a result, are yours alone.

There is a shortcut, if you want it. And it is pain free. Death free: Two thousand years ago Christ established the sacrament of Communion for the express purpose of assisting all to advance along their own, unique evolutionary paths. The Church permits you to take of this marvelous elixir once a day, starting at the age of 7. Should you do this, each and every day of a long life, the result will be that in your next life you will have moved ahead of your peers in the evolutionary scheme of things. You will be a leader. Should you do this for two or three lifetimes, you will be among the greatest beings on the planet. If you are serious, you will take ordination as a priest, or vows as a nun, as these people take the Host daily as a matter of course. If the Catholic Church is not to your liking, then any of its branches, which have retained direct Apostolic Succession, will do as well (among them, Lutherans and Anglicans). In fact, there are many among us who have already finished a series of such lives and are now, not Church fanatics, but leaders in their fields. Leaders in all fields. Am I proselytizing for the Church? If you wish. I am merely reciting what I know to be true. I am fully aware the Church is not acceptable to many. Not acceptable to me, alas. Or rather, I am not acceptable to it.

I want to be perfectly clear. For every successful initiation, there are a dozen failures. Perhaps a hundred. Each one, a life lost. A life cut short. A life wasted. Fated to reincarnate only to start all over again from the beginning, having gained nothing and lost all. Murder is murder. Groups that murder candidates do not write books, they are not found in towns and cities, they do not place ads of any sort. If, despite my ghastly story, you are willing and eager to sacrifice yourself and seek them out, you will never find them. They are hidden away in poor, sparsely populated countries, tucked away on lonely mountain tops, living in old and dilapidated buildings, where there are no roads, no nearby towns of any sort. They are not to be found in any guidebook. Whenever these groups come to the attention of the authorities, they are promptly broken up. So they hide.

As for achievement via suicide, know that even fourth degree initiates come to regret the deed. Suicides always destroy the friends and family they leave behind. In many cases, the suicide posthumously causes the actual deaths of his family and friends, one way or another. And even if he thinks he is prepared, thinks he has thought it through, thinks that he has perfectly hidden it from the world, the process is so strange, the energies so powerfully uncontrolled, that he will likely create only pain and suffering, for himself and for many others.

If you wish this boon, this greatest of all gifts, the one safe route, open to virtually all, is the Church. Regardless what you think of it, regardless of your own experiences, regardless of what you may have heard. Grit your teeth, smile nicely at the priest, and early every morning, jog over to your parish church and let him put the host on your tongue. You don't have to like him and he doesn't have to like you. You can, and I think, should, ignore everything he and his Pope says from their pulpits, as they often are, in fact, as mean and as petty and as stupid as they come. Remember you're not coming for them or their sermons. You're coming for the host itself. Establish a direct relationship with it, and be patient, and be happy. Ultimate liberation is a long, slow process. Perhaps someday the Church will not be the ultimate Yin-Yang.

Back to the book at hand. I did not expect it to be very good, but I was disappointed it was merely a shill for an existing esoteric school. No, that's wrong. The Servants of the Light is not esoteric, but magical. The degrees of initiation offered are not of the cosmic, eternal level, but merely stages in the formation of a magician. As such, the authors are correct in saying their degrees of initiation are elective, optional, at the discretion of the candidate, or of the initiator. Ashcroft-Nowicki may be telling the truth in saying there has never been a book quite like this before. (Crowley might have done it, but I am unfamiliar with most of his work. Ashcroft-Nowicki and Norris both studiously avoid all mention of him.) Viewed in this light, you can practice Ashcroft-Nowicki's magic, or Crowley's magic, or Dion Fortune's magic, or that of a number of other schools.

And if you go down that route, you will, in your next life, learn the fate of reincarnate magicians. To be cannibalized by one's own, long forgotten spells and enchantments. To be compelled to again be the town shaman, or the nadi reader, or the magus. Over and over again.

Why would anyone do this? Want to be initiate? Because he wants to be a big shot and has heard this is the way to go. If he only knew the path ahead of him, either magical or cosmic, he might not be so cocky. The final question: Does an initiate know he's initiate? With almost no exceptions, an initiate can pass through all four stages and not have a single clue. This is actually a mercy.

I've heard said that the Tibetans teach that if you make a good death, you are immediately liberated from the endless cycle of death and rebirth. Which is initiation, no more, no less. Myself, I have long been curious about these strange creatures, these initiates, hence my lavish notes.

January 31
1606 – Guy Fawkes executed.
1747 – First VD clinic in London
1849 – Corn laws abolished in UK.
1929 – Leon Trotsky exiled.
1930 – 3M markets Scotch tape.

More Fun with Houses

If angular houses (1, 4, 7 and 10) are Where You Go Out and Get the World, and if cadent houses (3, 6, 9 and 12) are Where The World Comes to Get YOU!, then succeedent houses (2, 5, 8 and 11) are where you Find Repose. Retreat from the world. Seek refuge, via money or children or sex or friends (2, 5, 8 and 11, respectively).

While it's not possible, or at any rate, darn rare to have a planet in each house, a well-rounded chart will have planets angular, planets succeedent, and planets cadent. But if not, then we get something in houses that resembles Marc Edmund Jones's famous Planetary Patterns, i.e., Bucket, Bowl, Splash, Splay, Bundle, Locomotive, etc.

Specifically, if all your planets are in angular and cadent houses (no succeedent), then you have a Push-Pull sort of chart. You push on the world, it pushes back on you. Lacking succeedent, you have no repose, no rest. Which perhaps you don't want, or perhaps you sorely miss, I don't know which.

With these empty houses it's important to note where the planets disposing those cusps happen to fall, as that's where these houses will play out. No planets in the 5th??? Does that mean No Children or No Sex?!

No. It means that you get children / have sex by means of the house where the planet owning the 5th house is found. Ruler of the 5th in the second? Maybe you need to have money to woo the charming maiden. Or maybe you make your living in the sex trade. Ruler of the 5th in the 4th? Your father may have final say over who you see and when, or perhaps will raise your children for you. Ruler of the 5th in the 9th? You meet your lovers at religious retreats, or at universities, etc. — This is how unoccupied houses work. All houses, occupied or not, work this way, but the process is most easily understood if one looks first at the unoccupied ones. Now back to my subject of the moment: —

If all your planets are in cardinal and succeedent houses (no cadent), and if the ruler of the horoscope as well as the Sun and Moon are in angular houses, then you are a terror set loose on the world (no, not a terrorist!!! Come on, now!) who retreats from time to time to recharge his batteries.

If all your planets are in angular and succeedent, but the chart ruler, Sun and Moon are in succeedent houses, then from time to time you leave the safety of your nest to ravage the countryside around you. (Well, you get the idea.) In neither case does the world ever seem to catch up and get back at you, since the cadent houses which would permit this are unoccupied. Does this mean that you're stupid (3rd empty), have no morals (9th empty), or will live forever (6th empty)? Of course not. As with the example of the 5th house, it only means the affairs of these houses are subordinated to the houses in which the rulers of these unoccupied houses may be found.

If angular houses are unoccupied, the individual will appear to have no outward drive, no ambition. This often frustrates his friends, who see his talents wasted but do not know why.

All planets in succeedent and cadent make for one or another form of paranoid. The world is a strange place, we have no power (i.e. angularity) over it. Refuge is the best we can hope for. If the ruler of the chart, the Sun and Moon are all in cadent houses (as in my case) we are continually on guard that we not be ensnared in some mindless trap. In the other case, chart ruler, Sun and Moon in succeedent houses, we are a wary recluse.

Both of these cases may be attributed to a past life which failed in some spectacular way. When such an individual reincarnates, he is more interested in knowing about his past, about why things failed, than he is in making any new mark on the world. Hence he is withdrawn, and, when challenged, may have a nasty sting.

It would not surprise me that individuals with empty angular, or succeedent, or cadent houses, would seek partners who have those houses occupied in their own charts. The person who lacks angularity would much profit from someone who has planets in them. Such a partner would be his window to the world. This again reminds me of M.E. Jones, who postulated that people with complimentary planetary patterns took up with each other and made each other "whole". Someone who was lacking succeedent would find a partner with an abundance of succeedent to be a welcome person to come home to.

Houses are endlessly fascinating to me. I can read a chart, start to finish, with little else. Of course I sacrifice the predictive side of astrology, but with a cadent-heavy chart, I'm more than a little wary of what's out there and am more than a little dubious if there is such a thing as a good forecast.

— *January 26, 2010*

Neptune Returns

Neptune returns to what? I hear you ask. To where we found it. Long, long ago, in a land far, far away. Neptune, the planet of fairy tales, myths and adventure, was discovered September 23, 1846, at 25 ♒ 53ʀ. As if an omen, Saturn was dead conjunct at 25 ♒ 09ʀ. I always thought that Saturn was the best thing that ever happened to Neptune. (The Moon, if you're curious, was in Scorpio.)

I think we've done rather well with it. Neptune started life as a nasty malefic, but a lot of people now think of it as a close companion. Planetary interaction is a two-way street. For the last 164 years, we've been messing up Neptune, just as much as it's been messing up us. (Imagine what Earth Logic is doing to those poor Neptunians!)

So now it's returned to 25 and change Aquarius. Neptune first got there April last year. It's now about to pass that point for the third and last time.

Sunday, February 7, is the Super Bowl. Who will win? Don't look at me. I haven't watched a football game in decades. But you can use astrology to find out. Specifically, John Frawley's book, **Sports Astrology**. Frawley expressly tackles the problem of making money with sports wagers. He's just about the only person to ever attempt that. I wonder if you could use John's techniques to beat the stock market. Heaven knows, it needs a beating rather badly just now.

— February 2, 2010

Climes

The third book of the new Masha'alla treatise (**Six Astrological Treatises**, translated by James H. Holden) deals with climes, and as climes have been mysterious to me, I Wickied it. Climes are bands of longitude based on the longest day of the year (summer solstice), in half-hour intervals. Here in Bel Air, latitude 39N32, the longest day of the year is 14h46m from sunrise to sunset, which puts us in the 6th of 33 climes, but in the system of seven climes, we're in the 4th, ruled by the Sun. The fifth, a bit to the north, is ruled by Venus. The first clime, which starts about 16 degrees north of the equator, is ruled by Saturn. I'd tell you more, but I've sold all my copies of Masha'allah for the week. More will arrive on Wednesday.

Ptolemy takes climes and divides them into east and west. The division is along the Red Sea and up the Adriatic. He uses the Mediterranean as a north/south division. The result is four quadrants of very different peoples. The quadrants, in modern terms, are:

1. Europe, of the northwest.
2. Africa, of the southwest.
3. Northeastern Asia, including Russia.
4. Southeast Asia, including the Middle East.

The northwest, i.e., Europe, is ruled by Aries, Leo and Sagittarius, which is to say, the triplicity of Sun, Mars and Jupiter. Europeans are, consequently, impatient, industrious, warlike freedom-lovers.

Opposing Europe, from the southeast, is an area ruled by Taurus, Virgo and Capricorn. Which is Venus and Saturn, more than Mercury. Ptolemy says such peoples because of their proximity to Europeans, have certain European traits, and have favorable temperament of mind and body, courage and impatience with restraint. Further out in this quadrant, India, Persia, Mesopotamia, etc., are known for obedience.

The northeast quadrant, which is to say, Russia, is under Gemini, Libra and Aquarius, which is Mercury, Venus and Saturn. They are rich, dainty in diet, and skilled in magic. Don't look at me, I'm just copying what Ptolemy says. He gives lots more details in the second book of **Tetrabiblos.**

Another Birthtime for President Obama

MR emails to propose a late degree of Gemini rising for Mr. Obama's chart. Set in Hawaii, that would be a rectified birth time of 2:50 - 3:00 AM, AHST, on August 4, 1961, Honolulu. MR likes this chart as it puts his Saturn-Uranus opposition just past the MC/IC axis. The chart can be tweaked to put transiting Uranus (retrograde) conjunct Obama's MC on Election Day.

My feeling is that Senator Obama's win was widely expected and so therefore not Uranian at all, but on the other hand, during the campaign Mr. Obama had a most strange succession of successful voids, so the possibility of a backwards Uranus producing an expected result cannot be ruled out. (Dewey Beats Truman, that's a Uranian outcome. Remember?) Uranus initially hit 19 Pisces in March, 2008. By which time it was already clear that Obama had won the nomination and probably the big prize at the end as well.

I saw something else in the chart. I relocated it to Chicago, but I did it as if he was actually born in Chicago. In other words, I keep a late degree of Gemini on the ascendant. Relocation is justified, as Mr. Obama has called Chicago his hometown for many years, but I cheated the calculations.

I used 2:25 am CDT, Chicago, and got 28 Gemini rising, and 3 Pisces on the MC. Uranus hit that in the early spring of 2004 and was still in the neighborhood when Obama had his breakthrough at the Democratic National Convention on July 27, 2004. Which was a truly Uranian moment.

But you will say, Wasn't Obama's birthtime settled long ago? Did Mr. Obama not publish his actual birth certificate, did it not state the time of birth as 7:24 pm, and should not that have settled the matter?

Well, no. To anyone who could read a chart, it settled nothing at all. With the 7:24 pm chart you have an abstract, impractical, futuristic Aquarius rising, coupled with a flighty, fidgety two-faced Gemini Moon, along with a chart that screams out its need for a partner to lead him. Which is all the stuff in Leo in 7th/Virgo in 7-8. Which is before we start reading the 4th house for daddy or the 10th for mommy. Fifteen years ago Obama wrote a book about his parents (**Dreams from My Father**), which is odd as the 7:24 pm chart's 10th house (Mom) is completely empty, and while the 4th has the Moon, the Moon's sign does not match the sign on the IC, which means the Moon has little interest in the father.

The book the 7:24 chart would write, with Uranus in Leo on the descendant, Mars on the 8th house cusp, Venus in 5, would be How to Get Girls to Pick You Up — so you can get all their money.

But look what we can do with a Gemini rising chart: The ruler, Mercury, is in the 2nd, but wants to be in the 3rd. Mercury puffs himself up in Leo, and as the extended meaning of the third is Everyday Life, a puffed up Leo Mercury in 3 wants to be a Big Man Around Town. A community leader, perhaps. This agrees perfectly with the Sun's position and is why I cheated with the relocation.

But what's more interesting is this also describes Obama's father, as the same Mercury rules the 4th, which is the father. Since a puffy Mercury rules both the ascendant, as well as the father, the son will tend to idealize the father, very possibly confusing his own identity with his father's. A "Junior" by his very nature.

Since the 4th also rules ultimate outcomes, we see that with both Mars and Pluto in the 4th, the fate of Obama's father was not good. He was killed in a car crash in 1982.

So what about the Birthers? Those who say that Obama was not born in Hawaii? Are they right? I will put it to you this way:

My experience has been that popular beliefs, in the form of instincts, ruled by the Moon, are **usually right**. But also,

My experience is that the public gets the reasons for their beliefs wildly **wrong,** and for precisely the same astro-

Another birthtime for President Obama

logical reasons. Lunar instinct lacks all intelligence, which comes from Mercury. That Mr. Obama was not born in Hawaii is possible. That he was born in Kenya is flatly absurd. If you're looking for an alternative birth place, first try Obama's "home town" of Chicago.

As there is very little of Gemini left on the ascendant, Obama's de facto Cancer first house implies, just under the surface, that he's sensitive and that he cares. While we think of him as a Gemini (mistaking his ascendant for his Moon), with Venus at 0 Cancer, not far underneath his Gemini facade, he is a Cancer we really want to like.

— February 9, 2010

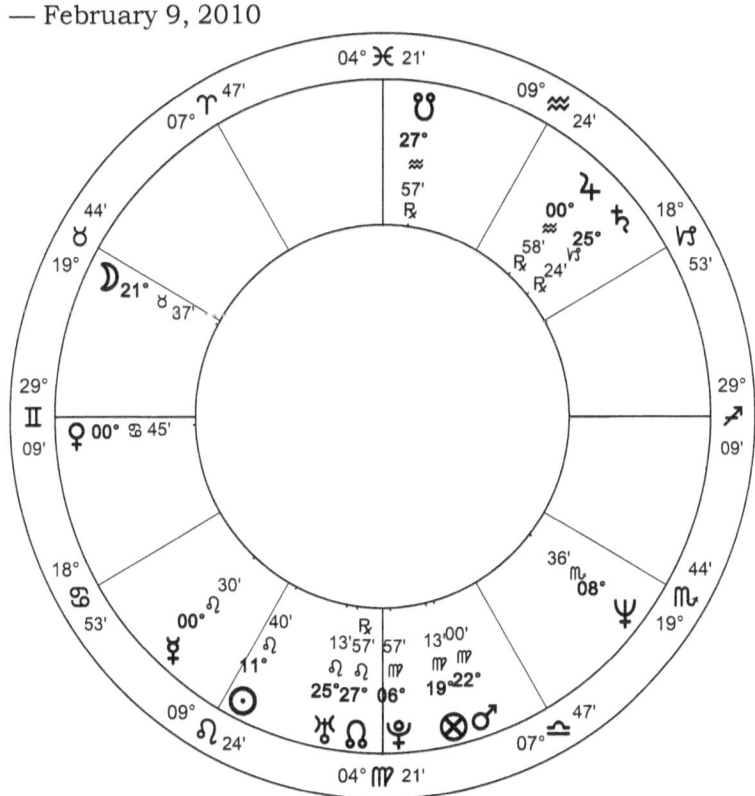

Proposed natal chart for Barak Obama
August 4, 1961, 2:25 am CST, Chicago

George Washington's Birthday

If you asked George himself, he would have told you he was born February 11, 173**1**. Tell him he's mistaken, that the date was really February 22, 173**2**, and he will Tut, Tut and remind you of the great change of 1750.

And it's the same for all the other Founding Fathers. Thomas Jefferson, born April 13, 1743? Not according to the clock on his wall. It read April 2nd. Ben Franklin? History says he was born on January 17, 1706. Benjamin, an almanac maker (which means he knew time) would correct you and give the actual date as January 6. Samuel Adams never drank the beer named in his honor, which is to say he was sane and sober in saying his birthday was September 16, 1722. Not September 27.

Astute readers will know where I'm going with this, but wasn't the change from Julian to Gregorian calendars, wasn't that in, like, 1582 or something?

Well, yes it was, but in England the Gregorian reform was seen as an Evil Papist Plot. Which is to say there's nothing especially modern about being blinded by ideology. England spent 182 years blinded by just this one idiocy. If a generation is 20 years, that's nine generations of not too terribly brite. England changed from Julian to Gregorian in 1750. At which point they added eleven days to their daily life.

As for George's year of birth, a further reform in 1751 changed the first day of the year from March 25 to January 1. Which was already the custom in many other countries. Prior to that, the English gave dates in March using both years, such as, March 15,1743/4.

Well, this was all a long time ago and we don't have to

worry about it anymore, right? WRONG. Consider the curious case of Ehrich Weiss, better known under his stage name of Harry Houdini. He has two birthdays. His real one, in Budapest on March 24, 1874, and the one he himself claimed, which was April 6, in Wisconsin. You look at this and think, Aha! Was Budapest a secret Julian hangout? But then you do the math and discover that in the 19th century the Julian and Gregorian differed by 12 days and Houdini has 13. And then it dawns on you that Ehrich was a very clever boy and accounted for his birth in Hungary early on the morning of the 24th by factoring in the actual time in Wisconsin (the previous day), thereby accounting for the 13th day. He "relocated his chart," in other words.

Nicola Tesla was Serbian. He was born July 10, 1856, but when you set up the chart it looks like nothing at all. Add twelve days to get July 22, and the chart will knock your socks off. Run it for, say, 4:00 am and you will get Moon/Neptune as well as Sun/Venus conjunctions, the four planets/two conjunctions in trine to each other. Effortless electro-magic, you can't do better than that.

Mother Teresa, another Serbian, was born August 26, 1910, and, again, if you calculate the chart, you get nothing much. Add 13 days (the Julian slipped another day behind when it marked the nonexistent February 29, 1900), and you get September 6. Run that chart and you get the Sun applying to a conjunction of Mars, both in Virgo (good for abrasive hard work), and a new Moon sandwiched between Venus and Jupiter, all in Libra. Which is darn good for divinity.

WHAT IS GOING ON HERE? Was the Austro-Hungarian empire so decayed and corrupt that it was running TWO calendars? How could any bureaucrat possibly keep track? I learned the answer while on a train in 2002.

I was travelling from Baltimore to New York, returning to what was at that time the home of the World Headquarters and Chief Administrative Offices of The Astrology Center of America, and found myself sitting next to a recent Russian immigrant. And I asked him, Was Eastern Europe crazy enough to use both calendars?

And his answer was, yes, sort of. And it was quite

simple. Even though the Communists had outlawed the Orthodox Church right from the start, citizens continued to baptize their children in the Church, which not only conferred Julian birthdates upon them, but, in fact, **still does to this day**. Because the Russian Orthodox Church, to this day, uses the Julian, not the Gregorian, calendar. So if the Church was solidly Julian, but the Party Gregorian, as well as widely reviled and despised, then the ONLY Gregorian births in the former Soviet block would have been the children of party apparachnicks. What this means to data collectors is obvious (*hello Lois!*). What it says about the ability of astrologers to read the charts in front of them is less flattering.

— February 16, 2010

February 18
3102 BC — Kali Yuga starts!
1841 — The first Senate filibuster begins
1884 — Huckleberry Finn published.
1957— Vanna White born.

Sun versus Moon
which is stronger?

I am going to revisit a recent statement, that a Sun-Moon conjunction is a good time to get married, as it's a good example of how astrological analysis is done.

The Sun represents the male, the Moon represents the female, of this there is no disagreement. Marriage puts the two into a formal, permanent relationship, so, astrologically speaking, it's a good idea if the Sun and Moon are, in fact, in a recognized aspect on the day in question.

I will immediately discard the square (stressful), the opposition (confrontational), the inconjunct (too glancing), the sextile (too weak), as well as the semisquare and the semi-semi square and their various cognates, which are all stressful by definition. Marriage is a crap-shoot, if we can't get favorable conditions, at least we can strive for neutral ones.

Which leaves the trine and the conjunction. We already know the trine of Sun to Moon is about the most wonderful thing that can happen in astrology, so I will focus exclusively on the conjunction.

In the conjunction, the two energies merge and become one. Is this what happens in a marriage?

Well, no, frankly. Husband and wife retain their individualities, often to their mutual detriment (think, affairs and divorce). Nor is this unexpected. In real life, whenever we see two factors merging, we see a third emerging. Combine flour and water, you get pasta. Combine black and white, you get gray. Combine hydrogen and oxygen, you get water. Combine a male and a female, you get babies — which, in fact, you will get with or without marriage, and with every possible combination of Sun and Moon. As we all know.

Save for offspring, males and females cannot actually be combined, so, when they are represented by a new Moon — which is the case when the wedding falls on a new Moon, one or the other will win. Which?

Myself, I would have said, The man wins, since planets conjunct the Sun are said to be combust and burned up. The woman looses. But since I have books all over the place, I thought I would look it up and have my hunch confirmed.

To my surprise, I learned it was the man who looses. I've had a week to think about that, and here is what I've puzzled out:

Astrological tradition (Vivian Robson: **Electional Astrology**) says that a wedding on a new Moon is fatal to the husband. What this means is the Moon is stronger than the Sun. Is it?

The most extreme case of Sun conjunct Moon is a total solar eclipse. At such a time, the Moon's shadow falls directly upon the Earth. Astrologers are in universal agreement that such an event is always malefic, that places directly shadowed will suffer in the months and sometimes years that follow. (See any good book on mundane astrology.)

If the Moon's shadow is malefic, then the Moon, which is the source of the shadow, is also, in the end, at least a little bit malefic itself.

Which reminds us of old metaphysical stories, which says the Moon was our mother, and that the Moon is now a corpse, Earthlings (when we were Lunatics) having killed her. The Moon's known abilities in fertility, sexuality, emotions, etc., being, presumably, the remnants of her earlier glories.

Which then reminds us of more of the old metaphysics, which says that to the extent the Moon has any good qualities at all, is because of the solar energies which she reflects. It is therefore said, in all of these same treatises, that the reason the full Moon is the most intense part of the lunar cycle is not be cause of anything the Moon herself is doing, but because when she is full, she is as fully out of the way of the Sun as she can be. "Full Moon stress" is, in reality, nothing more than the full force of the Sun itself, helped, aided and assisted by whatever solar energies the Moon inadvertently kicks back at us.

Which, by process of elimination, means that when the Moon is new, she is as much of a blamed nuisance as she can be.

Which, if the Sun represents the groom and the Moon represents the bride, means that in a new Moon wedding, it will be the bride, not the groom, who will, in the end, win out. Whether this is physically fatal to the groom (seems kind of extreme to me) or merely helps persuade him to give up the union and go elsewhere, depends on the two people concerned.

We thus see that analysis confirms what was mere astrological hearsay. Such is the power of — I can't resist — E.F.'s "pseudo astrology." May your planets always wave cheerfully.

— February 23, 2010

Born February 29
1792 — Gioachino Rossini
Frederic, in the Pirates of Penzance

Help Save Astrology!

A couple of days ago David Huff, of North Carolina, forwarded an email from Lynn Koiner, of the Baltimore/Annapolis NCGR, that an elderly astrologer in Philadelphia was retiring and needed to find a home for his extensive collection of astrology books and magazines, going back to the 1940's, comprising some 30 boxes.

It amounts to 70 years of Who we are, Where we've been, What we've done. It is an irreplaceable historical archive, especially the magazines. It needs to be preserved, cataloged, organized and made available to the larger community.

Don't think it's just going to happen. The typical fate of such an archive is to be thrown in the trash, wholesale, either immediately, or after ten years of sitting in a damp garage or basement, by which time it will be a wet, mouldy, useless mess.

As astrologers, we are fated to reinvent the past for the simple reason that so much has been thrown away and is still being thrown away and lost forever. I was disheartened this request came by way of the national NCGR, as it is the national astrological groups (including the AFA, AFAN, ISAR and others) who must, as a matter of course, make every effort to preserve our past. They have the resources, or they should.

England has the Bodleian Library and the Ashmolean Museum, where you will find much. So far, the best we have is Michael Erlewine's Heart Center, which is fine, but only if you happen to be in a small town in central Michigan. We need more. We need to save our history, any way we can. God Bless Us if we can scan and put it on the internet for the benefit of all. Right now, that seems like an impossible dream. I am ashamed of us. — *March 9, 2010.*

Mozart's Birthday

This past week, V, of Rome, emailed to say he had read my remarks on Mozart's death and wanted to add that, according to Vedic astrology, Mozart should have lived longer than he did.

I replied that while I had never looked at Mozart's birth chart (January 27, 1756, 8:00 pm, Salzburg), I was certain it was wrong.

At the time there were a great many "child prodigies" touring Europe, all of whom pretended to be five or more years younger than they actually were. Beethoven himself did not find out his true age until he was around 40. His father subtracted five years to pass him off as a prodigy, but lacked the means to get them out of Bonn. This is documented.

Even if Mozart was actually born in 1756, his father would have tried to pass him off as younger. That's just how things were done with "prodigies". Since there is no evidence he did that, we automatically presume that Mozart was born before 1756 and that his birth records were falsified, one way or another. The likely years are between 1748 and 1753. We are looking for a person who would act out via sex, who would be the victim of authorities, who would face the possibility of imprisonment, who would be dominated by his father. Like as not there will be at least one fixed star prominent, Mozart's life has that kind of flavor. The overall frustrations of his life point strongly to squares being dominant. With squares, no matter how hard you try, things just don't seem to work. And that's Mozart, to a T.

Mozart's mother, Anna Maria, gave birth to seven children, only two of whom survived infancy. One possibility is that Mozart was an older child who was passed off as his younger (deceased) brother. This would be easy to do. "Helmut" (I invented the name) is born in, say, 1750, but when daddy seizes on the idea of making him a prodigy (around 1759, by the look of things), he is passed off as "Wolfgang", a child born in January 1756, who died at, say, six months.

Looking at Mozart's accepted birth data, the Moon is separating from a conjunction with Pluto, which is not good for health. The Sun is separating from a conjunction with Saturn, which is not good for health. Mercury, ruler of the ascendant, is combust, which is not good for health. Both Sun and Mercury are tightly opposed by Neptune, which is not good for a lot of reasons.

On March 17, 1756, transiting Saturn conjuncted Mozart's Sun. At which time Pluto was ten minutes of one degree from exactly conjunct his Moon. Ten days later Saturn passed over Mozart's Mercury, which is his chart ruler/ hyleg. That's both lights, and the chart ruler. All nailed, all at once. I've not studied death in charts, but it seems to me the child born on January 27, 1756, at 8 pm, was most likely dead by April of that year. A life of two months.

Mozart's name at birth was *Joannes Chrysostomus Wolfgangus Theophilus Mozart*. So where did "Amadeus" come from? It's said to be the Latin version of Theophilus, but if we should find a "deceased" brother with "Amadeus" in his name, we may have the real man. And, as it turns out,

Among the children of Anna Maria was Johann Karl Amadeus, born November 4 1751 or '52, "died" February 2, 1753. (There seems to be confusion as to the year of birth.) Note that Leopold's first-born, Johann Leopold Joachim, died on February 2 of 1749.

Let's presume that when Johann Amadeus was to be passed off as Wolfgang Theophilus, he was "given" a death on a day that was already a family tragedy. But kept his middle name, a tell-tale clue. Younger brother's first name, his own middle name: A composite name, a compromise.

So was Wolfgang really Johann? Is Mozart's real date of birth November 4, 1752, Salzburg? Let's set a chart for 1 am (humor me) and have a quick look at it.

The chart gives a Moon/Mars conjunction in Libra: headstrong and willful, squared by Jupiter in Cancer. Sun/

Mercury in Scorpio is squared by Neptune in Leo. There is no aspect between Sun and Moon, (general confusion). One a.m. gives Virgo rising, lots of planets in 2 and 3 (money, and travel), with daddy/Saturn in Sag in 4.

The chart for November 4, 1751 is just as interesting. Here we have powerful oppositions. The Sun is conjunct Venus in Scorpio, opposite the Moon in Taurus. The north node, Pluto and Saturn are all conjunct in Sagittarius, opposite Jupiter and the south node. Jupiter/Saturn in opposition are said to indicate bankruptcy, in other words, an inability to keep money. If we set the chart for 1 am (Virgo rising), we get Venus, Sun, north node and Pluto all in the 3rd, with the Moon in the 9th. In signs of water and earth, these house placements can indicate a restless, roving nature.

This will have to do until someone comes up with the parish's original birth register. (If they recorded Wolfgang's birth time, they recorded Johann's.) In the meanwhile, you tell me if either of these charts works for his alleged death on December 5, 1791, or his actual death on March 24, 1826.

— March 16, 2010

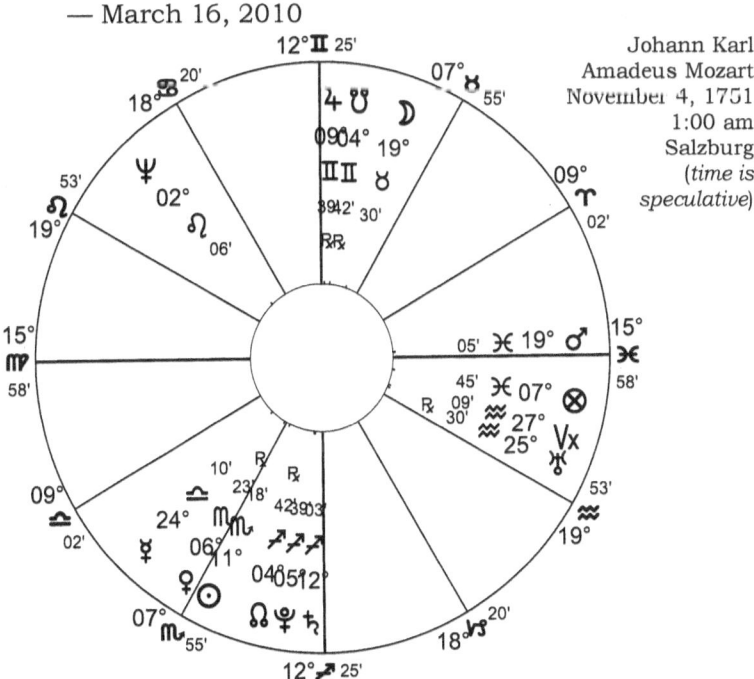

A Dream

I had a dream recently. I was in a room with some nice people. I wanted to go outside, but they wanted to stay indoors. It was nice inside, but I didn't understand why they would want to stay there.

I went outdoors and the houses were the sort of droopy melted things that Dr. Seuss used to draw. All sorts of bright colors. There were windows, big black ovals, but I don't remember seeing any doors. Reminded me of the tenements on the lower east side of New York. All sorts of sounds were coming from them. I could hear people talking, singing, music being played, but mostly I heard a lot of shouting and fighting. Whenever I got close to any of the windows, there was such a stink coming out of them. People seemed trapped inside, they couldn't get out into the fresh air and sunshine. Mostly, they didn't know how, but a lot didn't even want to. I had been inside a lot of the houses, I knew there were some very nice places, but I also knew there were a lot that weren't. I knew that if I went back into one, it would be hard to get out again. I also knew a lot of my friends were stuck inside those houses. I thought about going to visit, but didn't want to get stuck. I thought about going in and dragging a few of them out, but I knew they would refuse and I would only get stuck inside, all over again. So easy to go in, so hard to get out.

So I decided to wait until they came out of their own accord. Everyone comes out eventually. That made me happy. Outside there was wonderful, clear, golden sunshine. Everything scintillated, like that famous light the Impressionists found in Normandy. (Also along the Rio Grande in S. New Mexico). The air was crisp and clean. There were a lot of people in the streets, all enjoying themselves. A beautiful spring day. No, I don't think I will bother with those houses. Better to live in the open air!

That, to me, is what heaven looks like. A wonderful outdoor world full of amazing people and places.

Easter

Last week Sam called. His mind was made up. "I'm not a Christian," he said, "so why am I celebrating Easter?" Sam, I replied, you're 40-something and have been chowing down on chocolate eggs for how many years, and you just noticed?

He has a cute daughter, 8 years old, I think. What should he tell her? Heck, when you're 8 years old, crosses and nails and thorns and blood and gore is all a bit much (wait til she's 13, she won't be able to get enough of it), even if Catholics think 7 is old enough. Until then belief in the Easter Bunny will do fine. As long as you keep the chocolate coming.

"Why can't we just celebrate the Equinox?" he wailed. Well, okay, I said. How? It's the International Day of Astrology, did you know that? (The spring Equinox, I mean. Not Easter.) So what do astrologers do to celebrate?

No, I'm asking you, dear readers. What do astrologers do to celebrate? What did you do, last Saturday? Whip out charts and try to out-read each other? (Take ten paces, turn your 12th houses and Fire!?) Go to boring conventions and listen to soggy speakers? (Heaven knows, there's no sex at those shows.)

Well, okay. Astrologers just aren't the partying sort. So how should we celebrate the Equinox?

For those who are fuzzy, the spring Equinox is when the Sun, by declination, appears to stand directly over the equator, going from south to north. By declination, the sun appears to move from 23° 26' 17" south latitude at the Winter Solstice, to 23° 26' 17" north latitude at Summer Solstice, and then back, in an endless cycle. The Equinoxes are when it's halfway between here and there, standing directly over the equator. The northern extremity is known as the Tropic of Cancer (because the Sun is in the sign of Cancer when it reaches it), and the southern point is known as the Tropic of Capricorn. The entire area between is known as the Tropics, a band about 47 degrees wide.

What this means is that if you're in the Tropics, the Sun will, at one time of the year or another, shine on all four sides of a building. Including the north side, in northerly latitudes, and the south side, in southerly latitudes. North of the Tropics, the Sun never shines on the north side of things, while south of the Tropics, the Sun never shines on the south side of things.

The Spring Equinox, or a date very near it, has been the official start of the year in many northern cultures. And if not, it's the unofficial start of the year. I think it's a much better New Year than January 1.

Easter, on the other hand, is a fertility rite that Christians took over, because the best way to displace the old is to replace it with the new. If pagans have a spring festival, you have a spring festival. If pagans have a winter festival, you have a winter festival (Easter and Christmas, respectively). After a few years, no one will be able to tell them apart. After a few more years, no one will be able to remember the old.

Easter is defined as the FIRST Sunday after the FIRST full Moon after the Spring Equinox. Got that? By definition, the Sun will be in Aries. Aries is ruled by Mars, which is to say, that sexy hunk. In Aries, Venus is debilitated, which is to say, Mars gets to have his way with her. That's a fertility rite to me.

Venus doesn't wait long to turn the tables. May 1 is May Day. The Sun is in Taurus. Venus rules. Mars is debilitated. Which means Venus has Mars stuck in the earth where she can get herself all over him. Hey! That's the meaning behind the Maypole and the long streamers twined around it.

So let's put it together. Spring Equinox is the New Year. Get dressed up in party clothes, break out the champagne, sing Auld Lang Syne, kiss the one you're with.

At Sun hour on a Sunday (sunrise on Easter), the Hero

bursts forth from his mother's womb. This is graphically shown in no less than two places in many Gothic cathedrals: The Lady Chapel and the Tympanum. (Do "three days" equal "nine months"? Anyone want to try that arc out?) Because she's a virgin, an angel must roll away the stone, i.e., break through the hymen in order to do so. The angel was Mars, in a burst of energy, clearing the way for the Sun: All Aries. Just like the daffodils that are bursting out all over.

Suitably "uncorked" (it's a French thing), a couple of weeks later Venus/Moon gets her very own phallus, and proudly sets it up in the town square, decorated.

It's the happy, sexy time of year. Mars/Venus. Venus/Mars. Get out and enjoy yourselves! (Just barely kept my PG-rating!)

How to Calculate a Chart

Okay, okay, you wanna know my secret method. Here it is:

The Requirements:

Midnight Ephemeris
Table of Houses (any will do)
An atlas of some sort (Shanks' are excellent)
For a birth **NORTH** of the Equator, and,
WEST of London, e.g., somewhere in North America. Later you can adapt these rules for anywhere.

First: *Convert clock time to GMT.* Essentially, add 5 hours for EST, 6 hours for CST, 7 hours for MST, and 8 hours for PST.

Example 1: Birth at 10:40 am, New York, November 14, 1965: Add 5 hours to get 3:40 pm GMT.

If it's a summer birth in the US/Canada, add 4 hours for EDT, 5 hours for CDT, 6 hours for MDT, 7 hours for PDT.

Example 2: Birth on June 14, 1976, 1:27 pm, Los Angeles. Add 7 hours to get 8:27 pm GMT.

If the GMT time is in the afternoon, convert to 24 hour time (eg, add 12). So 3:40 pm GMT is 15:40; 8:27 pm is 20:27.

Go to your atlas. Look up the city of birth. You will

How to Set Up a Chart   163

find the difference between local time and GMT listed for each city. Take this number and SUBTRACT it from GMT. This will give you LOCAL MEAN TIME (LMT). Our examples:

The New York Example: Birth at 15:40 GMT. New York time difference: 4:56. Subtract 4:56 from 15:40 to get 10:44 am LMT, New York.

The Los Angeles Example: Birth at 20:27 GMT. Los Angeles time difference: 7:53. Subtract 7:53 from 20:27 to get 12:34 pm LMT, Los Angeles.

(Notice this method automatically corrects for daylight time, but you still have to know if daylight was in use.)

Go to your ephemeris. Look up the sidereal time shown for the date of birth. If the GMT time is for the next day, look up that day, not the original day of birth. ADD this sidereal time to the LMT. Our examples:

The New York example: Ephemeris sidereal time for November 14, 1965: 3:32 (the ephemeris gives seconds, I've rounded). ADD this to the New York LMT of 10:44 am to get a Sidereal Time for your chart of 14:16.

The Los Angeles example: Ephemeris sidereal time for June 14, 1976: 17:30 (rounded). ADD this to the Los Angeles LMT of 12:34 to get 30:04. As this is greater than 24, subtract 24 to get a Sidereal Time for your chart of 6:04

The Fudge Factor: Go to your Table of Houses. Find the nearest Sidereal time for your chart. Then **skip to the next greater Sidereal time.** This is the fudge factor, a rounding up one notch in time. Look down the table to find the latitude of birth. Those are your house cusps. They will generally be accurate within one degree without any further calculation. Our examples:

The New York Example: The sidereal time is 14:16. In the AFA Placidus Table of Houses, I found 14:16 on page 109. I skipped to the next table for 14:20. New York is 41 degrees north (from your atlas). At the top of the column a midheaven of 7 degrees, 21 minutes of Scorpio is given. The 11th house is 0 degrees, 53 minutes Sagittarius, the 12th is 21 degrees 13 minutes Sagittarius, the Ascendant is 12 degrees, 25 minutes of Capricorn, the second house is 24 degrees, 50 minutes of Aquarius, the third house is 6 degrees, 13 minutes of Aries. The computer gives an ascendant of 12 degrees, 11 minutes Capricorn, and a midheaven of 6 degrees, 55 minutes Scorpio. The difference between a fudge and the computer? A mere 14 minutes of arc.

The Los Angeles example: The Sidereal time for the chart is 6:04. I found 6:04 on page 46 of the AFA Placidus Table of Houses. I skipped to page 47, where I found a table for 6:08. It gave a midheaven of 1 degree, 50 minutes of Cancer. Los Angeles is 34 degrees north. I went to that line and found the 11th house to be 3 degrees, 11 minutes of Leo, the 12th house to be 3 degrees, 43 minutes of Virgo, the ascendant to be 0 degrees, 50 minutes of Libra, the second house to be 28 degrees, 4 minutes of Libra, the third house to be 28 degrees, 33 minutes of Scorpio. The computer gives a midheaven of 1 degree, 37 minutes of Cancer, an ascendant of 1 degree, 29 minutes of Libra. Here the difference between fudge and computer was 39 minutes of arc.

Can better hand calculation be done? Of course. The sidereal time "fudge factor" is a cover for the interval between midnight GMT and birth, combined with the shift westward from London to the birth location. If you want that, here they are: Add ten seconds for every 15 degrees west of London, add 20 seconds for every hour past midnight. Then you will need to interpolate the chart's sidereal time to the standard sidereal times shown in the table of houses, as well as interpolate the exact latitude of birth. New York is really 40 degrees, 45 minutes north of the equator. And remember that I rounded the sidereal time shown in the ephemeris. Do all this and you should be within a few minutes of a degree of the computer.

But for those of you completely in a fog, this should help.

How to Calculate Tertiary Progressions

The late Rick Houck was one of the first to really promote tertiaries (P3's) in his book, **Astrology of Death**, but he gave scant instructions on calculating. Here they are:

One day equals one lunar month. There are two possible values: A sidereal month (0 degrees Aries to 0 degrees Aries again) is 27.3217 days. A synodical month (one full moon to the next full moon) is 29.5306 days. I'm not sure which one is used, it might depend on what you want.

Find the Julian day of your birth, find today's Julian day, subtract the two, divide that by your month value (27.3217 or 29.5306). The result is the number of tertiary days that have passed since your birth. Add that number to your date of birth and you have tertiary progressed positions. You can do that by hand, but I'd prefer a calculator.

For angles, take your natal Sun, count forward in the zodiac until you come to the tertiary Sun position, add that number of degrees to the angles. For example, if you're born with the sun at 15 Capricorn and the P3 sun is at 15 Libra, you add 270 degrees to the angles. The years that have passed between the two dates (complete revolutions of the Sun) simply drop. A variation of this technique works with ordinary progressions and solar arcs: From one birthday to the next, you add 361 degrees per year. If you want progressed angles for any other date, you count the number of degrees between your sun and the desired date and add that number of degrees to the angles. So six months from your birthday, the angles are 180 degrees different. This gives real meaning to solar arc and progressed angles, though is rarely used.

Anyway, Rick Houck said the proof is that P3 aspects exactly time real world events. He says a one minute change in birthtime equals a one week difference in events, so he found it helpful in rectification.

Spring Planting

On Wednesday we planted flowers: Waxing Moon in Cancer. Early Saturday morning, the temperature dropped to the upper 20's (-2°C). I covered the most fragile with tea towels. I think they survived.

A standard almanac will tell you when the best planting days are, but those almanacs were all sold out months ago and if you don't have one and don't know the rules, you're stuck. So here's some help:

Plant with the Moon waxing, from new to full. If possible, in the second quarter, in other words, the week before full, but avoid the quarters themselves.

The Moon's element is important, and it's straightforward. Water signs (Cancer, Scorpio, Pisces) are fertile. Earth signs are so-so, fire and air are no-no's, so far as planting is concerned. (They have other uses.)

Root crops — potatoes, carrots, beets, turnips, onions, garlic — are planted in the dark of the Moon (waning) because you want the underground growth.

Then there are special cases. Plant flowers under Taurus and especially Libra, because Venus, goddess of prettiness, rules both. The late Louise Riotte said to plant trees under Taurus and vines under Virgo, which is to say that earthiness promotes woodiness. Plant berries under Scorpio, though why escapes me at the moment (intensity of flavor?). Virgo also rules grain, which is what lawns are, and Capricorn is said to rule herbs. Riotte was a master of signs and quarters of the Moon, selected for quite specific purposes.

A waning Moon in fire signs is good for weeding, and preparing the soil in general. Harvesting (never too early to think about it) is best with a waning Moon in air, as it helps prevent rot.

— March 30, 2010

The new health care legislation:
Easy Astrology

This week brought the signing of new Health Care act, on March 23, 2010, at 11:56:40 am EDT, Washington (exact time the President finished signing the act, as extracted from the C-Span video). That the bill is hopeless should be clear to all Americans. It does not lower premiums (which was supposedly the reason for the bill in the first place) and it only extends medical coverage by coercing those who have no money to buy what they do not want. Which makes us wonder how long this will last, and what its fate may be. Which is forecasting.

We first notice the Sun has just passed beyond the opposition to a retrograde Saturn in Libra. This is always unfortunate, for it means that transiting Saturn will soon oppose it — which it will do around the 21st of August, and that, by direction, it will again do so in approximately 21 months. Sun being alpha, Saturn being omega, when the two are in opposition we have already covered all possibilities and are now stretched to the breaking point. Which makes the upcoming transit all the more unfortunate.

The Moon in Cancer hangs directly on the ascendant. To my shock, Pluto in Capricorn is eleven minutes from exactly opposed to it. To give an idea how precise this is, it means the signing ceremony began at the moment the opposition was precisely exact.

Sun in Aries represents the head of state, in other words, the President. Saturn in Libra opposing it, that many in his own party (his natural partners, i.e., Librans) oppose him, but, retrograde, they could not find their "voice". When Saturn goes direct, they will.

The Moon in a mundane chart always represents the

people. Sun-Moon in square, people feel the president has misled them, but do not know how or why. But, Moon opposed to Pluto, this is a bill they hate. As in, HATE. The loathing that comes from the opposition, both planets being strong and angular, is frightening. That they are part of a larger grand cross in cardinals is ominous. National opposition to the health care act is trending to hysteria. National hysteria is like a person going into shock. There's no point saying he's "not really hurt" and that he should just "get over himself." The patient's life is at stake. You must administer emergency treatment. In other words, you drop the matter and wait for a better time. Do something else in the meanwhile. People are broke and out of work. A round of $1000 bribes, I mean, checks to every household in the country, wouldn't be a bad idea. Have I mentioned lately what fools there are in DC?

We have enough stressful aspects coming this summer, we did not need any additional provocation, but this chart has arrived anyway. With a strong focus in cardinals, it is bold and aggressive. Sun and Mars are in close trine as well as in mutual reception (the Sun exalted as well) giving the President great force and power. Note Cancer on the second house cusp — taxes. People with Cancer there natally are touchy about their money. Mars in Leo in the second appears like a thief: Pay the President what he demands, or else. Neptune in the 9th in Aquarius says we are dreaming and that the overall concept of the Health Care bill is flawed. Jupiter at the MC will side with the people, as his exaltation is in Cancer, the ascendant.

Of the planets and angles, even the nodes and Fortuna, only Mars and Neptune are in fixed signs. So, no surprise that before the week was out, Congress amended the act. The oppositions in this chart look to be a feast for the opposition party, the Republicans, who have promised to repeal it. This is a hollow promise. Legislation is not so easily undone.

But the nice new Health Care act will not change anything. Oppositions are like the trenches of World War I, they create stalemate. In this case, those who refuse to buy insurance are to be penalized by the IRS. If this act is as hated as Richard Nixon's 55 mph speed limit of 1974, it could spark a nationwide tax revolt, the IRS's nightmare.

But coercion was required if there was to be any relief from ever higher insurance premiums. If ever rising premiums force more to drop insurance altogether, if general economic malaise leads to continued low wages and high unemployment, if governments are unable to fund the welfare aspects of the bill ("if you 're not rich enough, insurance will be provided for you"), then the net result, the very likely probable result, one the signing chart strongly indicates, is no change. And rage, from all sides. Nasty? Yes.

I looked for significant fixed star positions, but there were none. (Thank your favorite deity for small mercies.) Like I said. This is easy. The chart is obvious.

—March 30, 2010

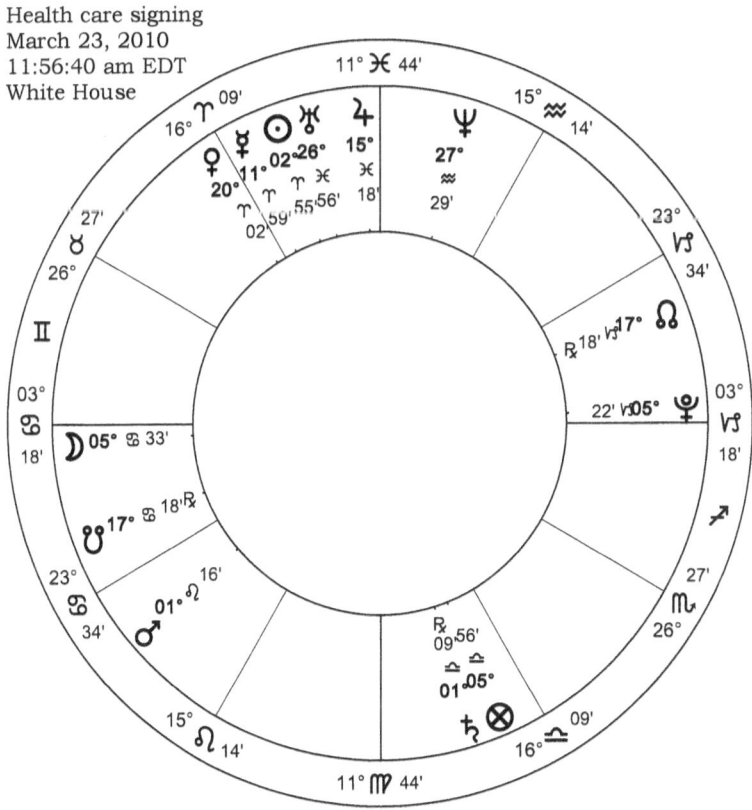

Health care signing
March 23, 2010
11:56:40 am EDT
White House

New books for Spring

This week saw the third edition of Dietrech Pessin's **Lunar Shadows**. As I wrote in my notes, Pessin says that the sign and degree of a new moon (or solar eclipse) turns up, a few degrees more or less, nine months later as the first quarter moon. Nine months after that, the same degree turns up as a full moon, and a further nine months later, it turns up as a third quarter moon. The Sun/Moon cycle is orderly enough that anytime a phase of the Moon hits a sensitive point in your chart (for example, the ascendant), that same point will be hit, nine months later, by the next phase in the sequence. A fascinating book.

In **Astro Graphology**, Darrelyn Gunzburg shows how to analyze handwriting and then confirm the analysis with the natal chart. She tends to reach extreme conclusions, but it might be she needs exciting conclusions to make a good read. While you can't change your natal chart, you can change your handwriting and thereby change your life.

Richard Idemon's second book is now back, **The Magic Thread**, joining **Through the Looking Glass**, which reappeared a month ago. Magic Thread is a better read than Looking Glass, which is entirely due to a better editor, Gina Ceaglio. But in reading it, I remembered why I didn't like Idemon when he first appeared 15 years ago: He sets up chart examples as an excuse for character assassinations. Not my cuppa.

Of late we are blessed with good books on eclipses. Last month saw the arrival of Bill Meridian's **Predictive Power of Eclipse Paths**. And don't forget Celeste Teal's **Eclipses: Predicting World Events and Personal Transformations**.

And I have a nice new edition of Carter's **Astrology of Accidents**. In a day or two it will be joined by a new edition of **Symbolic Directions in Modern Astrology**. Within a month, new editions of Carter's **Essays on the Foundations of Astrology**, and, **Zodiac and the Soul**. All fascinating books.

Time to get out and plant!

VOTE

In America, Tuesday, May 4, 2010, is Election Day for many local and state offices. You haven't heard? You weren't told? Welcome to the American Shrinking Democracy. Let me explain.

Many years ago when I was in school I was taught that as a result of corrupt mayors, in the 1950's local governments shifted to town councils, which hired City Managers to run things. But instead of eliminating corruption, this merely hid it. Council members were typically elected at large, which meant they were responsible to no one, while City Managers, no slouches them, quickly realized their jobs depended on catering to the every whim of the Councilors, their family, and their friends.

I don't know exactly when it came about, but sometime in the 1980's or '90's local elections were shifted from the first Tuesday in November, to the first Tuesday in May. This is puzzling until, as astrologers, we realize the shift was from Scorpio, to Taurus. Whereupon it becomes easy to remember. The "First Tuesday in Scorpio" is now The First Tuesday in Taurus.

On Wednesday the papers will be full of stories of apathetic voters. Turnout is typically under 10% of those registered (who are, themselves, around half of those eligible). Never mind that not the slightest effort is made to inform the public of the election going on. A decade ago, candidates felt obliged to at least make a pretense of yard signs and campaign cars, but this season I have seen only one car and no signs at all.

And the reason is simple: Whichever candidate has the most family and friends (and/or "muscle") wins. So why waste money? Which is pathetic.

No surprise the people who get "elected" have so little experience with the voters that the least citizen discontent results in the police being called out, tasers in hand.

So I thought it my duty to remind you.

Porphyry the Philosopher

This week saw the arrival of James Holden's latest translation, Porphyry's **Introduction to the Tetrabiblos**.

Ptolemy's **Tetrabiblos** was a century old when Porphyry came to write his Introduction to it. Porphyry's book looks a lot like a condensed version of Al Biruni's book, written 8 centuries later. That Porphyry stuck Ptolemy's name on it tells me several things. One, that Ptolemy wrote his book in verse, not prose, because only books in verse circulated. (Ptolemy's original text was lost, he exists only in the paraphrase of Proclus, of the 5th century. Which, to Porphyry, was centuries in the future.) Next, it tells me that despite books by Vettius Valens, Rhetorius, Dorotheus and others, Ptolemy's book had already become a standard reference — at least as far as Porphyry's immediate neighborhood was concerned. A reference that was flawed, in that it (Ptolemy) lacked essential details, the necessary twiddly bits, that make the rest of it work. Hence, Porphyry to the Rescue!

In his Preface, Holden notes that parts of this book turn up, verbatim, in books by Antiochus, Rhetorius and Sahl Ibn Bishr. This leads Holden to speculate that Porphyry's book was a composite patched together by Demophilus around the year 990. *Dear Mr. Holden*, should you chance across these notes, it is critical to know if these sources are all in poetry, and if so, if they were all written in the same language and used the same meter, which, if so, would indicate they were not copied from one manuscript to another, but were recited, independently, from memory onto paper, by each of the people concerned. Just as I might recite *Row, row, row your boat / Gently down the stream* or Poe's The Raven, from memory. In my view, it is critical to establish how knowledge was transmitted from one generation to another, to better understand how ancient society worked.

Which brings me to Porphyry's book itself. In brief, some of the details will be familiar to students, but many will not. It will repay study. Study the list of contents closely.

Charles Carter versus Adolf Hitler

I've just finished reprinting four of Charles Carter's books, and in two of them he expresses his frustration with the chart of Adolf Hitler. This was a real feat, because one of the books, **The Zodiac and the Soul,** was written in 1928 and had to be revised to put Mr. Hitler in it.

While Carter had an excuse — he was, after all, a contemporary of Hitler and lived in the London that Hitler's planes bombed, there is in our day, I am sad to say, a certain unending fascination with dear Adolf which is difficult to explain and which I am ashamed to watch. On History International, there is, on average, a program a day that showcases him, or his work. No other person, living or dead, not even Jesus himself, gets that kind of worshipful adulation. (Let's not kid ourselves. The youngest WWII vets are now 85 years old. TV has never catered to the extremely elderly and is not doing so now.)

Adolf Hitler was born on April 20, 1889, Braunau, Austria. The stated time was 6:30 pm CET (*from* **Essays on the Foundations of Astrology,** *p*g. 56), or **6:17** pm LMT (**Zodiac and the Soul**, *pg.* 112). In either case, 24 or 25 Libra ascends.

Carter is so frustrated by this chart that he writes, *it may be doubted whether the psychology of Hitler can be understood by reference to his natus alone. For one thing, much may be learnt from comparing his geniture with the map of the German Empire, established at Versailles on 18 January, 1871, at about one hour past noon, local time.* (**Foundations**, pg. 57)

Yet, the previous page, underneath Hitler's chart, Carter tells of a report that it was difficult to establish respiration and that Hitler could have been born with Scorpio rising. And I thought, Given the inaccuracy of the local cuckoo clocks, why not try a Scorpio ascendant. What could it hurt? So I changed the time to 6:54 pm LMT. Gave Hitler 1 degree Scorpio rising.

Well, dang it all. Doesn't Hitler look like a Scorpio rising? Piercing eyes? Doesn't he have the intensity of a Scorpio rising? Wasn't he a sneaky, ruthless bastard, like, I dunno, Scorpio rising? With a good, strong nose, like an eagle? (The high side of Scorpio.)

Hitler's traditional Libra rising was ruled by Venus in Taurus, intercepted in the 7th. Which by sign is a double-dose of Venus. Mr. Nice. Backed up by the conjunction with a debilitated Mars, both at 16 Taurus. (Tight.) Which is, Be Nice or I'll go pout, or something! And he'd have to go pout, since Venus, ruling Taurus while retrograde, will always be frustrated in its efforts at World Beautification.

Now look at the chart with Scorpio rising. Mars rules from the 7th in Taurus. Debilitated, Mars wants to be in the first (all debilitated planets want to be in the house opposite, one of *Dave's Rules*). Mars wanting to be in the first makes Hitler want to be the Man of Action! The Ruthless Hero.

Mars conjunct Venus made him sexually magnetic, but Venus, being retrograde, made Hitler The Man Your Mother Warned You About. In spades. He's a no-good. He will seduce you, lead you up the garden path — and then murder you. Or, at the very least, be profoundly strange at your death (Maria Reiter, Geli Raubal, Ernst Roehm). Dysfunctional/debilitated chart ruler Mars killing the object of affection (Venus retrograde, ruler of the 7th) who just wasn't good enough.

But, trine to the Moon, a long 16 degrees away from the Sun, and opposed to the ascendant, Hitler could keep his love-death nature away from the populace in general.

Mars/Venus conjunctions, in signs of Mars or Venus, especially when they rule the ascendant/descendant, always show people who are adored, loved, mobbed by thousands. Which Hitler was. (Not to mention Casanova.)

Elsewhere, you've heard that a 10th house Saturn means ultimate failure. Why? Because it takes on responsibilities until it is overwhelmed. That's why. In Hitler's case, Saturn was disposed by his Sun. When a 10th house Saturn disposes, or is disposed by, the Sun, it makes for a born leader. This isn't a matter of aspect. It is inherent in the nature of the planets themselves. Not only is the Sun-Saturn person the man you will trust, it's the person you instinctively look to for fathership itself. The qualities inherent in the very word, *führer*. This is Hitler, the leader.

Saturn ruling the 4th (where it would rather have been), the fourth being land and ancestry, Hitler would compulsively tackle German land problems. Which meant war.

To the radiant, evil sex appeal and the unquestioned leadership, add Hitler's Moon/Jupiter conjunction in Capricorn in the 3rd. Capricorn is practicality, Moon/Jupiter is instinct combined with intuition, 3rd house is verbal ability: A phenomenal speaker, with great intelligence.

Adolf Hitler was one very dangerous man. Danger that came from a Scorpio rising, a debilitated Mars and a retrograde Venus. What was wrong with Charles Carter?

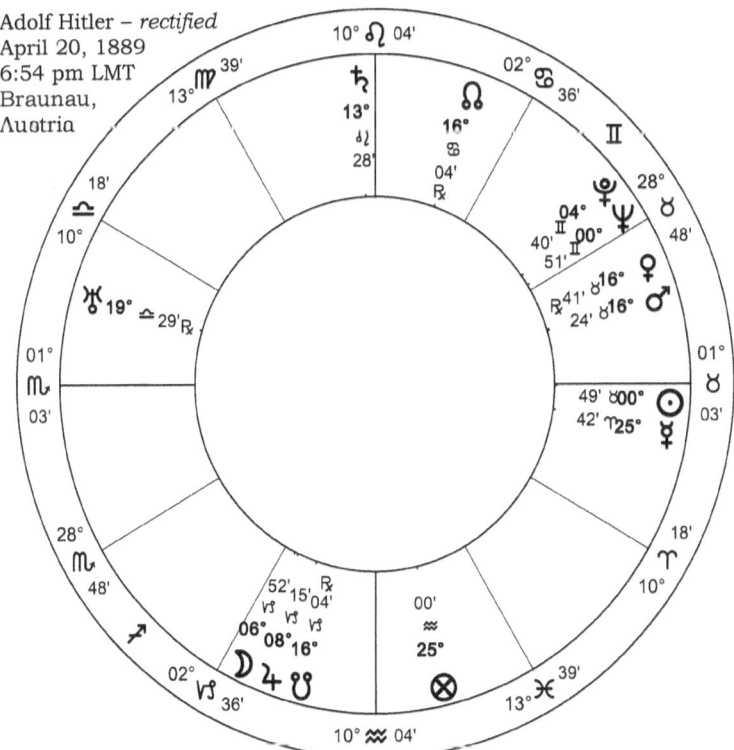

Odds and Ends

What did you do during the retrograde? Just before it started I was informed three of Charles Carter's books were to go out of print immediately. Looking closely at one at one of them, I determined that people in London had the rights if they wanted to claim them. I emailed and waited tensely to hear. They declined. So I immediately reprinted four of Carter's classic books: **Astrology of Accidents**, **Symbolic Directions in Modern Astrology**, **Essays on the Foundations of Astrology**, and, **Zodiac and the Soul**.

I am pleased to say that all nine of Carter's books are now in print, and proud that I publish eight of them.

Out-of-sign aspects, revisited. If you have a planet at the end of one sign, and another at the beginning of the next, are they conjunct? I think signs of the Zodiac are like rooms in a house. They have walls. But a friend disagreed. She has Uranus late in Virgo, with the Moon just over the hill in Libra. She's always felt they were conjunct, and since it's her life, I take her opinion seriously. So how about this: If a planet has more affinity in "that other sign" than it does in the one it's in, then I think it could "smear" its way into an aspect with an out-of-sign planet. In other words, some walls are brick and mortar. Some are Japanese rice paper. In this case, the Moon has more affinity for water and earth signs than it does for fire or air. You can work out the rest, but note Charles Carter's discussion of sign-to-sign aspects in **Foundations**. He has some surprising findings.

— May 18, 2010

A Charles Carter Festival

LEAVING aside a 40 page monograph, Charles Carter, 1887-1968, wrote nine books. Seven of them amount to an interconnected series. Carter refers to these books in his other books, adding details, cross-referencing, etc. So here's a handy guide to some of the best astrology books of the past century:

We start with **The Principles of Astrology**, from 1925. Of it, Carter said, *"The present work is designed to give a clear and concise presentation of the essential facts of modern Astrology."* In other words, the basic primer, suitable for beginners. But Carter immediately goes beyond that to include fascinating details and shrewd observations not normally seen in books of this type. I often hear it said of books, that they're suitable for beginners as well as advanced students. This is one of the few books where that claim is true. It also contains condensed versions of *Astrological Aspects, Essays on the Foundations of Astrology,* and *Symbolic Directions in Modern Astrology.* A lot in one book.

In the next book in the series, **Some Principles of Horoscopic Delineation**, Carter tackles one of the hardest problems in any profession: How do you go beyond mere rote learning? How do you, finally, master the subject and become your own authority? Anyone who's ever attempted that knows it's a gift that not everyone has. Carter offers this book as a useful stepping stone, a "borderland" between outer and inner sanctums. After a careful re-examination of astrological basics, Carter launches into topics, such as, two people born on the same day with quite different lives, longevity in the horoscope, insanity, crime, outstanding ability and failure. Carter himself said this book was a follow up to

Principles of Astrology and was to be used in conjunction with his **Encyclopaedia of Psychological Astrology**.

Next, we come to **Symbolic Directions in Modern Astrology**. Astrology is known for its forecasting ability, in this book Carter seeks to find reliable and simple means to do that. He has four principles in mind:

1. No important event should pass without a direction.
2. No direction should pass without an event.
3. Events and directions should correspond narrowly in time.
4. Events and directions should correspond in character. *(from page 10)*

It's unclear to me if Carter thought that Primaries qualified, but it was very clear to Carter that some other system was needed. The systems that Carter proposes are, frankly, lying around in your astro-software, ignored. (Or they should be!) In this book, Carter tackles the subject of death in the horoscope. Carter discovers the Measure of Death, a specific sort of direction. It does not always indicate death, but it is always present at death. You'd think he would have put this in one of his two Principles books, but no. In Symbolic Directions, you will find it.

Going beyond death, Carter takes a stab at pure metaphysics in **The Zodiac and the Soul**. Carter was never quite happy with this book and was still revising it the year of his death, 1968. This book is most notable for Carter's base-12 system of numerology. Considering there are 24 principle letters in the alphabet, this is a remarkable innovation.

We now turn to two books of chart analysis. In the first, **An Encyclopaedia of Psychological Astrology**, Carter chops up a lot of charts, looking for distinct astrological signatures. Others have tried and failed, Carter was one of the few to succeed and produce compelling results. In addition to the strictly psychological (including oratory, literature, boredom, love of land and sea, etc.), Carter found signatures for a great many illnesses, among them, epilepsy, diabetes, spinal curvature, alcoholism, goitre, appendicitis, rheumatism, and much more.

An outgrowth of that book was **The Astrology of Accidents**. This was tougher as the nature of accidents is itself vague, with much overlap. Among various classifications, Carter found signatures for Crushing, Scalding, Burns, Gunshots, Blows, Motorcars, Falls, Machinery, Poisons, and more. This is a difficult book. I have added a List of Local Influences (similar to that in *Psychology*), as well as a most useful Index.

Essays on the Foundations of Astrology is pretty much what it sounds like. **Astrological Aspects** (published by the AFA) is an essential expansion of a key detail from the *Principles* books. Bedeviled by mundane astrology, Carter wrote **An Introduction to Political Astrology** after WWII. And, what was the 10th, that got away? **Seven Great Problems of Astrology**, a precursor of *Zodiac and the Soul*. Someday it might get reprinted. — May 18, 2010

Charles Carter (*Carter's rectification*)
January 31, 1887
11:01:25 pm GMT
Parkstone, Dorset

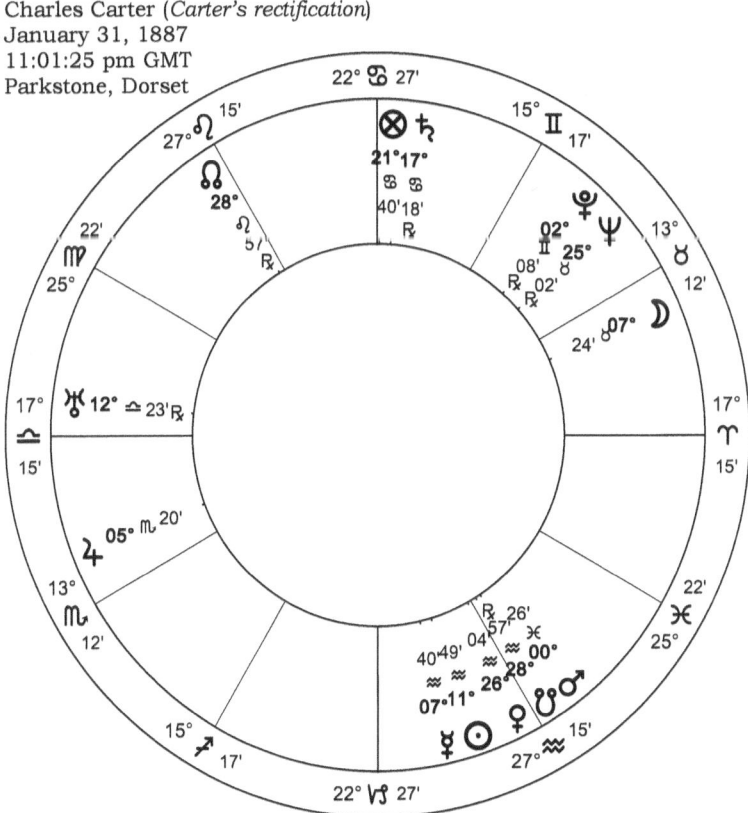

Towards a new theory of Astrology

I have scattered pieces of this here and there. It's time to make an organized statement.

Astrology has multiple variables, and they are not exactly obvious. We start with fundamentals:

The Zodiac

A Primary Zodiac is defined as the relationship of a star to one of its orbiting planet(s).

A Secondary Zodiac is defined as the relationship of a planet to one of its moon(s).

It is therefore clear that each star/planet pairing has its own primary zodiac, and each of the planet's moons will have its own, unique, secondary zodiac. As we live on a planet with a rather large moon, both of which orbit around a star, we will use the Sun, Earth and Moon as examples.

The Earth's relationship to the Sun is known as the Tropical Zodiac.

Zero Aries is known as the Vernal Equinox, defined as when the Sun, by declination, crosses the Earth's equator going north.

Zero Cancer is defined as the Sun's maximum northern latitude, known as the Summer Solstice.

Zero Libra is known as the Autumnal Equinox, when the Sun, by declination, crosses the Earth's equator, going south.

Zero Capricorn is defined as the Sun's maximum southerly declination, known as the Winter Solstice.

This is the Earth's Primary Zodiac.

This is not new. It was expounded by Ptolemy in **Tetrabiblos**, c. 140 AD, but even then it wasn't his idea. It had already been in use for some time prior.

So far as the Tropical vs: Sidereal controversy is concerned, you can pick up the entire solar system, Sun, planets, moons, asteroids and everything else, and drop them into a distant galaxy far, far away, and, so far as the Earth is concerned, the Tropical Zodiac will still be exactly accurate, since it will still be based on the Earth-Sun relationship. Which is fundamental. The Sidereal zodiac, based on the Earth's wobble, will need to be completely restructured.

Using the same principles, you can construct valid zodiacs for Mercury, for Mars, for Saturn, for Pluto, and for each and every body in orbit around the Sun. Each zodiac defined by the relationship of the individual planet to the Sun. The Sun being not only the single biggest object in the solar system, but the one which, uniquely, gives light, heat and life itself to each of the others. (Each planet having its own forms of life. On Earth, life has uniquely physical characteristics.)

How will these planetary zodiacs be structured? Will they have 360 degrees and twelve signs of 30 degrees each? Most likely, no. The numbers used to construct the Earth's zodiac, 2, 3, 4, 6, 12 and 60, are unique to the Earth. The numbers unique to the other classical planets (Sun, Moon, Mercury, Venus, Mars, Jupiter, Saturn) were known to medieval magicians, as they were essential to their work.

The Lunar Zodiac

Our theory says that a celestial body in orbit around another celestial body produces a zodiac, which means the Moon, which orbits around the Earth, must have its own zodiac. Which it does, though it has never been recognized as such. It has been given a variety of names. In the west we know it as the Lunar Mansions. In India, Nakshatras. In China, Lunar Mansions are known as Sieu. In all cases, a Mansion/Nakshatra is defined as the distance the Moon travels in one day, as it goes from New Moon to New Moon.

As the Mansions have never been recognized as an independent Zodiac, there is dispute as to the number of mansions ("signs"), 27 or 28, and their exact extent: 12°51', or 13°20'. The confusion is due to the number of days from one new moon to the next. The result is a Lunar Zodiac that expresses lunar energies from the point of view of the Earth.

Which explains the necessity of dividing the Moon's orbit by something other than twelve. Twelve is an Earth number. Not lunar.

What is surprising about the Lunar Zodiac is that it is based, not on the Tropical Zodiac, as one would expect, but the Sidereal Zodiac.

The Sidereal Zodiac is touted in many quarters because it is "based on the movement of the stars." This is untrue. The Sidereal Zodiac is based on the Earth's axial wobble, which takes some 26,000 years for one cycle. To better comprehend how a spinning body can have a wobble, spin an ordinary top. You will see the top itself spins rapidly, while its tip slowly describes a small circle under it. That slow small circle is a wobble.

The Earth's wobble, divided by twelve — a number which has significance to the Earth itself — usefully divides the 26,000 year period (known as a Great Year) into Astrological Ages, with each Age qualified by one or other of the various twelve-fold signs. There is nothing unusual with the Ages-as-Signs analogy. Any group of twelve — twelve Apostles, a dozen brothers (Joseph, et al), a dozen knights seated at a round table, twelve houses in a natal chart, a dozen donuts, if you will, can be described as a sequence starting with Aries and ending with Pisces. And, in fact, often are.

But in its traditional role as a zodiac of twelve signs, the Sidereal Zodiac, as it is generally understood, fails, because the Earth's wobble, on which it is based, is self-referential. If we do the same test as before, drop the solar system into some other galaxy, the Sidereal Zodiac promptly collapses. Measuring systems work by showing the difference against a mean, a relative value. To establish my worth, I measure myself against my peers and members of my family. I do not measure myself against the President of the US or the Premiere of Russia, or Julius Caesar or William Shakespeare. Likewise, the Earth measures its position relative to the Sun, not to stars billions of miles away.

The Sidereal Zodiac comes into its own in the construction of Secondary Zodiacs, where the Earth's wobble is applied to the Moon, a secondary body in orbit around it. Thus, the starting point for Lunar Mansions / Nakshatras precesses through the Tropical Zodiac, with which the lunar zodiac otherwise has no relationship. In other words, the Earth/Sun relationship is not appropriate to the Earth/Moon relationship. The lunar zodiac requires a strictly non-solar yardstick, hence the Earth's wobble as a starting point.

This brings up a number of points. One, the Sun's view of the Earth, the Helio-Earth zodiac, will not be based on the Tropical Zodiac, but presumably on the Sun's own axial wobble, as it relates to the Vernal Equinox. (A new idea of heliocentric astrology, if you will.) The Moon's conception of its own zodiac is likely based on lunar eclipses.

Another is a matter of scale and purpose. If the signs of the Tropical Zodiac are good for general astrological purposes, then the Lunar Zodiac of 27 or 28 mansions should relate to matters governed by the Moon and should provide for amazing detail. In India, each Nakshatra is divided into four Padas of 3°20'. I have seen some sketchy delineations for each of these 108 divisions.

Signs

Because the Earth does not have a perfectly circular orbit, some seasons are longer than others, and over the centuries, the dates of the Earth's perihelion (closest distance to the sun) and aphelion (furthest distance from the sun) change. In 1838, perihelion was at 4:00 am GMT on January 2. In 2020, perihelion will be at 7:49 am GMT on January 5. (Source: **Tables of Planetary Phenomena** 3rd edition, Michelsen/Pottenger, Starcrafts Publishing, 2007.) The tropical zodiac reflects this. The sidereal zodiac does not.

This means that from the Earth's perspective, the Sun moves faster in winter and slower in summer. Which means that winter signs, Capricorn, Aquarius and Pisces, are shorter in time than the opposite summer signs, Cancer, Leo and Virgo. As the Tropical Zodiac divides the earth's orbit into four quadrants of 90 degrees each, this means the value of a single degree in the winter quadrant (0° Capricorn to 30° Pisces) is different in elapsed time from a degree in the summer quadrant (0° Cancer to 30° Virgo). This, by the way, is another way in which the Tropical Zodiac is superior to the Sidereal. A degree in the Sidereal Zodiac is merely the annualized mean.

Which brings me to signs. Signs are not measured from

the Sun's longitude — which is how they are usually expressed — but from the Sun's declination. This was how the Sun's position was measured in ancient times, and how you can still measure it today. Every morning at sunrise, mark the Sun's first appearance on the horizon. From the Winter Solstice to the Summer Solstice, you will see it move, day by day, to the left (north). From the Summer Solstice to the Winter Solstice, it will move steadily to the right (south). This lateral distance on the horizon is trisected (in time) to form signs. Long ago it was projected against a backdrop of stars merely as a convenience. The twelve signs of the zodiac have no relation to the background of stars whatever. Because this is true, then it is also true the 27 or 28 Lunar Mansions, while appearing to remain constant in a given range of stars, have no relationship to them. For if the Earth's 12 signs do not relate to the background stars, then the Moon's mansions do not relate, either. The lesser cannot be superior to the greater.

The result, the longitudinal projection of the Sun's declination which became the Tropical Zodiac of twelve signs, is transposed onto the other planets in the solar system. I am not exactly certain how this is done, but I am satisfied with the proof that others can give. Those who study declination tell us that parallels and counter-parallels of declination, as well as when planets cross the Earth's equator, are all of great astrological importance.

Houses

Having defined a primary and a secondary zodiac based on the relationship of Sun, Earth and Moon, we next come to houses, which shows the daily relationship of the spinning Earth to the Sun.

Because all circles found on the Earth are divisible by twelve, we divide the Earth's rotation by twelve. This gives houses a superficial relationship to signs, as well as all other sets of twelve. So far as the direct relationship of houses to signs, consider that signs are formed by the Earth/Sun relationship and are therefore "of the air", while houses, which are formed "of the earth", are therefore of a lower, denser, "earthier", more practical vibration. This, in a manner of speaking, is how I myself view the differences between houses and signs, as, to me, houses and signs have no obvious rela-

A new theory of Astrology: Resonance

tionship, save having the same number.

Note that 13, in the Earth system, is always given as twelve plus one. Thirteen is never given as an organic whole, which is why a "thirteenth sign" is an impossibility.

We have, therefore, an annual cycle of Earth and Sun which gives us the signs of the zodiac, a monthly lunar cycle of New and Full Moons, and finally a daily cycle, that of the Earth's diurnal rotation. We have a machine, in other words. It only remains to add fuel to it.

Astrological energies and their source

The greatest puzzle is where astrological energies come from. This, too, has a solution.

The mistake has been to personalize astrological energies. Jupiter is shining upon me, it is shining upon you. Just as the sun shines on the plants in my window box. We believe we have a personal relationship with each of the planets, asteroids and all the other wonderful bodies in our natal charts, but **this belief is wrong**. The planets, individually and collectively, are not mini-suns, shining down upon us. The planets are coequals to the Earth. They are the Earth's peers.

Therefore I say that planets, including the Sun and Moon, "vibrate" each other, they **resonate** each other. In other words, the whole mass of Venus resonates the whole mass of the Earth, and vice-versa. The same is true of all planets, their moons, the asteroids, comets, Transneptunians, Kuiper belt objects, Centaurs, etc. In the case of moons (of Mars, Jupiter, Saturn, etc.) their individual resonance is part of their planet's overall resonance. So far as we on Earth are concerned, the resonance of moons of Jupiter are part of Jupiter's overall resonance and cannot be separated from it. I mention these details as there are those who do not understand hierarchical structure.

This is a new way of looking at the cosmos, and it is also plainly true. Jupiter gives me no personal "vibration". It gives the Earth as a whole its vibration, as do all the other celestial bodies found in the solar wind, which defines what does, and does not influence us.

The mass of the Earth accepts, contains, subsumes all the many vibrations which can be found in the solar wind. Note the solar wind does not itself transmit planetary resonance, instead it merely defines the area in which resonance exists. Mechanical clocks give a useful analogy. If two or more clocks are put in the same room they will ultimately synchronize their ticking, but the air in the room is not the means by which they do so. The clocks do this despite the fact that their relative gravities are nonexistent, so the process is not gravitational. Mechanical clocks produce no light, nor any electromagnetic radiation of any kind. Nor does the effect fall off with the inverse square law. Clocks placed on opposite sides of the room will synchronize just as well, just as fast, as clocks placed next to each other.

The Earth's collective melange of resonances soaks and pervades everything upon the this planet. Just as water wets everything with which it comes into contact. There are no exceptions, nor can there be exceptions.

But there are beginnings and endings. If I should cut a branch from a tree, then as soon as that branch is physically separated from the tree, it will immediately take on the prevailing vibrations as of that moment. Which will be on top of and in addition to, the original vibratory resonance it had before it was cut, when it was a part of the tree and had its original resonance.

What happens next is of interest. If the branch has "free will", in other words, if it is placed in the ground and encouraged to go on living, it will start a new life based on the moment it was cut. Even with the crude physical instruments we have, we can tell if a newly planted tree is "happy" or not, and we can often puzzle out why. Branches stuck in the frozen ground of January rarely survive. We may therefore conclude that Sun in Capricorn is an unhealthy time for a tree to be "born". Lunar gardeners can give more accurate reports as they have more sensitive tools.

The analogy is with human births. The birth-moment is important because at birth the newly born infant becomes independent of its mother's vibration. Which means that the first phase of birth happens when the cord is cut.

The second phase happens when the fetus — for it is still that — draws its first breath, at which time it literally sucks its soul into itself. I offer apologies for this metaphysical intrusion, but it should be noted that birth is a two-fold affair. First the infant becomes independent of its mother, then it becomes properly alive. Memory, as well as the ascendant, starts at the second phase, not the first. Both times are of equal importance, but there is normally no more than a few seconds between them.

This repeats, in reverse, at death. First the soul leaves, resulting in the death of the body, then, at some later date, the body itself disintegrates. Ivy Goldstein-Jacobson (and others) have noted the tendency for the dead to go on having events (*see* Your Chart Goes On, *from* **All Over the Earth**, 1963). This is presumably based on the physical body having its own, independent, astrological signature and, save for the very famous, would presumably end only when the body has physically decayed and returned to dust.

The prenatal epoch is therefore useful as it determines the kind of body one will have: Tall, short, healthy, or not, etc. To the extent that some, though not all, souls interact with their bodies before birth, the prenatal epoch can, in some cases, also indicate the kind of personality the individual may have.

There is an analogy to be made with small boys throwing stones from the back of a pickup truck as they speed down the highway. The boys are "mothers", the direction and velocity of the truck is the Earth's prevailing resonance, moment by moment, and the stones they throw are "newborns". Each stone follows a unique trajectory, based on the exact moment of release, the speed and direction of the truck, and the thrower's height above the road, direction of throw and strength of arm. The time the stones spend in the air is their lifespan, death is when they land. Regardless of the stones themselves, no two of them will end up in the same place. Each stone will have its own unique experience.

Parallax

Parallax is the difference in the Moon's apparent position based on the observer's location on earth. For example, observers in Alaska will see the Moon a certain number of degrees above the southern horizon, while observers in South Africa will see the Moon as a certain number of degrees above the northern horizon, the two positions being a number of degrees different. Astrological theories based on line-of-sight observation demand that the Moon's influence will therefore be different to these two observers. Which, given the line-of-sight theory, would be logical and expected.

Yet a number of independent studies have failed to find any notable parallax effect. If astrology is actually based on resonance, where whole planetary bodies resonate other whole planetary bodies, then there should be no parallax.

David Cochrane, at Cosmic Patterns Software, has investigated very high harmonics (in the 100's). I once explained my resonance theory to him. If I understood his reply correctly, he said he had been puzzled he could find no evidence for parallax. Very high harmonics magnify tiny differences. If parallax existed, harmonics should find it. The exception would be objects approaching the Earth's Roche Limit. Which is extremely rare.

Aspects

With a framework established, we can now look at aspects.

Aspects are the result of incoming planetary energies acting on the Earth in harmonic resonance. It is as if the Earth is a giant bell that is being struck in different places simultaneously by all the many different objects in the solar wind.

Bells are useful analogies. Bells are struck in a narrow band near the rim, a "sweet spot". Planetary energies (i.e. resonance) strike the Earth-as-bell in its "sweet spot", which is a band extending from roughly 28° north of the Equator, to roughly 28° below. The Sun's part of this range (23° 26' N and S of the Equator) defines the Tropics. This may partially explain why many visible stars seem to have little astrological impact. The Earth may well not be receptive to the influence of stars that fall outside the maximum planetary declinations.

Having established the numbers 2, 3, 4, 6 and 12 are significant to the Earth, we now see these are also the numbers of the Ptolemaic aspects, with (12 = 0) being a conjunction:

    2 = Opposition, 180°
    3 = Trine, 120°
    4 = Square, 90°
    6 = Sextile, 60°

Additionally, we can also relate the twelve signs of the

zodiac to the twelve notes in a musical octave. This parallel set of 30° aspects should have values, in terms of "good" or "bad" that are roughly similar to musical intervals in terms of harmony and dissonance. C to D-flat is a minor second. Is this a way of thinking about aspects between Aries and Taurus? I am borrowing the musical analogy, I regret that I have forgotten where I found it.

In any case, with regard to aspects we consider the Earth to be like a giant bell which is continually being "struck" in the region of the tropics by the energies of the other planets. Where the strikes are spaced in the customary intervals (aka Ptolemaic aspects) a given resonance is created, which is sometimes harmonious (sextile, trine), and sometimes discordant (opposition, square). This is in keeping with the underlying solar nature of the Tropical Zodiac.

When two "strikes" fall an equal distance from a known sensitive point – such as a natal planet – the result creates a midpoint structure.

We also have a lunar zodiac, of 27 or 28 signs. Twenty-seven reduces to 3 by way of 9. Twenty-eight reduces to 4 and 7. Curiously, in the extended aspects given to us by Kepler, we find Noviles (40°) and Septiles (51°26'). Proper delineations of these two aspects might be found by considering the lunar mansions / nakshatras that represent them.

There is a third set of aspects, based on 5 (quintiles) and 10 (deciles). These numbers do not seem to be part of the Earth system, but they are part of human anatomy, representing fingers and toes. H.P. Blavatsky noted the human head has seven openings (eyes, ears, nostrils, mouth). The male has two additional openings in the groin, for a total of nine. The female has three openings in the groin, for a total of ten. One could therefore consider "fiveness" (the 72° aspect) to be unique to humans, that noviles relate to males, while deciles are of importance to females. In practice these distinctions will be murky, since humans, both males and females, have entangled themselves thoroughly with the rest of the planet. Based on the testimony of number, one might also consider humans to be the Earth's guests and then wonder what it is that the Earth could want of us. If ten is the human number, and twelve the number of the Earth, then their product, 120, is also of interest. Which happens to be the "human life span" as it relates to Vimshottari Dashas, which are 120 years in length.

Aspects operate in parallel with dispositors and lords. I must now approach the subject dynamically. A planet in a given sign has, because of the Earth's own mass and its inherent resonance (a quality of mass), an affinity to other resonances, based upon rulership. The Earth is a large body and has, as is hinted with the Lunar Zodiac, more than one set of resonances. Rulerships follow a distinct pattern. Study the following, which I have borrowed from Al Biruni's **Book of Instruction**:

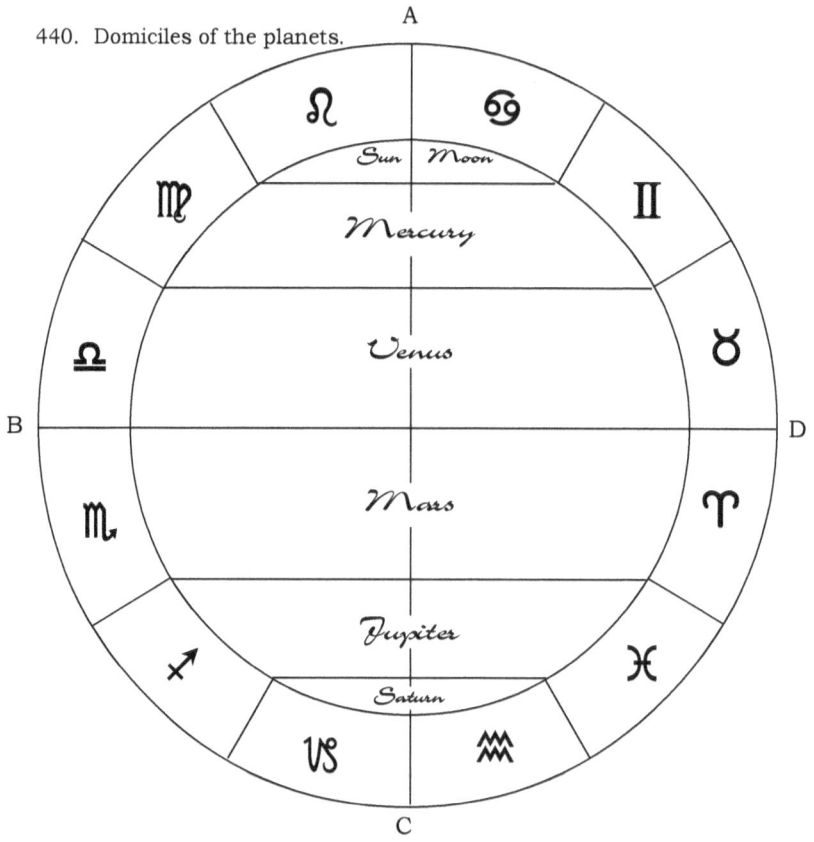

440. Domiciles of the planets.

ABC - The Sun half.   ADC - The Moon half.

Instead of looking at this wheel as a sphere of stars, think of it instead as the physical earth. Astrology can be considered as a study of the Earth's own resonance, and the Earth itself considered as but one of many bodies which resonate each other. As applied to individuals, the combined resonance becomes the natal chart.

Uses for a clockwork mechanism

The result of birth is that we are sensitive, by transit, to changes in the Earth's overall resonance, as the Earth's resonance changes in response to changing planetary resonances. This is already a better theory than "Jupiter made me do that," since our individual resonance is largely similar to the Earth's overall resonance, such that small changes in the Earth's resonance may produce notable changes in individual "units", which is what we humans are.

With the inherent "twelveness" of signs and houses, combined with the number of days in a year being nearly exactly divisible by 12, we have a purely mechanical mechanism that directly relates days to years, thus accounting, in slightly different ways, for both Secondary Progressions and Solar Arcs. When this machine aligns us with transits (defined here as the Earth's raw resonance), we note spectacular results. This would not be unexpected. An analogy would be Nikola Tesla's earth-based resonance experiments, where a small vibrating object, attached to a building and then left to run, would, when properly tuned ("progressed"), result in very powerful vibrations being generated in the building as a whole.

If it sounds as if I am trying to make astrology to be a physical or near physical thing, I am. What operates on the physical world must be physical or near physical. I agree there are more rarefied levels of astrology, that there are spiritual dimensions I do not doubt, but we must first find the basement of our building before we can describe the whereabouts of its 101st floor.

Primary directions are one degree increments of Right Ascension (on the horizon), which are paired with one year in life. Again we see a direct, mechanical relationship, in this case, with the Earth's daily rotation on its axis.

Minor progressions (one lunar month equals one year

of life) and Tertiary progressions (one day equals one lunar month of life) have rarely been used, presumably because they do not relate to the basic Earth/Sun relationship. I expect that if Minors and Tertiaries were related to Lunar Mansions/Nakshatras (the Lunar System), the results might be better.

Converse progressions look, to me, to be mangled Primaries. Which I suspect was Vivian Robson's view.

Conclusions

My goal has been to describe astrology in practical, concrete terms, because such terms are the only ones that can produce practical, concrete results, which astrology clearly does. Once a solid theoretical framework has been established, many puzzles can be solved.

Astrology amounts to the interplanetary resonances of spinning bodies in orbit around the Sun. As we live on the Earth, our study centers around the Earth's resonance and how it is influenced by the combined resonances of the other bodies in the Solar System. The Tropical Zodiac shows this resonance in one fashion. The Sidereal Zodiac, based on the Earth's wobble, shows the Earth's resonance in a another fashion. The resonance between Earth and Moon gives us a third point of view.

Will this make the scientists happy?

Of course not. They made up their minds long ago. Their egos will not let them change. Astrological prejudice—astrological envy—the fear of astrology itself—is as old as astrology. Fear of what is superior, the fear of God, if you like, is part of the human condition. Regardless of the existence of "God", as long as man is a fearful creature, excuses may – and have – changed, but hostility to astrology itself will not. But at least we can put a proper name to this affliction. We should otherwise ignore them. Astrologers and scientists each have their own work to do.

Finally, the famous maxim, "As above, so below" remains exactly true, even though I have given it a completely new meaning:

As above, so below, with man himself the intermediary.

Studies of "earth resonance" should focus on the human response, as humans are by far the most sensitive instruments on the planet.

The Pre-Copernican World

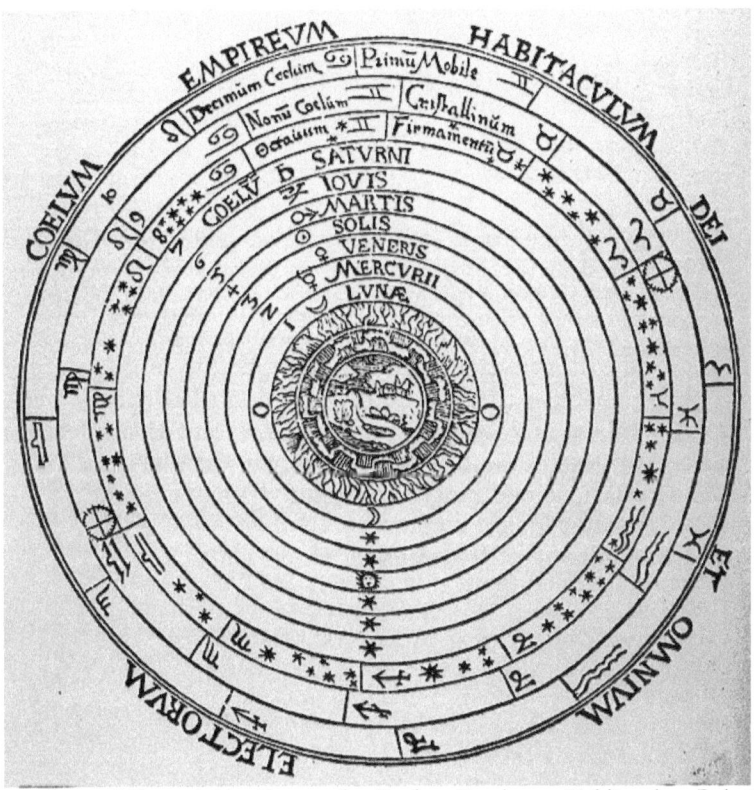

Around the outside, the words, *Coelum Empireum Habitacuium Dei et Omnium Electroum*: Heaven, the Supreme Abode of God and the Elect (i.e., Angels).

Inside the circle, ten concentric heavens. The outermost, the 10th heaven (*Decimum Coelum*), is the Primum Mobile, or First Cause, aka rapt motion. We know this as the Earth's daily rotation on its own axis. Inside it are the 9th (*Coelum Crystallinum*: Sphere of Crystal), the 8th (*Octavium Firmamentum*: Sphere of the Starry Sky), and then the spheres (in order) of Saturn, Jupiter, Mars, Sun, Venus, Mercury and the Moon. At the very center, the *Sublunary World*, i.e., the Earth.

❦ *Epilogue*: The author's Lament

I once wrote a book, long ago. It was wildly popular and is still quoted today. I came back to it a few years ago and read it again, as if for the first time. It was written in prose, so while I did not remember the words *per se*, once I had blundered into the theme, it all came back to me.

And to my surprise, I found my book had never been read. While many people had looked at individual words and had understood individual meanings, the book itself has, to this day, never actually been read. Except by me.

I may someday write a book about that book.

Natal Charts Mentioned in this Book
(arranged alphabetically)

Placidus houses
Mean node

Skeet Shooting for *Astrologers*

Tony Blair
May 6, 1953
6:10 am BST
Edinburgh

George W. Bush
July 6, 1946
7:26 am EDT
New Haven CT

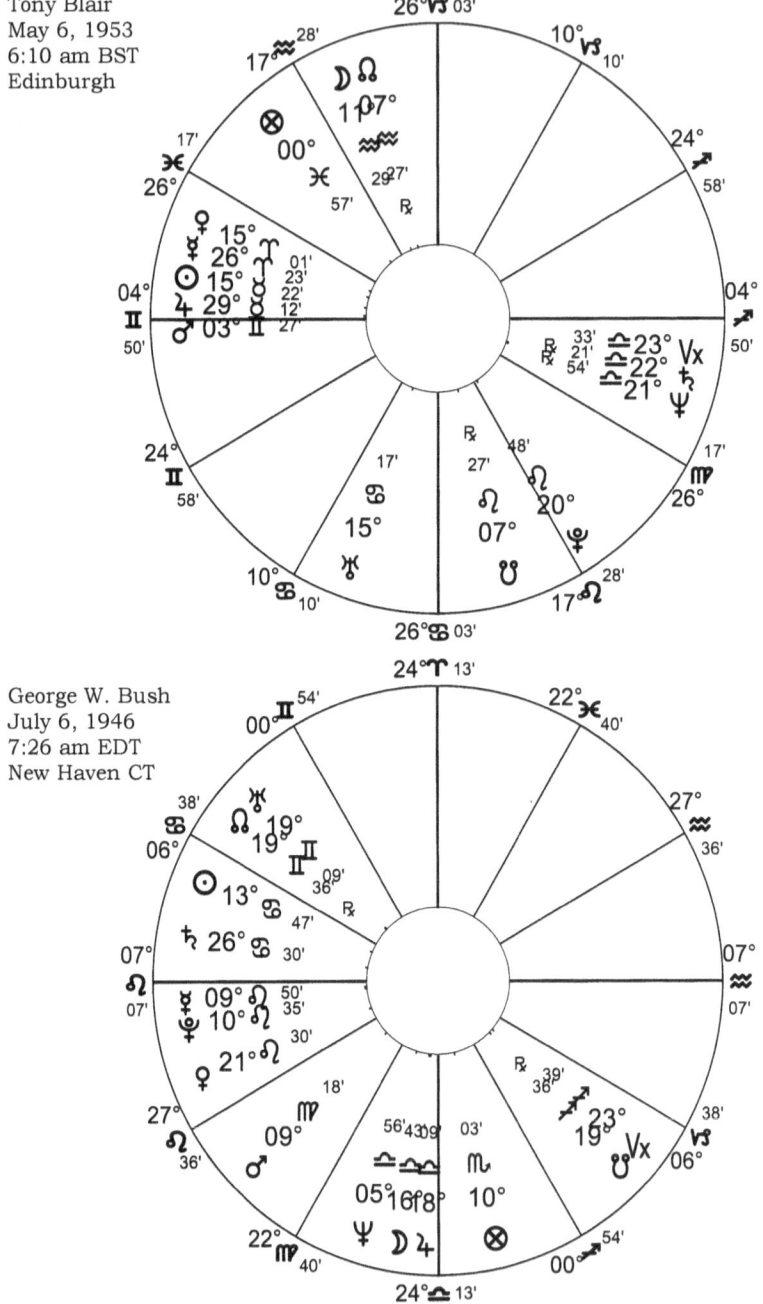

Natal Charts

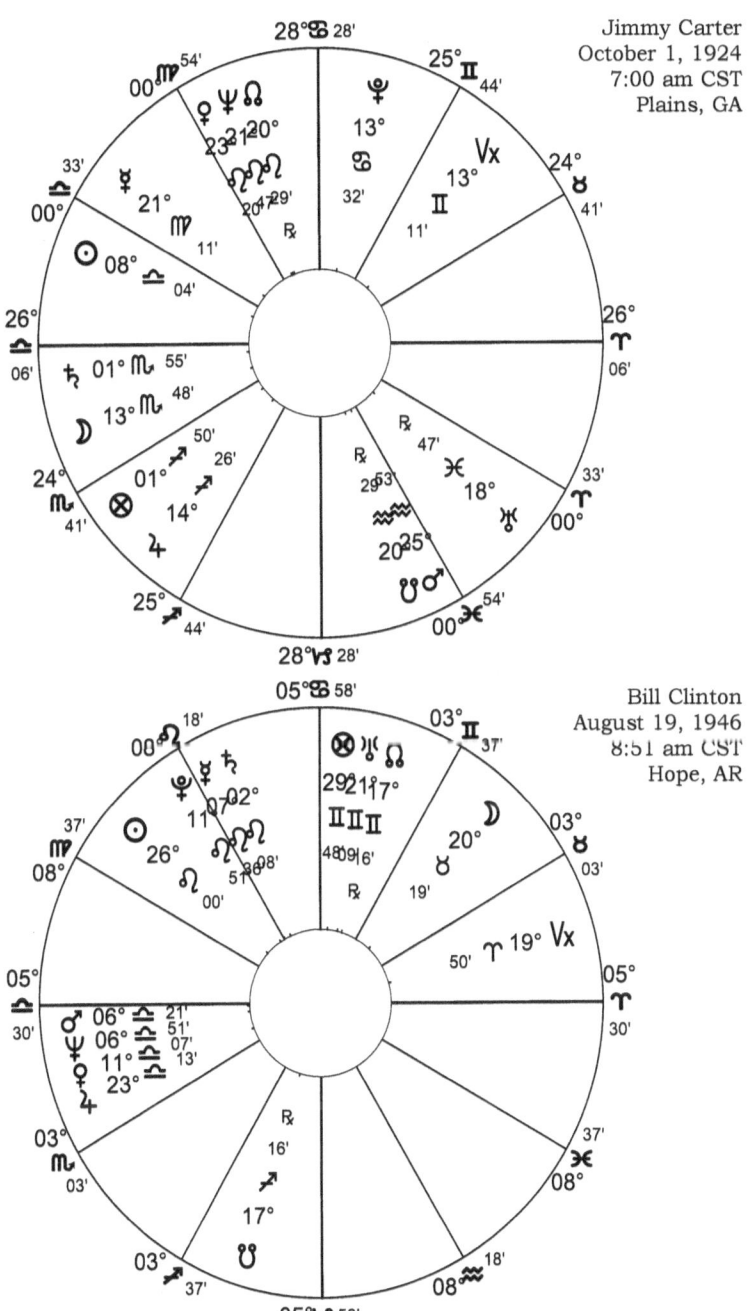

198   Skeet Shooting for *Astrologers*

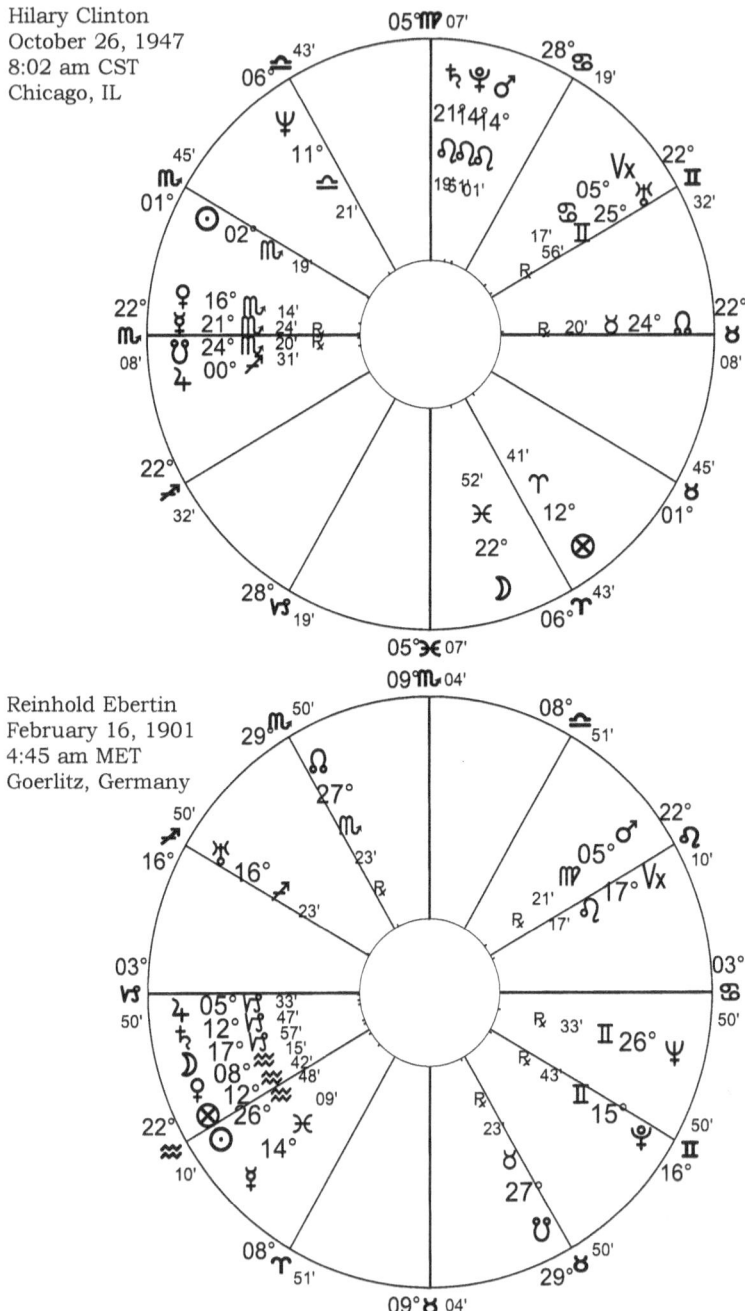

Natal Charts

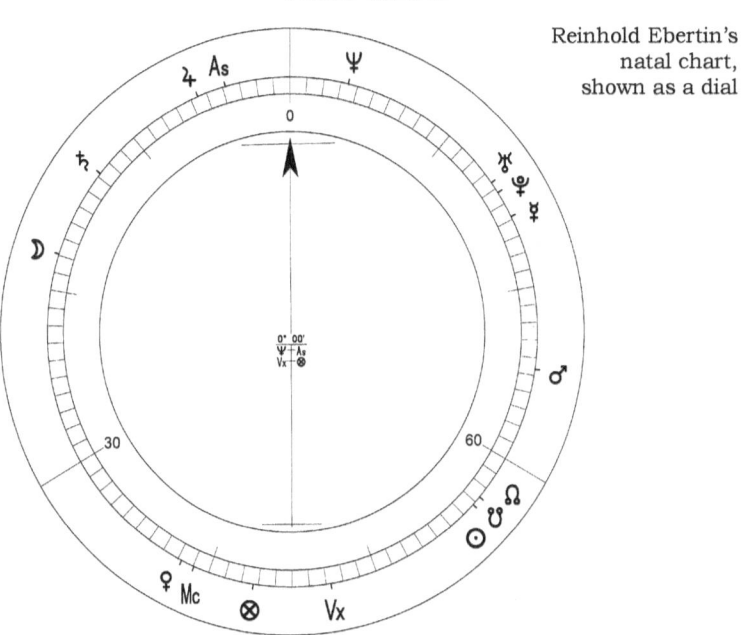

Reinhold Ebertin's natal chart, shown as a dial

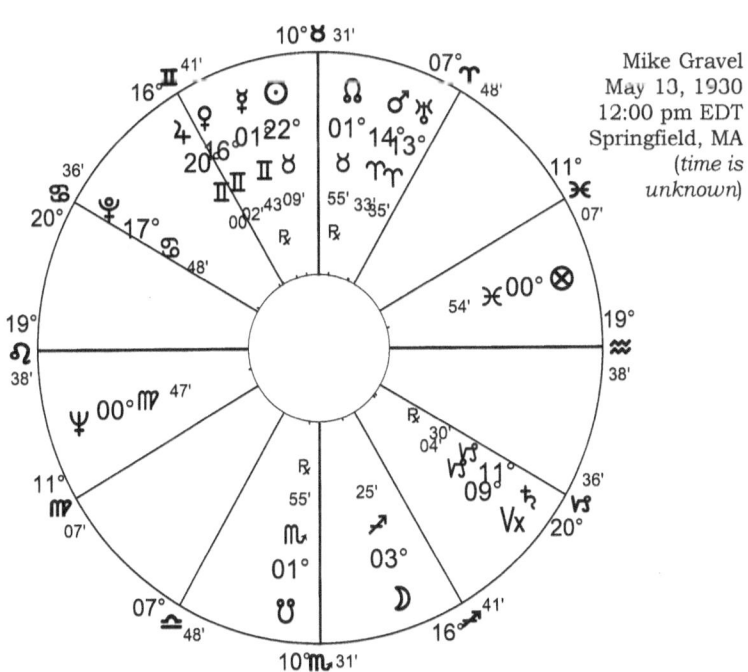

Mike Gravel
May 13, 1930
12:00 pm EDT
Springfield, MA
(*time is unknown*)

200   Skeet Shooting for *Astrologers*

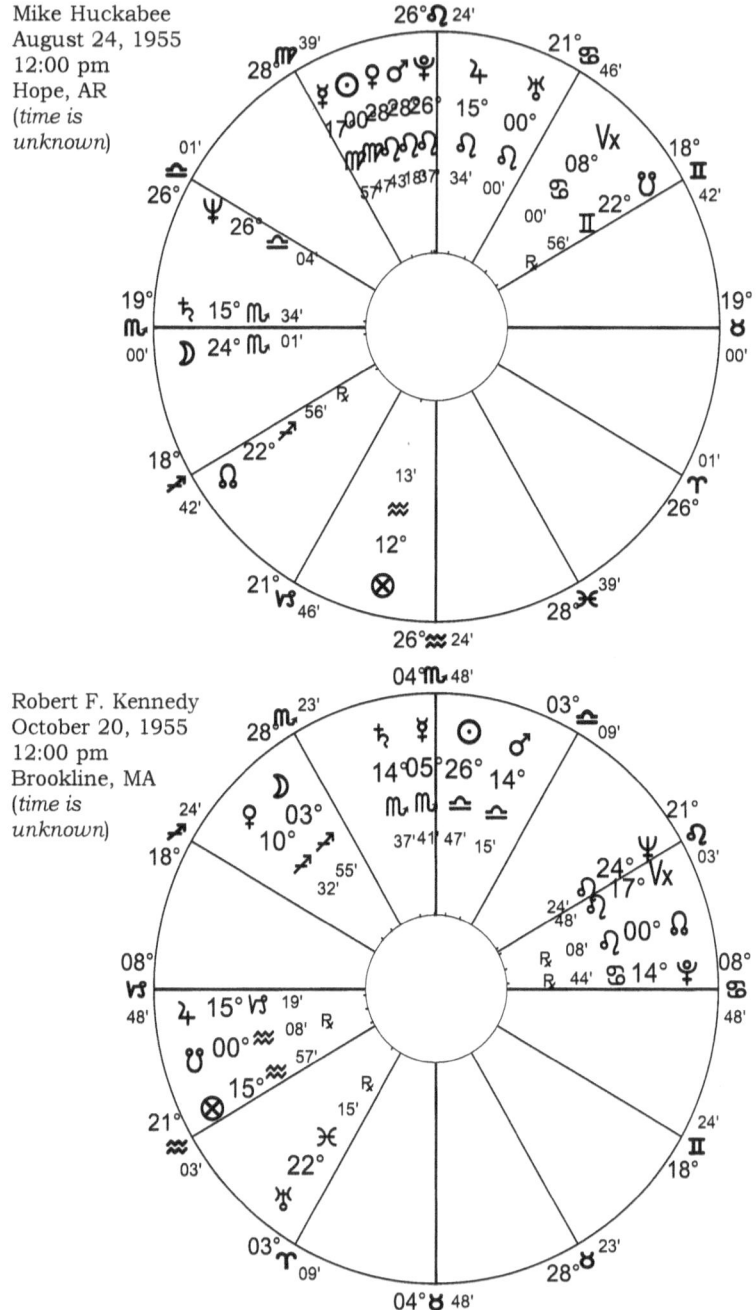

Natal Charts

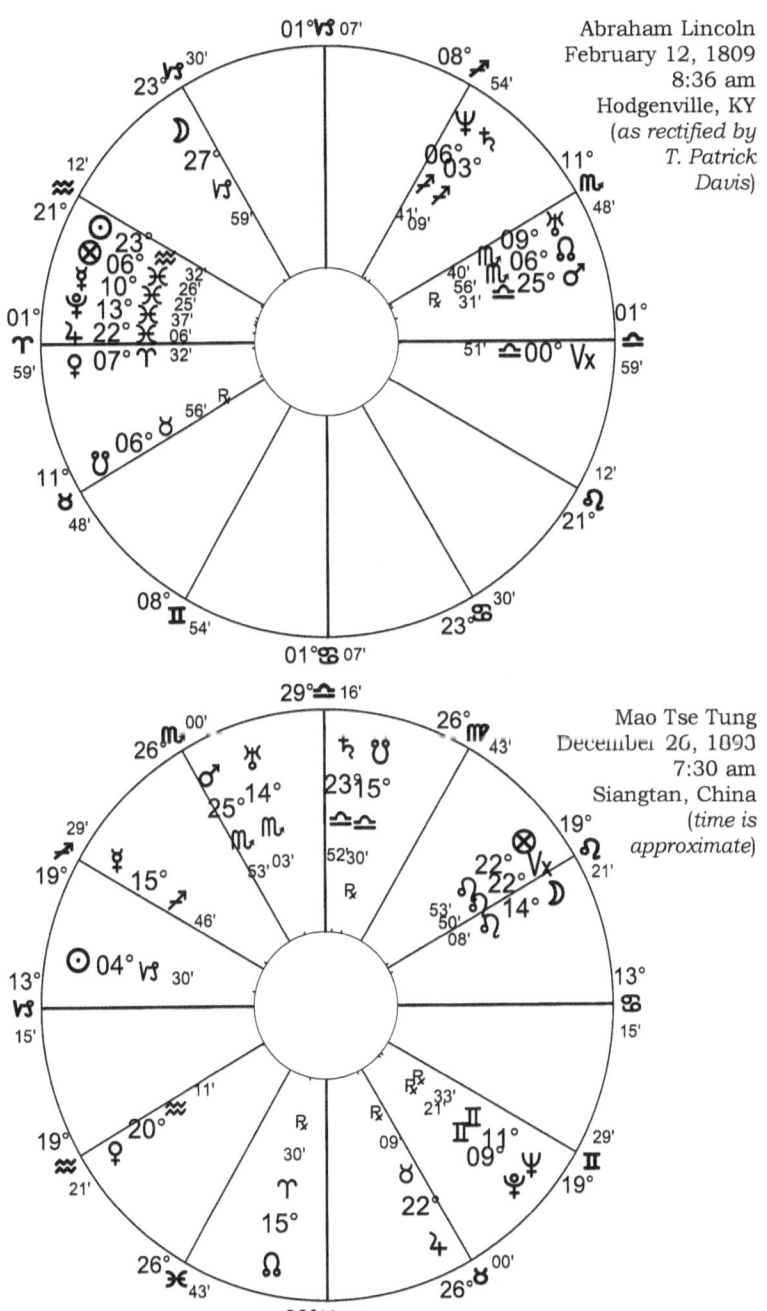

202   Skeet Shooting for *Astrologers*

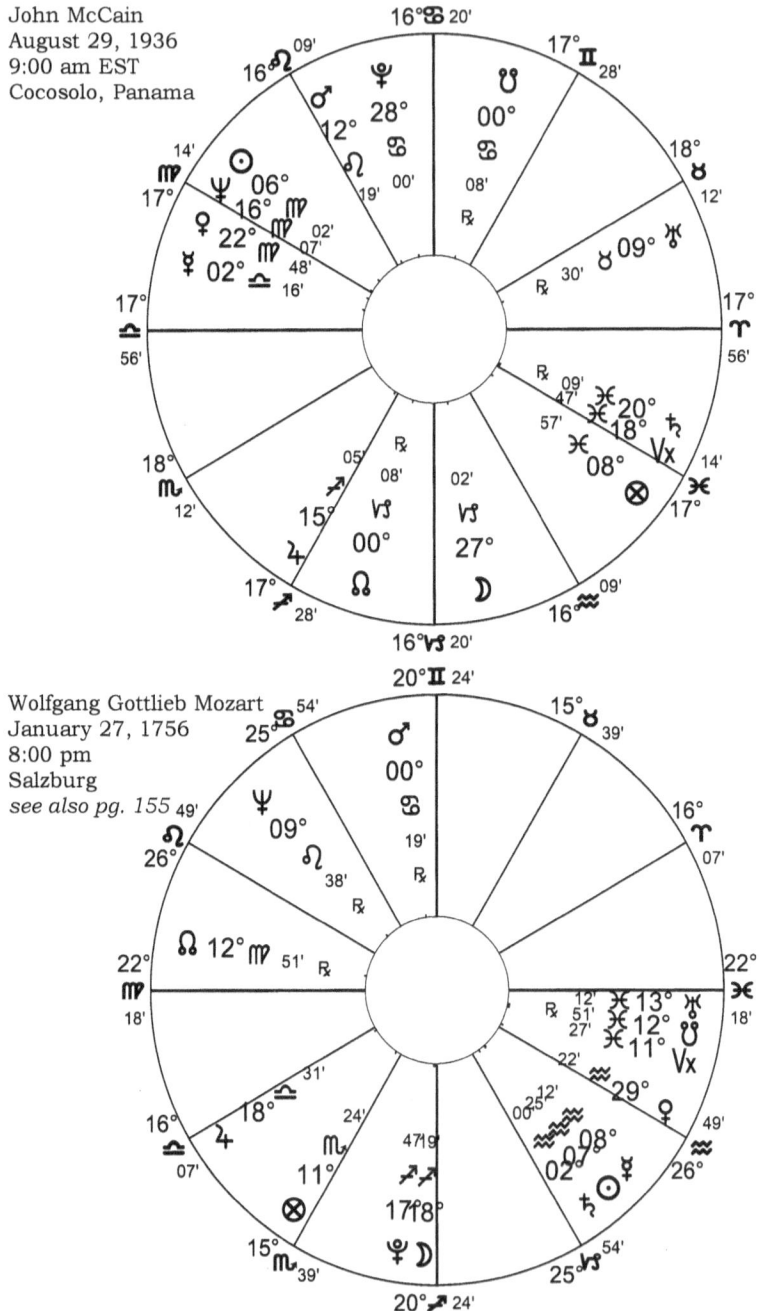

Natal Charts

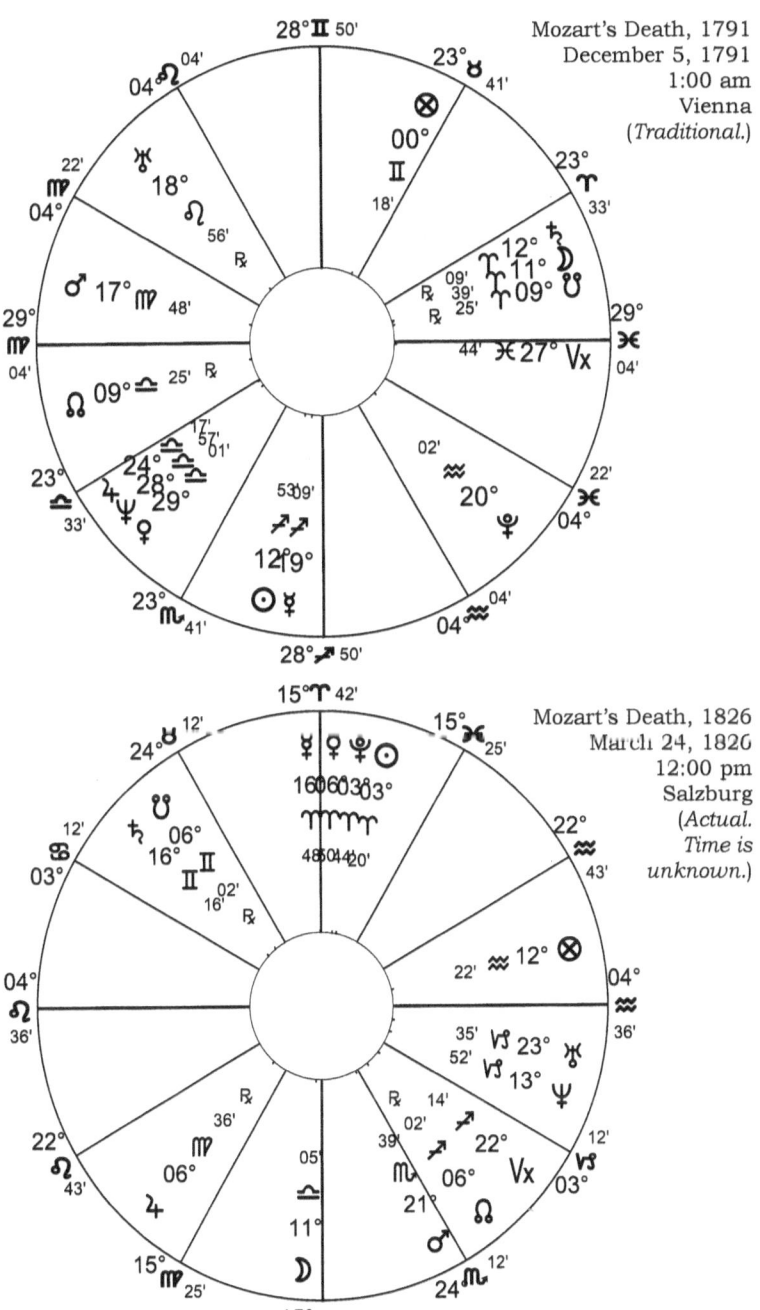

Mozart's Death, 1791
December 5, 1791
1:00 am
Vienna
(*Traditional.*)

Mozart's Death, 1826
March 24, 1826
12:00 pm
Salzburg
(*Actual.
Time is
unknown.*)

Skeet Shooting for *Astrologers*

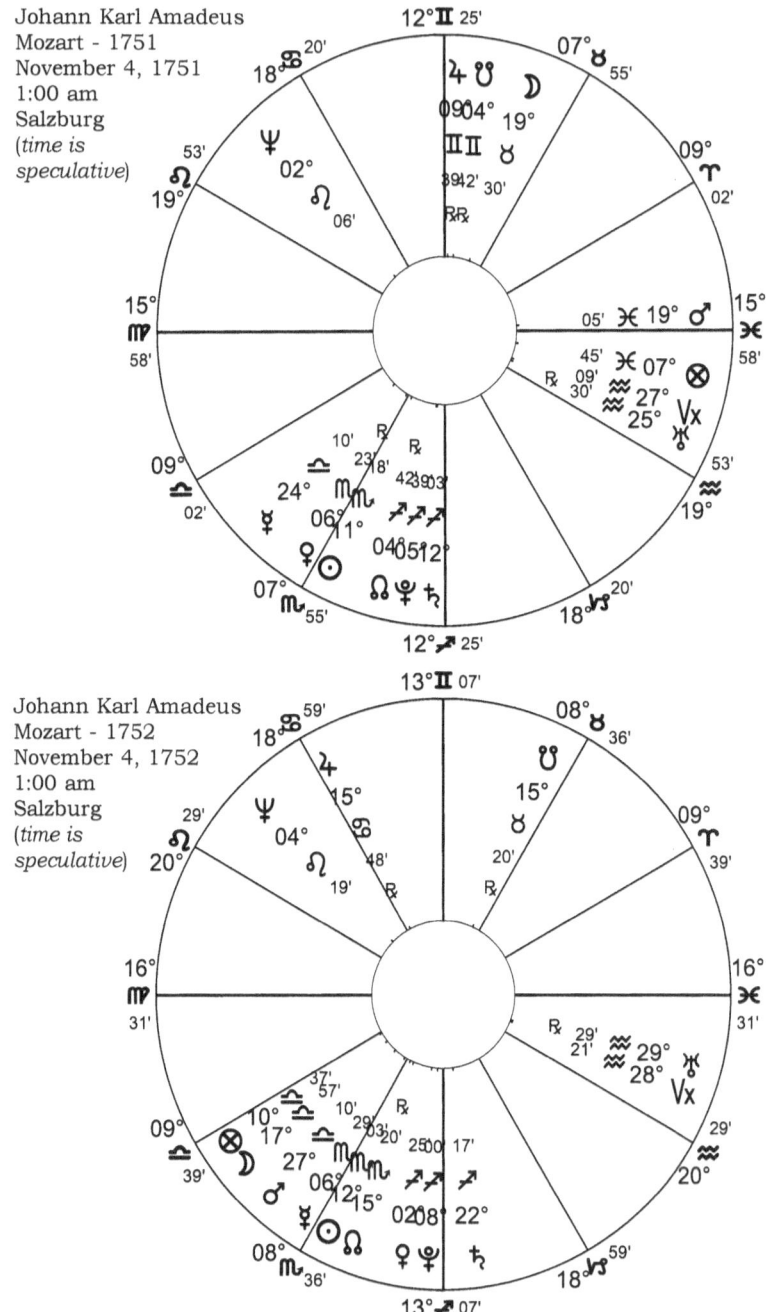

Johann Karl Amadeus Mozart - 1751
November 4, 1751
1:00 am
Salzburg
(*time is speculative*)

Johann Karl Amadeus Mozart - 1752
November 4, 1752
1:00 am
Salzburg
(*time is speculative*)

Natal Charts

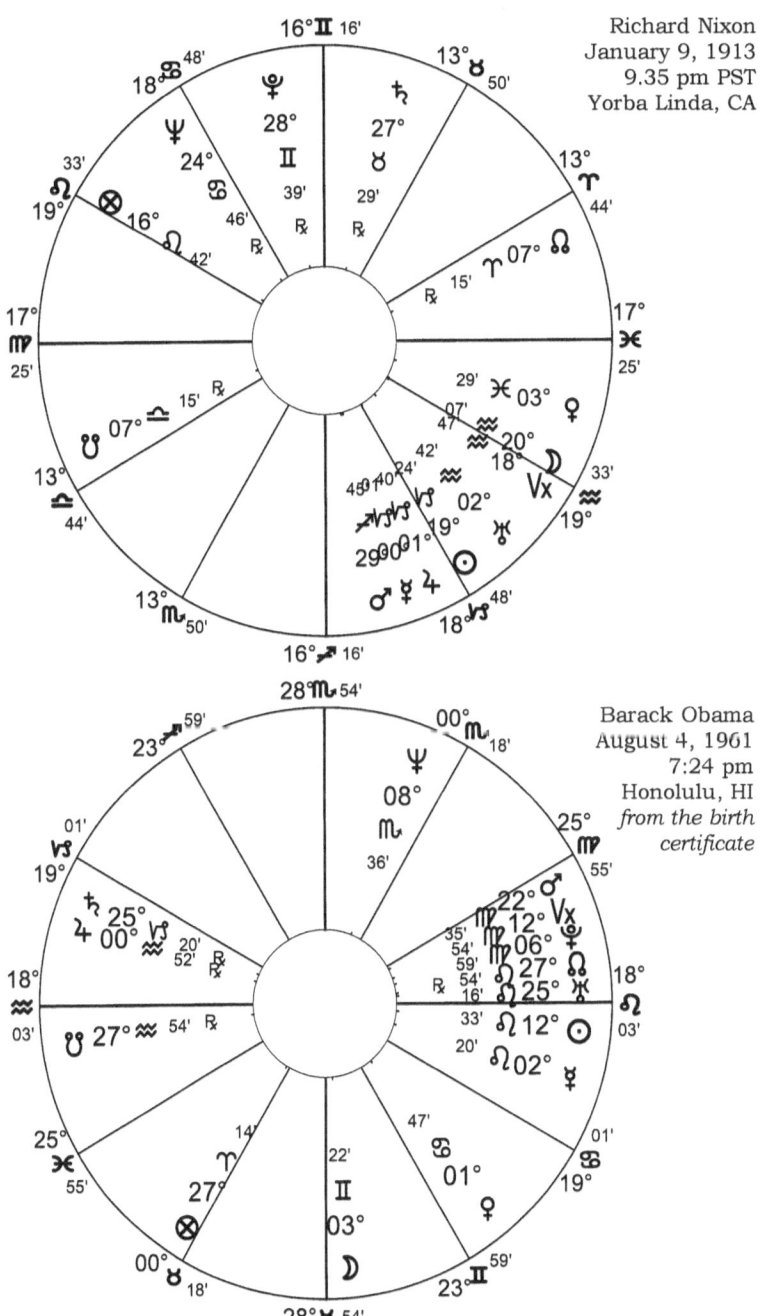

Ronald Reagan
February 6, 1911
1:15 am CST
Tampico, IL
Emma Belle Donath believed the year of birth to have been 1912. "Ronald subtracted a year, Nancy added a year, back in the 1950's." – to me, 1989.

Franklin Roosevelt
January 30, 1882
12:00 pm
Hyde Park, NY
(time is unknown)

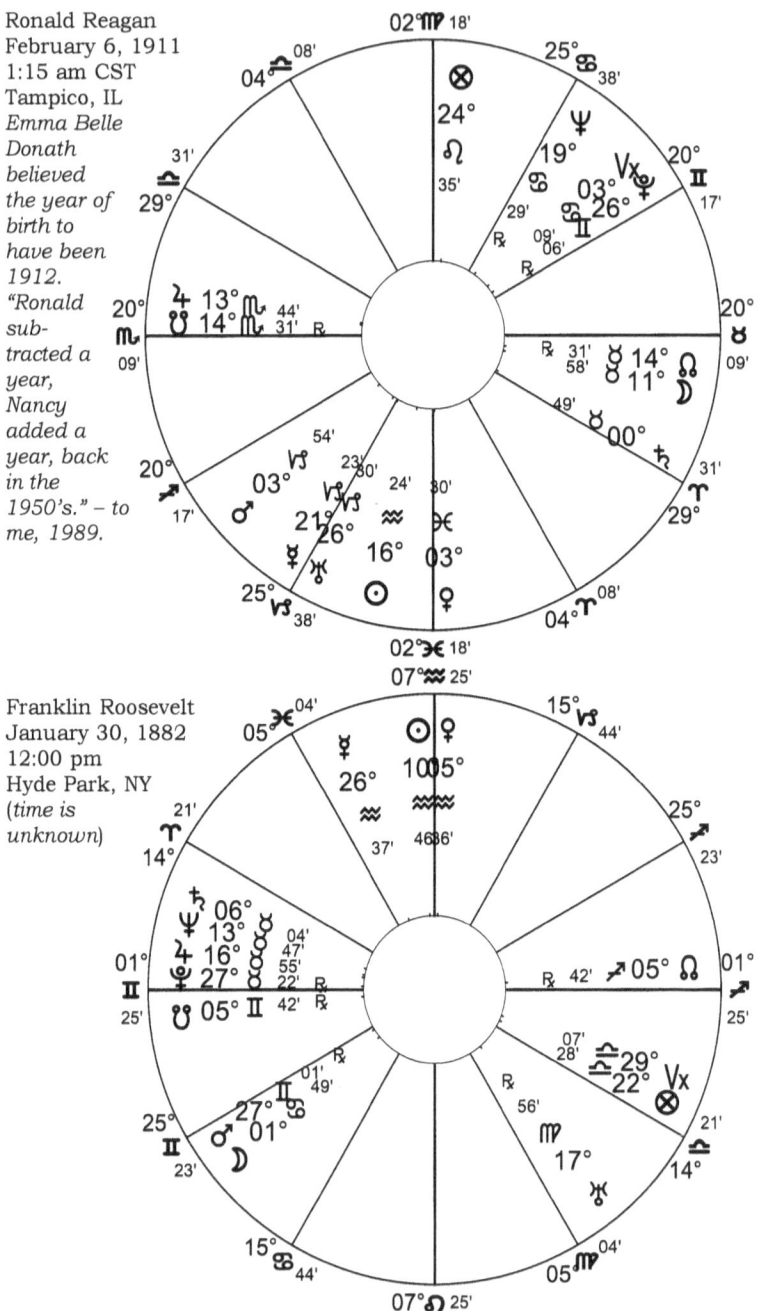

Bibliography

Books mentioned in this book:—

Al Biruni. *The Book of Instruction in the Elements of the Art of Astrology.* Bel Air, MD: Astrology Classics, 2006.
Ashcroft-Nowicki and Norris, Stephanie V. *The Door Unlocked.* Bournemouth, UK: Wessex Astrologer, 2009.
Astro Numeric Service. *AFA Tables of Houses Placidus System.* Tempe, AZ: AFA, 1977.
Bailey, Alice A. *Discipleship in the New Age*, vol. 1. New York: Lucis Trust, 1985.
────────── *Discipleship in the New Age*, vol. 2. New York: Lucis Trust, 1979.
────────── *Initiation, Human and Solar.* New York: Lucis Trust, 1997.
Blagrave, Joseph. *Astrological Practice of Physick.* Edited and with Introduction by David R. Roell. Bel Air, MD: Astrology Classics, 2010.
Blaschke, Robert P. *A Handbook for the Self-Employed Astrologer.* Santa Monica: Earthwalk School of Astrology, 2002.
────────── *Progressions.* Santa Monica: Earthwalk School of Astrology, 1998.
Brother Aloysius. *A Healer's Herbal.* York Beach, ME: Samuel Weiser, 1998
Campion, Nicholas. *The Book of World Horoscopes.* Bournemouth, UK: Wessex Astrologer, 2004.
Carter, C.E.O. *The Astrological Aspects.* Tempe, AZ: AFA, 2003.
────────── *The Astrology of Accidents.* Bel Air, MD: Astrology Classics, 2010.
────────── *An Encyclopaedia of Psychological Astrology.* Bel Air, MD: Astrology Classics, 2003.
────────── *Essays on the Foundations of Astrology.* Bel Air, MD: Astrology Classics, 2010.
────────── *The Principles of Astrology.* Bel Air, MD: Astrology Classics, 2009.
────────── *Symbolic Directions in Modern Astrology.* Bel Air, MD: Astrology Classics, 2010.
────────── *The Zodiac and the Soul.* Bel Air: Astrology Classics, 2010.
Charak, Dr. K.S. *Yogas in Astrology.* Delhi: UMA Publications, 1995.
Christino, Karen. *Forseeing the Future, Evangeline Adams and Astrology in America.* Amherst, MA: One Reed Publications, 2002.
Cornell, H.L., M.D. *The Encyclopaedia of Medical Astrology.* Bel Air, MD:

Astrology Classics, 2010.
Cozzi, Steve. *Planets in Locality*. Tempe, AZ: AFA, 1997.
Creme, Benjamin. *Maitreya's Mission*. Amsterdam: Share International, 1990.
Culpeper, Nicholas. *Astrological Judgement of Disease from the Decumbiture of the Sick*. Bel Air, MD: Astrology Classics, 2003.
Cunningham, Donna. *The Consulting Astrologer's Guidebook*. York Beach, ME: Samuel Weiser, 1994.
Davis, Martin. *Astrolocality Astrology*. Bournemouth, UK: Wessex Astrologer, 1999.
Davison, Ronald. *Synastry*. Santa Fe: Aurora Press, 1983.
DeVore, Nicholas. *Encyclopedia of Astrology*. Bel Air, MD: Astrology Classics, 2005.
Dorotheus of Sidon. *Carmen Astrologicum*. Translated by David Pingree. Abingdon, MD: Astrology Classics, 2005.
Ebertin, Reinhold. *Applied Cosmobiology*. Tempe, AZ: AFA, 1972.
———————— *The Combination of Stellar Influences*. Tempe, AZ: AFA, 2004.
Editors of Pensee. *Velikovsky Reconsidered*. London: Abacus, 1978.
Firmicus Maternus. *Ancient Astrology Theory and Practice, Matheseos Libri VIII*. Translated by Jean Rhys Bram. Bel Air, MD: Astrology Classics, 2005.
Francis, Therese. *The Mercury Retrograde Book*. Santa Fe: Crossquarter Breeze, 2000.
Frawley, John. *Sports Astrology*. London: Apprentice Books, 2007.
Gadbury, John. *Collectio Geniturarum*. London: James Cottrel, 1662.
Gansten, Martin. *Primary Directions, Astrology's Old Master Technique*. Bournemouth UK: Wessex Astrologer, 2009.
Garrett, Helen. *More About Retrogrades*. Tempe, AZ: AFA, 2003.
———————— *Understanding Retrogrades*. Tempe, AZ: AFA, 1980.
Goldstein-Jacobson, Ivy. *All Over the Earth Astrologically*. Pasadena: 1963
Green, H.S. and Raphael and Carter, C.E.O. *Mundane Astrology, The Astrology of Nations and States*. Bel Air, MD: Astrology Classics, 2004.
Gunzburg, Darrelyn. *Astro Graphology*. Bournemouth, UK: Wessex Astrologer, 2009.
Hamaker-Zondag, Karen. *The House Connection*. York Beach, ME: Samuel Weiser, 1994.
Hastings, Nancy. *Secondary Progressions, Time to Remember*. York Beach ME: Samuel Weiser, 1984.
Houck, Richard. *The Astrology of Death*. Gaithersburg, MD: Groundswell Press, 1994.
Idemon, Richard. *The Magic Thread*. Edited by Gina Ceaglio. Bournemouth, UK: Wessex Astrologer, 2010.
———————— *Through the Looking Glass*. Edited by Howard Sasportas. Bournemouth, UK: Wessex Astrologer, 2010.
Koparkar, Mohan. *Retrogrades*. Rochester, NY: Mohan Enterprises, 1980.
Leo, Alan. *The Progressed Horoscope*. Bel Air, MD: Astrology Classics, 2007.
Lilly, William. *The Astrologer's Guide*. Tempe, AZ: AFA, 2005.
———————— *Christian Astrology*, Books 1 and 2. Edited by David R. Roell. Bel Air, MD: Astrology Classics, 2006

Bibliography

———— *Christian Astrology*, Book 3. Edited by David R. Roell. Bel Air, MD: Astrology Classics, 2005.

Lutyens, Mary. *Krishnamurti: The Years of Awakening*. New York: Farrar Straus and Giroux, 1975.

Manilius. *Astronomica* (Loeb Classical Library No. 469). Translated by G.P. Gould. Cambridge: Harvard University Press, 1977.

Mason, Sophia. *Delineation of Progressions*. Tempe, AZ: AFA, 1985.

Masha'allah. *Six Astrological Treatises*. Translated by James H. Holden. Tempe, AZ: AFA, 2009.

McRae, I.I. Chris. *The Geodetic World Map*. Tempe, AZ: AFA, 1988.

Meadows, David. *Where in the World with Astro*Carto*Graphy*. Tempe, AZ: AFA, 1999.

Meridian, Bill. *Predictive Power of Eclipse Paths*. New York: Cycles Research, 2010.

Michelsen, Neil F. *Tables of Planetary Phenomena*. Revisions by Rique Pottenger. Exeter, NH: Starcrafts Publishing, 2007.

Milburn, Leigh Hope. *The Progressed Horoscope Simplified*. Tempe, AZ: AFA, 2009.

Miller, Alice. *Interceptions, Heralds of a New Age*. Tempe, AZ: AFA, 2000.

Obama, Barack Hussein. *Dreams From My Father*. New York: Times Books, 1995.

Oken, Alan. *Alan Oken's Complete Astrology*. New York: Bantam Books, 1980.

Orion, Rae. *Astrology for Dummies*, second edition. Hoboken, NJ: Wiley Publishing, 2007.

Paul, Haydn. *Gate of Rebirth*. York Beach, ME: Samuel Weiser, 1993.

Penfield, Marc. *Bon Voyage*. Tempe, AZ: AFA, 1992.

———— *Horoscopes of Africa*. Tempe, AZ: AFA, 2008.

———— *Horoscopes of Asia, Australia and the Pacific*. Tempe, AZ: AFA, 2005.

———— *Horoscopes of Europe*. Tempe, AZ: AFA, 2006.

———— *Horoscopes of Latin America*. Tempe, AZ: AFA, 2008.

———— *Horoscopes of USA and Canada*. Tempe, AZ: AFA, 1996.

Pessin, Dietrech. *Lunar Shadows III*. Tucson: Igloo Press, 2009.

Porphyry the Philosopher. *Introduction to the Tetrabiblos*. Translated by James H. Holden. Tempe, AZ: AFA, 2009.

Ptolemy, Claudius. *Tetrabiblos*. Paraphrase by Proclus. Translated by J. M. Ashmand. Bel Air, MD: Astrology Classics, 2002.

Rhetorius the Egyptian. *Astrological Compendium*. Tempe, AZ: AFA, 2009.

Riotte, Louise. *Planetary Planting*. San Diego: Astro Computing Services, 1975.

Riske, Kris Brandt. *Astrometeorology: Planetary Power in Weather Forecasting*. Tempe, AZ: AFA, 1997.

Robertson, Marc. *The 8th House*. Tempe, AZ: AFA, 1994.

Robson, Vivian. *Astrology and Sex*. Bel Air, MD: Astrology Classics, 2004.

———— *Electional Astrology*. Bel Air, MD: Astrology Classics, 2005

Roell, David R. *AstroAmerica's Daily Ephemeris of the Planets' Places 2000-2020*. Bel Air, MD: Astrology Classics, 2006.

Sakoian, Frances and Acker, Louis S. *The Astrologer's Handbook*. New York: Harper & Row, 1973.

———— *Decanates and Dwads*. Tempe, AZ:

AFA, 2009.
Saunders, Richard. *The Astrological Judgment and Practice of Physick*. Abingdon, MD: Astrology Classics, 2003.
Sellar, Wanda. *The Consultation Chart*. Bournemouth UK: Wessex Astrologer, 2000.
Sepharial. *Geodetic Equivalents*. Washington: AFA, 1972.
——— *Primary Directions, A definitive study*. Bel Air, MD: Astrology Classics, 2006.
Teal, Celeste. *Eclipses: Predicting World Events and Personal Transformations*. St. Paul: Llewellyn, 2006.
Tyl, Noel. *The Creative Astrologer*. St. Paul: Llewellyn Publications, 2000.
Velikovsky, Immanuel. *Ages In Chaos*. London: Abacus, 1973.
——————————— *Worlds In Collision*. London: Abacus, 1978.
Walsh, Patricia L. *Understanding Karmic Complexes*. Bournemouth, UK: Wessex Astrologer, 2009.
Wehrman, Joyce. *What Are Winning Transits?*. San Diego: Astro Communications Services, 1983.
Wickenburg, Joanne. *Your Hidden Powers*. Tempe, AZ: AFA, 1992.
Wilson, James. *The Dictionary of Astrology*. Bel Air, MD: Astrology Classics, 2006.
Zain, CC. *Weather Predicting*. Albuquerque: Church of Light, 1975.

Index

10th house Saturn, 174
120 years, 190
1202, 38, 48, 83
361 degrees per year, 165
Abacus, 46, 82
Adams, Evangeline, 8, 31
Adams, Samuel, 148
Adhi yoga, 2
AFA Placidus Table of Houses, 163
AFA, 154
AFAN, 154
Air movement chart, 68
Al Biruni, 172
Alan Oken's Complete Astrology, 32
Aldebaran, 61
Alexandria, 37, 83
Alexandria, library, 15
Alexandrian astrology, 48
All Over the Earth Astrologically, 187
American people, 25
An Introduction to Political Astrology, 179
Ancestor worship, 18
Angular relationships, 111
Angular, succeedent, cadent, 126
Antikythera mechanism, 63, 64, 81-88
Aphelion, 61, 183
Aphorisms, 3, 118
Apollonius of Tyna, 136
Apostolic Succession, 137
Applied Cosmobiology, 70
Aquarian Age, ix
Arabic numbers, 38
Arizona crater, 72
Around the neck, 97
Arthritis, 98
As above, so below, 192
Asexual Mercury, 4
Ashcroft-Nowicki, Delores, 139
Ashmolean Museum, 154

Aspects to rulers, 42
Aspects, 188
Astral infections, 96
Astro Computing Services, 64
Astro Graphology, 170
AstroAmerica's Daily Ephemeris, 100
AstroCartoGraphy, 89
Astrodice, 54
Astrolocality Astrology, A guide, 89
Astrologer's Guide, the, 118
Astrologer's Handbook, the, 1, 12
Astrological ages, 182
Astrological aspects, 179
Astrological energies: source, 185
Astrological house theory, 49
Astrological Judgment and Practice of Physick, 17
Astrological prejudice, 192
Astrology A Language of Life vol. 1: Progressions, 74
Astrology and karma, 115
Astrology and Sex, 2, 33, 118
Astrology and weather, 68
Astrology for Dummies, 7
Astrology of Accidents, 170, 176, 178
Astrology of Death, 165
Astrometeorlogy, 69
Astronomers, 77
Astronomica, 14, 16
Astronomy, 66
Astrophysicists, 78
Athens, 37
Attic numerals, 37
Aura of protection, 96
Bailey, Alice, 130
Base-12 numerology, 178
Bastille, 9, 58
Beethoven, Ludwig, 134, 155
Beijing, 46
Bible, 19

Big Bang, 67
Big Rapids, MI, 90
Birth, two-fold, 187
Birth-moment, 186
Black holes, 66
Blagrave, Joseph, 97
Blair, Tony, 5, *chart* 196
Blaschke, Robert, 44
Blavatsky, H.P., 189
Bodleian Library, 154
Book of Instruction, 190
Book of World Horoscopes, 34
Bordeux, 10
Brandenburg Concerti, 13
Brooklyn, 58
Brown, Alton, 99
Bruckner, Anton, 134
Bush, George W., 5, *chart* 196
Campanus, 38
Campion, Nicholas, 90
Cargo cults, 88
Carmen Astrologicum, 13, 14, 64, 81, 82
Carter, Charles, *chart* 179
Carter, Jimmy, 6, *chart* 197
Casablanca, 62
Celestial Influences wall calendar, 87
Centiloquy, 118
Charlemagne, 17
Charles Carter vs: Adolf Hitler, 173
Chart, how to calculate
Chicago home town, 147
Chinese astrology, 46
Christ, 136
Christian Astrology, 8, 83
Church, the, 137
Clepsydra, 36
Climes, 83, 144
Clinton, Bill, 5, 28, 30, 56, *chart* 197
Clinton, Hillary, 5, *chart* 198
Clockwork mechanism, 63, 191
Clothing, 103
Coal, 77
Coca-cola, 114
Cochrane, David, 188
Combination of Stellar Influences, 30, 70
Comcast, 75
Communion, 137
Communists, 150
Confucius, 135
Conjunct ascendants, 32
Consultation Chart, the, 8, 101

Consulting Astrologer's Guidebook, the, 104
Controlling planet, 121
Converse progressions, 192
Copper bracelets, 98
Cosmic Patterns Software, 188
Cosmobiology, 33, 70
Craters of the Moon, 71
Creative Astrologer: Effective Single Session Counseling, 7
Creme, Benjamin, 131
Crucifixion, 19, 136
Crusades, 16
Cunningham, Donna, 104
CycloAstroCartoGraphy, 90
da Ponte, Lorenzo, 58
Dark matter, 66
Dave's rules, 174
Daylight time, 163
Days to years, 191
Dean, Geoffrey, 39
Death penalty, 132
Decanates and Dwads, 130
Decans, 84
Deciles, 189
Declination, 184
Delineation of Progressions, 74
Dewey Beats Truman, 145
Dial, 70
Directions, 50
Discipleship in the New Age, 130
Dodecatemoria, 82
Doggerel, 17, 18
Dominant house, 31
Donuts, 75
Door Unlocked: An astrological insight into initiation, 129
Doppler dogma, 65
Dorotheus, 83, 172
Dreams From My Father, 146
Dvorak, Antonín, 134
Earth's axial rotation, 182
Earth's own resonance, 191
Earth/Sun relationship, 61
Earthiness promotes woodiness, 166
Easter, 159, defined 160
Ebertin, Reinhold, 39, 70, *chart* 198, *dial* 199
Eclipses, 56
Eclipses, mundane, 57
Eclipses, Predicting World Events, 170

Index

Edison, Thomas, 77
Eighth house, 106
Einstein, 65, 80
Election day, 171
Electional Astrology, 152
Electrical properties of the Sun, 78
Elemental spirits, 96
Elementals, 96
Elements, 34
Empty houses, 140
Encyclopaedia of Medical Astrology, 95
Encyclopaedia of Psychological Astrology, 178
Encyclopedia of Astrology, 56
Energy body, 97
Engineering vs: science, 92
Engineering, 66
English magician, 121
Enlightenment, 65
Entire sign, 36
Equal houses, 38, 46
Equinox, 159
Erlewine, Michael, 60, 90
Essays on the Foundations of Astrology, 170, 173, 176, 179
Evangelists, 19
Excrement, 99
Faces, 84
Fatalists, casuists, idealists, 107
Fertile signs, 51
Fertility, 52
Fibonacci, 38
FiOS, 75
Firmicus, Julius, 16, 118
First breath, 186
First cause, 193
First day of the year, 148
Flowers, 51, 166
flyswatters, vii
Foreseeing the Future, 31
France, 58
Franklin, Benjamin, 148
Free will, 186
Friedman, Hank, 87
Fudge, 72
Full Moon, 95
Full Moon birth, 31
Full Moon stress, 152
Gadbury, John, 55
Gardening, 51
Gate of Rebirth, 106

Gays, 30
Gemini Moon, 27
Genghis Khan, 17
Geocentric, 61
Geodetic World Map, 91
German school, 39
German sniper rifles, vii
Gettysburg Address, 14, 21
Gochara, 49
Gold crosses, 98
Gold ring, 97
Gospels, 19
Gould, G.P., 16
Grand trine, 35
Gravel, Mike, 6, *chart* 199
Great year, 182
Green, Jeffery, 130
Handbook for the Self-Employed Astrologer, 7
Harmonic resonance, 188
Harmonics, high, 188
Hawaiian lava, 72
Hazelnut trees, 98
Health Care Act, 167
Heart Center Library, 154
Hee Haw, 76
Helio-Earth zodiac, 183
Heliocentric astrology, 183
Heliocentric, 61
Hellenistic astrology, 13, 36, 38, 60, 88
Hermes Trismegistus, 18
Hindsight, 36
History of Astrology, 13
Hitler, Adolf, *chart* 175
Holden, James, 18, 172
Homer, 15
Homosexuality, 4
Horary, 7, 31
Host, 137
Houck, Richard, 165
Houdini, Harry, 149
House Connection, 2
House systems, 38
Houses, 1, 36, 140, 184
Houses as framework, 126
Houses to signs, 184
Huckabee, Mike, 6 *chart* 200
Human anatomy, 189
Humphrey Bogart, 61-2
Hydrogen bomb, 77
Iceland Weather Report, 114

Iliad, 14
Illiteracy, 19
Implacable Enemy of America, 67
Inaugural Charts, 22, *chart* 26
Incoming planetary energies, 188
Indiction cycle, 100
Initiation, 129-139
Initiation Human and Solar, 130, 137
Intercepted signs, 11, 120, 123
International Day of Astrology, 159
Introduction to the Tetrabiblos, 172
Inverse square law, 186
ISAR, 154
Jefferson, Thomas, 148
Jesus, 135
Jones, Marc Edmund, 140, 142
Juergens, Ralph E., 79
Julian Day, 100, 165
Julian to Gregorian, 148
Jupiter, retrograde, 112
Kennedy, Bobby, 6, *chart* 200
Kenya, 147
Kepler, Johannes, 33, 83, 189
Keywords, 54
Kinky sex, 128
Koch, 52
Koparkar, Mohan, 113
Krishnamurti, Jiddhu, 131, 136
Krishnamurti The Years of Awakening, 130
Krugman, Paul, 30
La Rentrée, 9
Latitude, 37, 83
LCROSS, 92
Lefeldt, Hermann, 39
Lennon, John, 134
Lilly, William, 17, 55, 57, 83
Lincoln, Abraham, 6, 21, *chart* 201
Literacy, 19
Local Mean Time, 163
Local space, 89
London, 38
Look at me!, 106
Lucis Trust, 130
Lunar domes, 72
Lunar mansions, 53, 181, 182, 192
Lunar Shadows, 170
Lunar zodiac, 181
Magic Thread, the, 170
Make money, 101
Mao Tse-Tung, 6, *chart* 201

Marchant, Jo, 63
Maria Therese, 58
Marie Antoinette, 58
Marriage, 151
Mars, debilitated, 175
Mars, retrograde, 112
Masha'allah, 144
Mathesoes Libri VIII, 13
Matthew, 135
Mayans, ix
McCain, John, 6, *chart* 202
Measure of Death, 178
Mechanical clocks, 186
Mechanical computers, 37
Medieval astrology, 50
Medieval Europe, 48
Medieval medicine, 97
Mercury Retrograde Book, the, 113
Mercury retrograde, 75
Metonic cycle, 100
Midpoints, 70
Milky Way, 66
Miller, Alice, 121
Mini-readings, 101
Minor aspects, 33
Minor progressions, 191
Miscarriage, 11
Moisture chart, 68
Money, 7, 43
More About Retrogrades, 113
Morin, 38, 49
Mother Teresa, 149
Mozart, 58
Mozart's birthday, 155
Mozart's death, ix
Mozart's death (actual), *chart* 203
Mozart's death (traditional), *chart* 203
Mozart, Johann Karl Amadeus, *charts* 204
Mozart, Wolfgang Gottlieb, *chart* 202
Mundane aspects, 33
Mundane Astrology, 23
Musical octave, 189
Mutual disposition, 44
Nakshatras, 53, 181, 182, 192
NASA, 92
NCGR, 154
Neptune, 5
Neptune oppositions, 5
Neptune returns, 143
Netflix, 76

Index

New lamps for old, 75
New Moon, 153
New Testament, 19, 136
New York Astrology Center, 63
Nixon, Richard, 5, 168, *chart* 205
Norris, Stephanie V., 139
North Korea, 67
Noviles, 189
Nuclear fusion, 78
Number, 46
Obama, Barack, 5, 12, 24 *et seq.*, *chart*, 147, *chart*, 205
Obama's father, 146
Occam's Razor, 88
Office of the President, 23
Oken, Alan, 45
Old Farmers, 68, 69
Operations dangerous, 96
Oral knowledge, 18
Oral transmission, 14
Orthodox Church (Russian), 150
Out of sign aspects, 176
Padhas, 183
Page, A.P. Nelson, 38
Parallax, 187
Parallels and counter-parallels, 184
Paris, 38
Party apparachnicks, 150
Paul's Letters, 19
Paul, Ron, 6
Penfield, Marc, 90
Perihelion, 61, 183
Philadelphia, 46
Photosphere, 78
Pickup truck, 187
Pingree, David, 81
Placidian, 38
Placido de Titis, 38
Placidus, 52
Planetary patterns, 140
Planetary trees, 70
Planets in Locality, 91
Pleiades, 53
Plutonians, 5
Poe, Edgar Allan, 20
Points of Evolution, 131
Polich, Vendel, 38
Politicians, 5
Porphyry houses, 37
Porphyry the Philosopher, 172
Prague, 58

Pre-Copernican world, 193
Predictive Power of Eclipse Paths, 170
Pregnancy, 52
Prenatal epoch, 187
Primary directions, 38, 49, 191
Primary Directions, A definitive study, 110
Primum Mobile, 193
Principles of Astrology, 35, 177
Printing press, 15
Proclus, 172
Progressed Horoscope Simplified, the, 74
Progressed Horoscope, the, 74
Progressions, 74
Pseudoscience, 65, 71, 77
Ptolemaic aspects, 188
Ptolemy, 16, 38, 95, 144
Push-pull, 140
Questions, 7
Quickie readings, 103
Quintiles, 189
Rabbi, 72
Raphael's Ephemeris, 87
Raphael, (Robert Cross), 57
Rapt motion, 193
Raven, the, 14, 20
Reagan, Ronald, 6, *chart* 206
Reconciling Celestial Mechanics and Velikovskian Catastrophism, 79
Rectification, 31
Red shift, 65
Regiomontanus, 38
Reincarnation, 115, 120, 123
Resonance, 185
Retrograde hangover, 111
Retrograde shadow, 111
Retrogrades, 111
Rhetorius, 172
Right ascension, 191
Riotte, Louise, 51, 166
Robertson, Marc, 106
Robson, Vivian, 192
Roche limit, 188
Rodden, Lois, 150
Roman Empire, 16
Roman numerals, 37, 82
Rome, 38
Roosevelt, Franklin, 6, *chart* 206
Rudhyar, Dane, 131
Ruler of the First, 40 et seq

Ruler of the second, 43 et seq
Rules for Operations, 95
Sacrificed for love, 134
Salzburg, 59
Sardines, 99
Saturn, retrograde, 112
Scaliger, Joseph, 100
Schmidt, Robert, 13
Second house, 1
Secondary progressions, 191
Secondary Progressions, Time to Remember, 74
Sepharial, 90, 107
Septiles, 189
Servants of the Light, the, 138
Seven Great Problems of Astrology, 179
Sidereal time, 163
Sidereal, Vedic, 49
Sidereal zodiac, 182
Sign of the Cross, 98
Signs, 183
Sikkim, 34
Six Astrological Treatises, 129, 144
Skeets, vii
Solar arcs, 191
Solar cycle, 100
Solar eclipse, 152
Solar herbs, 97
Solar wind, 185-6
Some Principles of Horoscopic Delineation, 177
Space aliens, 103
Spica, 60, 61
Sports Astrology, 143
Spring equinox, 60
Spring planting, 166
Squares, stressful, 34
Squares to Neptune, 5
Star Spangled Banner, 14
Stationary, 112
Strawberries, 51
Stream-of-consciousness, 55, 102
Sub-lunary world, 193
Sucker aspect, 5
Summer signs, 183
Sun vs: Moon, 151
Sun's declination, 61
Sun-Moon conjunct, 151
Sundial, 36
Sweet spot, 188
Symbolic Directions in Modern Astrology, 170, 176, 178
Synastry, 25
Table of Houses, 163
Tables of Planetary Phenomena, 61, 183
Teller, Edward, 77
Temperature chart, 68
Ten concentric heavens, 193
Tertiary progressions, 165, 192
Tesla, Nicola, 149, 191
Tetrabiblos, 13, 172, 180
Theosophists, 130
Thermonuclear theory, 78
Third Republic, 9
Thirteen Yule Lads, 114
Thirteen, 185
Three Stooges, 76
Through the Looking Glass, 170
Tibetan astrology, ix
Tibetans, 139
Topocentric, 38
Traditional Chinese Medicine, 99
Transits, 55
Trees, 51
Trojan War, 14
Tropical houses, 49
Tropical vs: Sidereal, 60, 181
Tropics, 188
Tycho crater, 72
Ujjain, 38
Understanding Karmic Complexes, 129
Understanding Retrogrades, 113
Unique zodiacs, 53
Uranium, 77
Vacation, 9
Vedas, 14, 38, 46, 48
Velikovsky Reconsidered, 79
Velikovsky, Immanuel, 79
Venus, retrograde, 112
Verizon, 75
Vettius Valens, 172
Vicenti, Massimo Mogi, 63
Vienna's public cemetery, 58
Vimshottari dashas, 47, 190
Vines, 51
Void Moon, 25
Voids, 12
Washington, George, 148
Water-clock, 36, 83
Waxing, 51
Waxing Moon, 166
Weather Channel, 69

Index

Weather Predicting, 69
Weingarten, Henry, 63
Weiss, Ehrich, 149
Wessex Astrologer, 60
What Are Winning Transits, 39
Where in the World with AstroCartoGraphy, 90
Wii, 76
Wiltshire plains, 88
Winter signs, 183
Witte, Alfred, 39
World astrology, 50
Yogananda, 134
Yogas in Astrology, 2
Yogas, 3
Yogini dashas, 47
Young Turks, 66
Your Hidden Powers, 113
Yule cat, 114
Zodiac and the Soul, 170, 173, 176, 178
Zodiac Within Each Sign, 130
Zodiac, primary, 180
Zodiac, secondary, 180, 182
Zodiacs, 52

Better books make better astrologers.
Here are some of our other titles:

AstroAmerica's Daily Ephemeris, 2010-2020
AstroAmerica's Daily Ephemeris, 2000-2020
   - *both for Midnight. Compiled & formatted by David R. Roell*

Al Biruni
The Book of Instructions in the Elements of the Art of Astrology, *1029 AD, translated by R. Ramsay Wright*

David Anrias
Man and the Zodiac

Derek Appleby
Horary Astrology: The Art of Astrological Divination

E.H. Bailey
The Prenatal Epoch

Joseph Blagrave
Astrological Practice of Physick

C.E.O. Carter
The Astrology of Accidents
An Encyclopaedia of Psychological Astrology
Essays on the Foundations of Astrology
The Principles of Astrology, *Intermediate no. 1*
Some Principles of Horoscopic Delineation, *Intermediate no. 2*
Symbolic Directions in Modern Astrology
The Zodiac and the Soul

Charubel & Sepharial
Degrees of the Zodiac Symbolized, *1898*

H.L. Cornell
Encyclopaedia of Medical Astrology

Nicholas Culpeper
Astrological Judgement of Diseases from the Decumbiture of the Sick, *1655, and,* **Urinalia**, *1658*

Dorotheus of Sidon
Carmen Astrologicum, *c. 50 AD, translated by David Pingree*

Nicholas deVore
Encyclopedia of Astrology

Firmicus Maternus
Ancient Astrology Theory & Practice: Matheseos Libri VIII, *c. 350 AD, translated by Jean Rhys Bram*

Margaret Hone
The Modern Text-Book of Astrology

Alan Leo
The Progressed Horoscope, *1905*
The Key to Your Own Nativity, *1910*
Dictionary of Astrology, *edited by Vivian Robson, 1929*

William Lilly
Christian Astrology, books 1 & 2, *1647*
  The Introduction to Astrology, Resolution of all manner of questions.
Christian Astrology, book 3, *1647*
  Easie and plaine method teaching how to judge upon nativities.

Jean-Baptiste Morin
The Cabal of the Twelve Houses Astrological
  translated by George Wharton, edited by D.R. Roell

Claudius Ptolemy
Tetrabiblos, *c. 140 AD, translated by J.M. Ashmand*

Vivian Robson
Astrology and Sex
Electional Astrology
Fixed Stars & Constellations in Astrology
A Beginner's Guide to Practical Astrology
A Student's Text-Book of Astrology,
  Vivian Robson Memorial Edition

Diana Roche
The Sabian Symbols, A Screen of Prophecy

Richard Saunders
The Astrological Judgement and Practice of Physick, *1677*

Sepharial
The Manual of Astrology, the Standard Work
Primary Directions, a definitive study
Sepharial On Money. *For the first time in one volume, complete texts:*
  • **Law of Values**
  • **Silver Key**
  • **Arcana, or Stock and Share Key** — *first time in print!*

James Wilson, Esq.
Dictionary of Astrology

H.S. Green, Raphael & C.E.O. Carter
Mundane Astrology: *3 Books, complete in one volume.*

If not available from your local bookseller, order directly from:
The Astrology Center of America
207 Victory Lane
Bel Air, MD 21014

on the web at:
http://www.astroamerica.com

www.ingramcontent.com/pod-product-compliance
Lightning Source LLC
Chambersburg PA
CBHW030138170426

43199CB00008B/118